Cultivating
Lasting
Happiness

A 7-STEP GUIDE TO
MINDFULNESS

SECOND EDITION

TERRY FRALICH, LCPC

D0097332

DEDICATION

To my Mom and Dad, who blessed my life in such
profound ways.

To Rebecca, who graces my days with kindness,
laughter, beauty and love.

Editor: Sandra Lindow
Book Design by: East Hill Page Composition & Design
www.pagecomposition.com

Published by: Premier Publishing and Media
PO Box 1000
3839 White Avenue
Eau Claire, Wisconsin 54702

www.pesi.com

ABOUT THE AUTHOR

Terry Fralich is a Licensed Clinical Professional Counselor with a private practice in Southern Maine and a former Adjunct Faculty Member of the University of Southern Maine Graduate School. He also is an attorney who practiced law in New York City, Los Angeles and Portland prior to becoming a counselor. During that time, Terry studied extensively with His Holiness the Dalai Lama, other leading Tibetan teachers and with some of the American pioneers of mindfulness work, including Jon Kabat-Zinn. Inspired by their teachings and his own study of psychology, mindfulness and meditation, he earned a masters degree in clinical counseling, left the practice of law and began his counseling and teaching activities.

Terry is a Co-Founder of the Mindfulness Center of Southern Maine. He has led many workshops at the Center and other Maine locations in mindfulness, emotional intelligence, stress reduction, meditation and the latest developments in neuroscience. He has taught more that 260 seminars on similar topics throughout the country. In addition, he taught mindfulness, meditation and stress reduction for six years at Maine Medical Center's cardiac rehabilitation program and the Cancer Community Center in Southern Maine.

Terry has pursued his own meditation and mindfulness practice for more than 34 years.

Premier strives to obtain knowledgeable authors and faculty for its publications and seminars. The clinical recommendations contained herein are the result of extensive author research and review. Obviously, any recommendations for patient care must be held up against individual circumstances at hand. To the best of our knowledge any recommendations included by the author or faculty reflect currently accepted practice. However, these recommendations cannot be considered universal and complete. The authors and publisher repudiate any responsibility for unfavorable effects that result from information, recommendations, undetected omissions or errors. Professionals using this publication should research other original sources of authority as well.

For information on this and other PPM publications and audio recordings, please call 800-844-8260 or visit our website at www.pesi.com

TABLE OF CONTENTS

PREFACE 1

INTRODUCTION 7

THE SEVEN STEPS TO MINDFULLNESS 19

CHAPTER 1— MINDFULNESS . . . WHY BOTHER? 23

CHAPTER 2 — MINDFULNESS: A PATH AND A PRACTICE 43

CHAPTER 3 — STEP ONE: NURTURING THE WITNESS 61

CHAPTER 4 — STEP TWO: BECOMING BRAIN SAVVY 93

CHAPTER 5 — STEP THREE: SELF-REGULATION 123

CHAPTER 6 — STEP FOUR: LIFE STORY 151

CHAPTER 7 — STEP FIVE: INSIGHT DEVELOPMENT 175

CHAPTER 8 — STEP SIX: NEW REALITIES 219

CHAPTER 9 — STEP SEVEN: A PERSONAL STRATEGY 241

CHAPTER 10 — FURTHER ALONG THE PATH OF MINDFULNESS . . 267

APPENDIX I 279

APPENDIX II 283

APPENDIX III 287

APPENDIX IV 289

ENDNOTES 291

INDEX 303

PREFACE TO THE SECOND EDITION

It has been six years since I wrote this book. As I begin to work on a second edition, I am even more convinced that mindfulness practice is not only a path to a more lasting happiness, but that it is also a fundamental life fitness program for nurturing greater sanity in ourselves and in the world. To be blunt, we live in crazy times. On a personal level, so many of us are stretched to the limits of our capacities by the responsibilities of our jobs and our families. We struggle with the challenges of parenting, finances, maintaining the household, health, family relations, sex and a long list of other issues. We are frequently over-stressed and under-rested, often feeling that we are swept along in a hectic, rushing energy but still not quite keeping up with the tasks at hand.

This experience is not the result of some defect in our character. It is a product of the conditions we face in the world today. Human beings have always had the challenge of providing for themselves and their families in a dangerous world; but our lives in the twenty-first century are very different from the lives experienced by most of our predecessors. Evolutionary psychologists remind us that for all but a very small portion of human history, we have been hunter-gatherers or primitive farmers. We lived in small groups or communities and were very socially interconnected. We hunted and farmed together, ate together and worked together to meet the challenges of our environment. Our lives had a natural rhythm with the light of the day and with the flow of the seasons. Exercise was an integral part of how we lived. We slept a lot more. In fact, as recently as the late 1800's, just 115 years ago, Americans slept an average of 10 hours a night. When was the last time you did that?

So much has changed and the rate of change continues to accelerate. Think of just one small example. As I write this, Facebook® is about six years old. In that short time, it has attracted approximately 800,000,000 subscribers – about one out of every nine people on the planet – and has dramatically changed how we interact with each other.

That example highlights two overall changes. We no longer live in small, relatively manageable environments; we live in a global community that, in its connectedness, is so much more complicated and much more challenging to understand or manage. Here is just one small example of what I mean by that: Rather than hearing the latest developments in our family, our clan or our small community, we are barraged by the latest news from all over the planet, hitting us with an intensity, speed and complexity that is overwhelming. To make things worse, much of that news is anxiety-producing.

Moreover, the Facebook® example reminds us of the on-going rapidity of change. I read a year or so ago that the speed of computing has doubled about every 18 months over the past 15 years. This impacts the speed of information flow, the speed of our work and the general speed of our lives.

To put it simply, our brains and our bodies did not develop, grow and mature under these conditions. It is no surprise that we struggle with the intense complexity of the conditions we face. It should be no surprise that we are pushed to the edge of our capacities by the many ramifications of these conditions.

It sounds so harsh, so daunting – at times so overwhelming. Yet, we all still have the basic yearning for happiness, not some fleeting pleasure that disappears like a bubble bursting in the sky, but a more lasting happiness that sustains us and is supported by more stable confidence, joy and love. As I reflect on my experience since writing this book, on my personal growth, my work with clients and my teaching of several hundred seminars on mindfulness, I realize that if we want to experience the lasting happiness we deserve, we have to be clear about some basic principles.

HONESTY ABOUT THE NATURE OF THE CHALLENGE

I wish that lasting happiness would emerge spontaneously from being a good person and trying to be conscientious in our lives. Unfortunately, it is much more complicated than that. We are complicated beings, with complex brains, emotions and conditioning. As briefly explored above, the conditions we face at this time of the human existence are intensely challenging and often a shock to our slowly evolving system.

There is no magic wand or magical fairy dust that will change all of that and transport us to a different experience. We have to be honest with ourselves that nurturing a more lasting happiness requires attention and effort.

CHOICES, CHOICES, CHOICES

We have a choice. We can continue on as we always have, trudging along and slugging it out, falling into bed at night exhausted and wondering why it is so hard to make it through the day. We are entitled to make that choice. If we do, however, we can be certain that our past will predict our future. The routines may vary somewhat, but the nature of our experience will not change a great deal and we will continue to wonder why happiness and satisfaction is so fleeting.

PATIENCE, ACCEPTANCE AND LOVING-KINDNESS FOR OURSELVES

If we are honest about the nature of the challenge and make the choice to bring attention and energy to cultivating a more lasting happiness, we need to support the process with patience with our pace, acceptance of the effort we can bring in the middle of already very busy lives and heart-felt loving kindness for ourselves when we fear that we don't know what we are doing, that we are not "doing it right" or that we are not making enough effort. In fact, the commitment to be kinder to ourselves, to be more accepting of our own human condition with all its inconsistencies and imperfections, is not only a support for the process; it is an essential foundation for a true and stable happiness. Take a moment and imagine how wonderful, how liberating it would be, to be more patient, accepting and kind – to others as well as to ourselves.

BELIEF, CONFIDENCE AND FAITH

I am not suggesting that cultivating more lasting happiness is dependent on a religious faith. Although if you have a sustaining religious or spiritual tradition, that can be an important support for this process. I am referring to a faith in practice. As I discuss throughout this book, my view of mindfulness is that it is a skill-based practice. We all have a sense for practice, whether it is in the context of a sport, an art, music, hobby or a profession. We know that if we return to the practice over and over again, something will change—most likely we will get better at what we are practicing. It may be slow improvement and it will undoubtedly be different from others around us who are also practicing, but there will be improvement if we keep practicing.

Mindfulness practice that leads to more lasting happiness is no different. We have to take a leap of faith when we begin the practice. We have to trust experienced practitioners that mindfulness practice actually leads to the happiness we deserve. As we continue, however, our belief in the practice grows, our personal confidence that we know what we are practicing slowly emerges and our faith in the practice strengthens. We begin to realize the blessings of mindfulness practice, that whatever life throws at us, we have a practice that will enable us to handle it with a certain amount of skill and grace. Put simply, the belief, confidence and faith in the practice becomes a sustaining force in our life.

Reading all this may seem dry and even academic. It seems a little like that to me and I wrote it! It is important to be honest with ourselves, to make difficult choices and to invest energy and attention even though at the beginning we don't fully understand what we are doing. The practice of mindfulness itself, however, is not dry or academic. It is fascinating, surprising, satisfying, confidence building and eventually, as I said, truly a sustaining force in our lives. It is daunting at times; but it is manageable, as we find our own pace with the practice.

Moreover, the vision of a more lasting happiness is not just some cute title that is designed to market a book. It is a vision that is lush and juicy, full of a diversity of experience that matches the complexity and uniqueness of our individual spirits. The vision is one that offers the ability to hold in our hearts the tremendous suffering in our personal environments and in the world generally without being blind to the incredible beauty and astonishing miracles surrounding us. It is a vision that opens us to our true capacity for joy and love. The foundation of a more stable happiness enables us to take on the big challenges of being human without losing ourselves in them. Nurturing this foundation enhances our own lives; but it also means we will be more patient, compassionate and supportive of others.

The vision of a more lasting happiness includes magical experiences that were previously beyond our imagination; but it also includes being full of delight and awe with simple, every day things. Just this morning, I was sitting on the dock that extends into the pond on our property. A light rain began. As the small drops fell onto the surface of the pond, they created hundreds of small circles, expanding into each other and fading into the water, as new drops fell, creating more circles, more movement and constantly changing patterns. It was a silent symphony filled with the beauty of smooth circles, playing with the movement of other expanding circles, dissolving, to be immediately followed by the precious notes of more circles moving across the surface of the water. There is so much joy when our strengthening mindfulness enables us to be present, to witness and connect with the simplicity and beauty of ordinary experiences. When this happens, the ordinary truly does become extraordinary!

I am so appreciative that you are curious about your growth, that you are bringing attention to mindfulness practice and what it may mean to you. As you read through this book, I encourage you to take your time, to take small bites of the material and be reflective about them. I hope that you will continue to clarify the question of what you are practicing—and that you will be patient with yourself when you realize that you have forgotten your practice altogether. When you recognize your forgetfulness, I encourage you to simply return to your practice in whatever way is possible and take some satisfaction that your mindfulness has once again awakened. With each awakening, your mindfulness inevitably gets a little stronger.

Throughout the book, you will hear my supportive voice and begin to know how much respect I have for your effort and for the beautiful being that you are. May you remember that I am practicing with you. May we realize that our mindfulness practice will not only enhance our own lives but will ripple out to others, making an important contribution to nurturing the sanity that is so badly needed at this challenging time of the human experience.

INTRODUCTION

I believe in the possibility of minimizing our suffering and cultivating a life enriched by consistent love, joy and true happiness. To be honest, I could not have said that in my early adult years. As the belief slowly emerged over the past three decades, it became increasingly clear to me that it is not only true, but that this possibility is one of the unique and precious opportunities offered by this complex condition of being human.

I wasn't very creative as a young adult. As the oldest son of Depression-era parents, I had a strong tendency to choose the safe route. I was always a good student, so a few years after college I decided to attend law school. I didn't have a grand vision, or even a strong desire to be a lawyer. I simply knew I could do it and that it probably would lead to a stable career path. There wasn't much imagination in my decision, or in the first few years of legal practice in New York City after graduation from law school.

In the mid-1970s, I moved to Los Angeles and joined what eventually became a 200-lawyer firm. For someone who was born in the Midwest and who lived in Maine during his teenage years, it was like moving to a foreign country. Virtually everything in the environment was different—the weather, the architecture, the vegetation, the diversity of cultures and that infamous Southern California attitude and lifestyle. It was an exciting transition for me, one that began to stimulate my curiosity more than ever before.

About a year after moving to L.A., my comfortable and somewhat narrow view of myself and my life path received a big jolt when I met Andrew DaPassano, my first meditation teacher. Andrew was an older, dramatically handsome man, probably in his early 70's, who had been involved with the study and practice of wisdom traditions for almost fifty years. In addition to all that experience, accumulated in Mexico, South America, Russia and the United States, he was a charismatic, mesmerizing and mischievous teacher. Female and male students alike, many forty years his junior, had huge crushes on Andrew, taking in his every word. Although it was thirty years ago, I remember one evening when he had been discussing some magical topic and, all of a sudden, he stopped, paused for a long moment, and said with a totally straight face: "Everything I have been telling you is a lie!" We were stunned. And that was exactly the point. Andrew had a way of shaking up your thinking, prodding you to be curious and question old beliefs.

By the way, there was a point to Andrew's comment. He wanted us to realize that just hearing from him about the grand possibilities available to us had no truth for us personally as long as we just took his word for it. The real task was to use his teachings as guideposts and pursue the practices that would enable us to create our own experience. Only then would his teachings be "true" for us.

One of the great blessings of studying with Andrew for several years was a solid grounding in a beginning meditation practice. Andrew often said that the constant activity of our mind is like having two excited monkeys on our back, furiously chatting away with little restraint. Meditation was the vehicle for settling the monkeys' nervous energy.

About a year after I met Andrew, I attended a public talk by the Dalai Lama. There are certain moments of grace in our lives when we know something important has happened, but we are not quite sure what it was or where it will lead. My first encounter with the Dalai Lama was one of those moments of grace. I don't remember anything he said, but his presence touched me in a profound way. The best way I can describe the impact of his presence is by telling a story from a retreat with him many years later.

In 1993, the Dalai Lama came to Tucson to give five days of teachings to several thousand students. I had the good fortune to have a seat in the front of the hall where the teachings were held. Sitting next to me was a woman from Tucson. She had no connection to Buddhism or the Dalai Lama. In fact, her tradition was Judaism. She came to the teachings because the Dalai Lama is, in one sense, an international celebrity. She lived in Tucson and she was simply curious. On the first morning, the Dalai Lama entered the hall from a door right at the end of our row. We weren't dummies, so the next time the organizers announced that he was about to enter the hall, everyone in our row crowded down to the end of the row to be closer as he passed.

The Dalai Lama always enters his public appearances with a slight bow to the audience and a radiant smile. This morning was no exception and he walked by about six feet away from us. As we returned to our chairs, the woman sitting next to me was weeping. Here was an individual with no investment in the person or his tradition, yet the power of the Dalai Lama's presence, his love and compassion, quite unexpectedly to her, had deeply touched her heart.

I don't know whether my neighbor's reaction changed anything in her life; but from my first encounter with the Dalai Lama, I was drawn into the study and practice of Tibetan Buddhism. Like many American students of this ancient Asian tradition, I didn't approach Buddhism as a religion, but as a philosophy and psychology of life, a path for opening to our greatest potential for love and compassion. Over the next several decades, I attended many teachings by the Dalai Lama and other highly respected Tibetan teachers. This led to contact and study with some of the pioneers of mindfulness in our country.

Along the way, there were significant events in my life. I left the practice of law and ran a residential real estate company for five years. My wife and I pursued our interest in Eastern wisdom traditions by travelling to the Himalayan region of Asia on several occasions. In one life-changing trip, we spent six weeks in McLeod Ganj, a small village hugging the side of a mountain in northern India and the residence of the Dalai Lama and the Tibetan government-in-exile.

The environment in McLeod Ganj is a powerful catalyst. Suddenly, after an arduous thirteen-hour bus ride through the northern Indian plains and up the steep side of a mountain in the Himalayan foothills (all on challenging Third World roads, of course), you are in a community with a unique emphasis on spirituality and spiritual study. At the heart of the community, and at the very center of its spiritual strength, is the Dalai Lama. Whether he is actually physically present or not, the power of his wisdom and altruism emanates from his residence and serves both as a symbolic and tangible guiding light for the thousands of monks and nuns there, as well as for the Western students.

For Westerners like my wife and me, there is rare access in Mcleod Ganj to great teachers, both Tibetans who have evolved from within the traditional Tibetan system of training and various Westerners who have been in extensive contact with many of the great Tibetan teachers of the second half of the twentieth century.

Inevitably, the teachings of Tibetan Buddhism lead to love and compassion, the essential and central themes of the tradition. In one way or another, our period of study and practice in McCleod Ganj led to reflection on these qualities. It was a wonderful opportunity, undistracted by TV, radio, newspapers, jobs, bills, house cleaning or even cooking, to explore the nature of love and compassion—what blocks our capacity for them, what nurtures and frees our natural abilities to be loving and compassionate and what incredible challenges we face in our competitive society to maintaining a consistently loving and compassionate heart.

Even with all the experiences of opening and investigation that flowed through my life, as I passed the midpoint of my 40s, I found myself back where I started professionally—practicing law. Thinking about hitting 50 in a few years wasn't terribly startling, but it led to the first real encounter with thoughts of being 60. That was a bit of a wake-up call. I realized that it was finally time to be more creative, more courageous, and to take steps to integrate more fully my personal and professional lives. It was a surprisingly easy decision once I reached that point. (Of course, it took me about a quarter of century from college graduation to get there!)

For many years, I had been fascinated by what supports growth, what leads to an experience of greater happiness in our lives. I wanted to bring that exploration into the center of my life—and to support others' exploration of the same questions. It took a few years to obtain a graduate degree in clinical counseling and become licensed as a Licensed Clinical Professional Counselor, but completing that journey enabled me to bring my legal career to a close.

At the time I was making my transition, there were dramatic and exciting events occurring in the field of neuroscience. In fact, the 1990s have been referred to as "the decade of the brain" because of the advances in neuroscience research. By the late 1990s, the accumulated research led to truly amazing paradigm shifts in neuroscience that affirmed, for the first time, the expansive capacity of the human brain, over the *entire* life span, to change in ways that maximize our human potential.

It was perfect timing for me. I had been immersed in the study of the mind and emotions from the perspective of Eastern wisdom traditions for years and now Western science was beginning to describe in greater detail what was happening in the brain with regard to states that both support and undermine happiness. My personal fascination with the interface of Western psychology and neuroscience, on the one hand, and Eastern wisdom traditions' exploration of the mind, on the other, mirrored the significant East-West dialogue that was rapidly emerging. Experienced researchers and practitioners on both sides were becoming increasingly interested in what the other had discovered. One of the many clear examples of this dialogue was an international conference of neuroscientists organized by the Society of Neuroscience in Washington, D.C. in 2005, attended by an astounding 36,000 participants—and the opening keynote speaker was the Dalai Lama.

There are many wonderful aspects of this East-West dialogue, but the primary theme is a shared passionate effort to understand the human mind. Although the methods of investigation and the descriptive language vary widely, the central message from both sides of the dialogue affirms the belief stated in the first sentence of this book—that the possibility of cultivating a life enriched by consistent love, joy and lasting happiness is available to anyone willing to bring effort and perseverance to the exploration.

My intent in writing this book has been to draw on all the sources that have been available to me in over thirty years of exploration—my wise and loving teachers, my exploration of Western psychology, Eastern wisdom traditions and neuroscience, my many fantastic clients, and the thousands of dedicated individuals in my classes and workshops. My entire motivation is to present what I have learned in a coherent and practical way to help you clarify your own possibilities and refine your approach to cultivating the lasting happiness you deserve.

It is difficult to talk precisely about the nature of happiness since we all have such varied experiences. Consequently, as a framework for this book, I want to define what I mean by "lasting happiness." There may be great masters in the wisdom traditions who can maintain happiness, a mental/emotional state of well-being or balance, all the time; but the great majority of us cannot. Through the practice of mindfulness, however, we can achieve a state of happiness that is more stable, enabling us to more consistently experience contentment, satisfaction, delight, joy, awe and love. The task is building a foundation and practice that makes it possible to experience well-being regardless of the circumstances in our lives or the events around us. This is what I mean by "lasting happiness."

"Cultivating" implies that this is a process requiring attention and initiative. It takes effort, of course; but the alternative of fleeting and short-lived moments of happiness is not very attractive. This process is facilitated by a growth of awareness, awareness of what is going on in our mind, emotions and body. You might say that mindfulness sharpens and refines an awareness of our awareness, a clear recognition of our state of being moment-to-moment.

Cultivation of lasting happiness, then, can be thought of as developing the skills to minimize our suffering and maximize positive states so that our overall well-being, or happiness, is more stable. Mindfulness also leads to the development of a clear strategy for returning to balance when we have slipped into some agitated, contracted, distracted or otherwise negative state.

In the end, the stability of our well-being becomes a continually re-playing cycle of the following:

- State of well-being or balance (happiness) →
- Disruption of well-being (loss of mental/emotional balance) →
- Prompt awareness of loss of balance →
- Application of strategy or practice for returning to balance →
- State of well-being or balance (happiness)

Even more simply, the equation for cultivating lasting happiness can be envisioned as:

- Happiness → mental/emotional disruption → dissolving disruption → happiness.

You may not have found the right conditions to begin your personal transformation, the right spark to kindle your imagination about what is possible or you may have been on a path of growth for some time. In either case, I am hopeful that the perspectives and techniques in this book can be an encouraging force, sustaining you in your personal process of growth.

There are many themes in the book, but the two that hold the process of transformation together are mindfulness and practice. Over the past thirty years or so, mindfulness has become an umbrella term in the United States that incorporates many ideas, skills and techniques. In a way, the term is not terribly helpful without a thorough exploration of what it means and how we actually nurture it in our lives. We will engage in that exploration and seek to determine how mindfulness can be an active force, guiding us insightfully through the rocky and often threatening terrain of the human landscape.

While reading this book, I encourage you to think of mindfulness as a path or vehicle for staying as close as possible to your best intentions. We all want to be kind to our loved ones and to ourselves. We all strive to make good choices that truly support our health and happiness. We all hope to be loving and joyful. Everyone could probably agree with that; but there are powerful influences inhibiting our ability to manifest our best intentions, influences that arise from our personal histories, the way the brain is hard-wired to function, the pressures of modern life and the unavoidable challenges of being human—just to name a few. Mindfulness offers a path that enables us to have a clear, realistic view of the landscape of our lives and to make affirmative choices that are consistent with our best intentions.

Practice is action. It is the energy that gives life to the ideas of mindfulness. Mindfulness and practice are such a powerful combination. With the clear view of mindfulness and the energy of practice, we are truly able to create something new, to transform old negative habits that cause so much suffering and to cultivate states of being that open us to joy and love.

If you stop and think about it for a moment, I bet that you have very useful thoughts about practice. At some time of your life, you probably have practiced a musical instrument, a craft, a sport or a skill set in a job. You already know that there are some basic elements to practice, such as the realization that you are still learning, an aspiration to keep refining what you already know, a commitment to bring consistency to your effort and a willingness to keep at your practice—or continue coming back to it—even when you feel confused, awkward or unsuccessful in what you are doing. Underlying anything you have practiced is the belief, or maybe just the hope, that you will eventually be more confident and more skillful in what you are doing.

Mindfulness practice shares all these elements, but there is at least *one* significant difference. Whereas other practices may apply to one aspect of your life, mindfulness is a vehicle for your *entire* life. Yes, for everything! It is a practice that supports manifesting everything you want to be. It enables you to make both moment-to-moment and life-altering decisions consistent with your best intentions for love, joy and lasting happiness.

In many ways, this book is a call to action. If it remains only an intellectual exercise, whatever seeds for growth you find here will most likely lie fallow and never blossom. In the Eastern teachings, it is often said that there are two tracks in the path of transformation: the track of insight or wisdom and the track of experience. Information and knowledge enable us to increase our understanding of ourselves and the complex world in which we live; but if we do not bring the energy of action to the process, we are very unlikely to create anything new. Once we acknowledge that our lives involve more suffering and less true happiness than we would like, the essential task, of course, is to create a new experience, not just to keep accumulating more information. The new experience then draws on our insight to make sense of it and to stabilize what is valuable in it. In this way, the two tracks of wisdom and experience make a seamless circle in our process of growth.

So I challenge you to read this book as a guide for action, not simply as an intellectual exercise. Use your intellect. As Albert Einstein once said, it has powerful muscles, but also use the energy of your heart to power action. Use your longing to really experience love and the lush beauty of the human experience to bring you back to practice over and over again. With that combination of insight and action, you will create a new experience and manifest the lasting happiness you deserve.

There are many calls to action in this book. Pick whatever appeals to you most and just begin there, bringing whatever effort you can make in the context of your life as it is right now. If you are consistent with your effort, however modest, you will experience the transformative quality of mindfulness practice— and you will develop more confidence both in your personal wisdom and your practice. Moreover, whatever happens, you will know yourself better and connect with beautiful aspects of yourself that have been hidden from your sight. They are like buried treasure waiting to be discovered by you.

At times, you may feel that the book is repetitious, as it frequently returns to topics that have already been explored. This is intentional. This is a huge project we are approaching. We are aspiring to nothing less than manifesting our greatest potential as human beings, to live more fully with love, peace of mind and happiness. In my own life and in working with the many people I have had the good fortune to support, I have discovered how important it is to keep connecting what we know and what we are learning. All the individual ideas about mindfulness and practice, for example, are not very useful as separate concepts viewed in isolation. Their great power emerges from seeing them as related parts of a whole. When we have this holistic view, all the disparate ideas, insights, skills, techniques and strategies reinforce each other and accelerate the refinement of our understanding and the creation of our new, more positive experience.

I think of esoteric knowledge not as something hidden away in some secret vault and accessible to only a few privileged beings, but as commonly known insights and concepts understood more deeply. In returning to themes and topics we have already explored, we are putting together the pieces of a beautiful mosaic. The individual elements may be marvelous in their own right; but when we can see their relationship more clearly, when the whole work of art emerges, the power to move or to touch something in us increases dramatically. So when we return to familiar themes once again throughout this book, we are seeking to refine and clarify our view of the whole. By deepening our understanding of ideas and concepts we have heard before, we are creating a personal esoteric wisdom.

I have been on the path we are exploring in this book for many years. I do not take any personal credit for that. It is so much more the inexplicable blessings of having had wonderful teachers and loved ones in my life who have brought to me such kindness, caring, creativity, inspiration and insight. I certainly am not done with my own work on the path of mindfulness, so I continue to listen to my teachers and, of course, keep on practicing. I hope that as you read this book, you will think of my travelling the path with you. I cannot do the work for you;

but I can be a dedicated and determined supporter, believing in you and in the possibility of you experiencing the lasting happiness you deserve. My first teacher in this magical process of nurturing our highest potential always encouraged us to call on his spirit when we felt confused or discouraged—to just pause, ask for help, leave some space in our mind and see what emerges. If it is helpful, don't hesitate to call on my spirit (or the spirit of any beings you have known or believe in) for encouragement and clarity. Be assured that I will be doing my best to send positive energy and to wish the best for you as you continue your exploration.

May our collective efforts benefit all other beings and add some modest energy to the nurturing of peace, love and sanity in the world.

The Seven Steps to Mindfulness

STEP ONE: THE WITNESS . . .

OPENING TO SPACIOUSNESS

It is a revolutionary concept for many people that we can have a thought and watch it at the same time, or that we can experience an emotional arising without it totally dominating our awareness. The heart of mindfulness is to develop the ability to witness our inner landscape without becoming fully immersed in the stream of spontaneously arising thoughts, emotions and sensations constantly flowing through us.

STEP TWO: BASIC BRAIN FUNCTION . . .

MAKING SENSE OF OLD PATTERNS

The latest developments in neuroscience offer us clear information about old patterns that continue to undermine our happiness. Becoming a little "brain savvy" is easy and offers us major advantages. First, understanding that our old patterns make sense in light of the way the brain works enables us to be kinder to ourselves and to realize that our negative patterns are not a result of some personal defect. Second, becoming brain savvy enables us to identify challenging emotional patterns and to work with them with insight. Third, learning about the brain's plasticity, its ability to "re-wire" over our entire life span, offers us hope that change is possible and that we do not need to be stuck in old, unhealthy patterns.

STEP THREE: SELF-REGULATION . . .
NURTURING THE ABILITY TO SETTLE NEGATIVE ENERGIES

We know now from neuroscience that strong emotional reactions frequently hijack our ability to think clearly and act in ways that are consistent with our best intentions. Learning how to effectively settle down—to self-regulate—is essential to minimizing our suffering and to building a foundation for lasting happiness.

STEP FOUR: LIFE STORY . . .
DISCOVERING CONNECTIONS

Developing an overview of our life story enables us to understand the connection between brain function and the negative emotional patterns that undermine our happiness. This overview helps us to see our life experiences and patterns in a holistic way and opens the door for healing.

STEP FIVE: INSIGHT DEVELOPMENT . . .
IDENTIFYING OLD MESSAGES
AND EXPLODING OLD MYTHS

Immersed in our life stories are negative conclusions and messages about ourselves that have been our reality since childhood. These negative messages and conclusions were an understandable reaction to circumstances we experienced as children, but they are simply not a true reflection of who we really are. Identifying these old messages and seeing them from the adult perspective enables us to dismantle them and begin to truly disengage from the belief systems that undermine our happiness.

STEP SIX: NEW REALITIES . . .

INVESTING IN A NEW VISION OF SELF

As we explode the old negative myths about ourselves, we have the wonderful opportunity to discover a new, healthier and true vision of who we are. Although we may be skeptical at first, exploration of this new vision eventually connects the insight of our mind with the emotion of our heart. As we begin to realize something deeper in ourselves, the vision of our radiant nature and basic goodness becomes our emerging reality and a powerful support for our happiness.

STEP SEVEN: A PERSONAL STRATEGY . . .

DEVELOPING A CLEAR PLAN
FOR MINDFULNESS PRACTICE

Each of the first six steps can be helpful when used individually or in combination with one or more of the other steps. Developing a clear plan for mindfulness practice incorporating all the steps enables us to maximize the potential benefit. As we weave together insights and techniques from each of the steps in a comprehensive practice, we create a beautiful and powerful foundation for cultivating the lasting happiness we all deserve.

CHAPTER 1

Mindfulness . . . Why Bother?

When the Dalai Lama speaks to Western audiences, he often begins by saying that we all share the desire to be happy. With the profound compassion and loving-kindness that radiates through his teachings, he also reminds his listeners that we all *deserve* to be happy. If we all wish to be happy and we all deserve it, why is a lasting experience of happiness so rare? Why is the sense of being happy so fleeting? One moment we are feeling good from a pleasant experience, and the very next moment we are plunged into a bad mood that totally overpowers our consciousness and dominates our experience. When this happens, as it often does, the happiness that seemed so real just a moment before feels like an illusion. The shift can be provoked in many ways: an unkind word from a spouse or child, a careless driver on the road, an unexpected demand at work, a dissatisfied colleague, client or customer, or simply not having things go quite the way we had planned or hoped. I am sure you could think of a hundred ways that the happiness or contentment of the previous moment simply evaporates in an instant and is replaced by a negative state of mind.

Depending on the perspective we chose, we could talk endlessly about why happiness is so fleeting. We could investigate the question from a spiritual, psychological, historical, political or even evolutionary standpoint and debate the issue forever.

And that's half the problem, isn't it? Where to start? In writing this book, my goal is to avoid the endless debates and begin work, here and now, with the one thing that lies at the heart of every aspect of our experience, happy or otherwise, with the one thing that we can influence in every remaining moment of our lives: *our minds*. I will be referring to our minds throughout this book in the inclusive sense used by Eastern traditions, meaning the mind *and* the heart. Accordingly, all references to the mind also include the heart and the emotions.

Although we will touch on many perspectives, we will keep our focus on the mind. The mind presents us with a vast topic, but we will maintain a determination to avoid getting lost in the theoretical or the incomprehensible. Our focus will be on the practical. We will explore our minds with the singular purpose of understanding, refining and practicing what we can do in our lives *right now* that will make a difference in every aspect of our experience. Our goal will be to create the happiness we deserve—not the illusion of happiness that disappears in an instant like a bubble in water, but a durable happiness that supports all aspects of this exciting, challenging and precious experience of being human.

If we are serious about working with our minds to achieve this ambitious goal, we have to honestly confront some initial obstacles. Why do we have to start with obstacles? It's so depressing! The obstacles give us guidance. They reveal important information regarding the issues we face. They show us the way. The good news is that the obstacles are surmountable. Just by having the courage to face the obstacles to our happiness, with curiosity and kindness, the alchemical process of transforming them into something valuable has already begun. So let's start by considering a few of the obstacles to true happiness.

OBSTACLE ONE:

THE ILLUSION THAT HAPPINESS SHOULD JUST HAPPEN TO US.

The first obstacle is the illusion that happiness should just happen to us. If we are a good person, treat our loved ones with some amount of decency and work hard at our jobs, happiness should simply flow into our lives as a reward or fringe benefit awarded for making a sincere effort. Maybe you don't live in this fairytale, but I think many of us do. Furthermore, it makes intuitive sense, doesn't it? If we are relatively conscientious in the kind of life we live, we should be rewarded. Shouldn't we?

I wish there were such a grand plan in the universe that we could count on; but the day-to-day experience in our own lives, and in the lives of those all around us, just doesn't support it. It's not that being a decent and conscientious person doesn't count for something. It certainly does. The harsh reality is, however, that it does not guarantee happiness. In fact, if we look at the evidence of our own lives, the truth is absolutely clear. Being a decent person, in itself, is not enough. It may seem unfair. We may have to struggle with our sense of unfairness and grieve the loss of an expectation; but sooner or later, we have to look at the evidence with a cool head and come to terms with the reality of the situation. Lasting happiness does not flow automatically from being a decent person. It is a much more complicated situation than that.

OBSTACLE TWO:

THE ILLUSION OF "IF-ONLY" HAPPINESS

Okay. So let's say we accept this hard reality. Let's say we are willing to acknowledge that we have to do something more that just be a decent person. Maybe you have done that already. Maybe you did it years ago and entered into a more active process of finding your own happiness. That leads to a second obstacle. It is fair to say that in our culture (and in other cultures, too, but let's just stick with what we know best), we are often looking for happiness in all the wrong places. We are certain that we will find it in the next romantic relationship, or the job promotion we have worked so hard for, or the new home that we are sure will work so well for our family, or in that car we have wanted for years.

You can think of many other examples with a similar theme. We will finally be really happy when we get this or that or when this or that happens. We almost promise ourselves we will be happy *if only* our expectation, our dream, our wish comes true; but it is a false promise. All those "if only's" we invest in too often fall short. We may feel excitement, contentment or gratification when they finally occur, but it doesn't last. In a very short time, we are constructing new "if only's" without recognizing that we are just beginning the cycle of ultimate disappointment or disillusionment all over again.

Harvard psychology professor Daniel Gilbert, along with his colleagues psychologist Tim Wilson of the University of Virginia, economist George Loewenstein of Carnegie Mellon and psychologist (and Nobel laureate in economics) Daniel Kahneman of Princeton, study the happiness question.[1] More specifically, over the past few years they have researched the decisions we make in our search for happiness. They have asked questions such as: "How do we predict what will make us happy or unhappy—then how do we feel after the actual experience?" Gilbert and his colleagues have concluded that we consistently overestimate the intensity and duration of our emotional reactions to future events. In other words, we invest a great deal in the anticipation of finally getting the new car or buying the new house in the belief that the acquisitions will significantly increase our happiness, but our new possessions will almost certainly be less exciting than we anticipated and any excitement we do experience will last a shorter time than we would have predicted.

Gilbert and Wilson call the difference between what we anticipate about these events and what we actually experience "the impact bias." Our if-only thinking leads us to believe that our lives, our happiness quotient, will really improve if only the next acquisition, the next promotion, the next relationship finally occurs; but the research strongly indicates that our prediction will turn out to be wrong. Because we have a consistent tendency to overestimate the impact of these events, we often experience some amount of short-term pleasure and then feel flat or disappointed. We invest so much hopeful energy in anticipating the object of our if-only thinking ("Things will be really great when . . ."). When we realize that our lives haven't changed that much, that we really aren't any happier, the disappointment can be quite severe. I witnessed a dramatic example of this many years ago before I had heard of the impact bias.

A dear friend of mine was an aspiring professional musician. She had studied music for years and had logged thousands of hours practicing her instrument. She dreamed of getting a record contract and performing before concert audiences. Over the course of less than three months, she suddenly, and quite magically, went from playing background music in a restaurant to being offered a recording contract and playing before large audiences in wonderful concert halls. It was a dream come true and a wonderful blessing for her. Although the circumstances of her career had changed dramatically, in a very real sense, nothing had changed inside her. She was temporarily thrilled, of course; but, as Gilbert and his colleagues would have predicted, the thrill was not as great as anticipated and was not durable. It just didn't last. Although it was many years ago, I still clearly remember how confused and disappointed my friend was when she realized that her dream had come true, but it had not had a lasting effect on her happiness.

Other recent research into the foundations for our happiness adds further support to the illusion of "if only thinking." Social scientists tell us that Americans are three times wealthier than we were fifty years ago, but we are no happier. Moreover, the research also shows that after attaining a quite modest income, earning more and more money does not at all guarantee that we will be any happier.[2]

Avoiding this cycle of expectation and disillusionment is very difficult to do. We are bombarded with messages that we will finally attain happiness if we make more money, obtain this product or another, or if only we could finally shape up and lose those few extra pounds—or, more recently, if only we take the latest pill. The modern advertising industry has been called the most effective brainwashing propaganda entity ever developed—and we are its constant target. The result: we increasingly believe the message. Make no mistake about it; the advertising industry's message is the "if only" doctrine. Billions of dollars are spent every year to convince us that we can be happy (or even okay), if only we acquire, see, taste, hear or experience in some way what the particular advertiser has to sell.

The advertising industry doesn't bear all the blame. As a species, we seem to have an innate tendency to look for happiness in these external events or things; but the advertising industry manipulates our tendency, strengthening our illusion that we can find happiness in this way. It is like overbreeding. We have this natural tendency to live in this "if only" way and the advertising industry exaggerates our natural tendency. Since this has been happening in the modern era for generations, our whole culture is infected with this "if only" way of thinking about our happiness. It is very hard for all of us not to be affected by it on a very personal level. So, to use the cliché one more time, we keep looking for happiness in all the wrong places, even though we are repeatedly disappointed in our search.

In the Sufi tradition, there are many stories about the wise jester and fool, Mullah Nasruddin. In one story, Nasruddin is out in front of his house, looking for something in the sand under a lamppost. One of his neighbors comes by and asks, "Nasruddin, what are you looking for?"

"I have lost the key to my house," he replies.

"Oh, then I will help you look for it." The neighbor gets down on his hands and knees and the two men root around in the sand for a very long time, looking for the key; but they find nothing. Finally, the neighbor asks, "Nasruddin, we have looked such a long time for your key and have not found it. Are you sure you lost it here?"

"Oh no," Nasruddin replies, with a big smile on his face. " I lost my key in the house, but the light is so much better out here!" ³ Like Mullah Nasruddin, we are often going through the futile exercise of looking for happiness in external things and events because "if only" thinking shines so much light on them.

Psychologist Frances Vaughn emphasizes that our futile tendency to look outside ourselves for happiness has a major negative side effect: it inhibits the type of change that can truly serve as a foundation for the happiness we seek:

> As long as men and women believe that someone or something outside them can make them happy, they usually fail to make the changes that can contribute to more pleasure and happiness and satisfaction in everyday life. The changes that actually do increase enjoyment and satisfaction are changes in perception, attitude, and consciousness.⁴

There is another variety of this obstacle to our lasting happiness. If what I have described above could be called "acquisition if-only thinking," this second type might be referred to as "elimination if-only thinking." It is the tendency to think that we would be happy if only something in our current conditions or the conditions in the environment could be eliminated. It goes something like this. "I would be O.K. if only I weren't so tired, didn't have this headache, or weren't so hungry." Another version looks to the immediate environment: "I would be just fine if it were warmer in this room, or if it weren't raining today, or if there weren't so many mosquitoes, or if that man over there weren't tapping his foot, or if my partner didn't snore at night."

I know what you are thinking. These are all natural and understandable reactions. You're right! They are, but let's look a little more closely. In each case, a person with this reaction is wishing against the reality of the moment and betting his happiness on the expectation that his wish will come true. Even though we all have done it, this is a fool's wish because the truth is that the condition or the situation we wish didn't exist does, in fact, exist — at least for the time being. Resisting it only undermines our peace of mind and the possibility of enjoying our current experience. I have a little equation for this very human tendency of ours:

The reality of the moment x resistance = suffering!

This doesn't imply that we should powerlessly resign ourselves to an uncomfortable situation. If we can change it (get something to eat if we are hungry) or remove ourselves from it (leave the room where the man is tapping his foot), that's fine; but that's not always possible and we are left to confront the reality of the moment.

I am sure we can all think of occasions in which we have succumbed to this elimination if-only thinking, or have witnessed others fall prey to it. Two instances immediately come to my mind.

I have the wonderful opportunity to lead a lot of workshops all over the country and they are generally held in hotel functions rooms. One of the challenges is to adjust the room temperature so that it is comfortable for the majority of the workshop participants. Frankly, it is not always possible to do that. Personal comfort temperature levels vary considerably. If the room is a little too cool, some number of people become quite upset. As I said above, it is a normal and understandable reaction; but here's the problem. When the elimination if-only thinking takes over ("I would be just fine if only it were warmer in here."), we contract. Our view becomes very limited and we start to miss a good deal of the possibilities inherent in our experience.

I was attending a workshop a number of years ago at Omega Institute, a beautiful learning center in upstate New York.[5] Jon Kabat-Zinn, one of the pioneers in mindfulness work in the United States, was leading the workshop and we had just finished a meditation session.[6] When he asked for questions or comments about the exercise, a woman in the group shared that she "couldn't stand the sound of the birds singing outside—they were just so distracting." Having fallen into elimination if-only thinking, the whole exercise was "ruined" for her. It was humorous to many of us because the singing of the birds seemed so wonderful, but I fully appreciated the nature of her reaction. We can make the presence of anything into a problem!

So how do we deal with this tendency? Another story points us in the direction we will be going. In the mid-1980s I was travelling in Nepal. One morning I hiked a few hours outside Kathmandu to visit a monastery where an Australian Buddhist nun was teaching Western visitors. At the end of her talk, she took questions and an American woman asked for her advice. She said she loved her husband, but "just couldn't stand the way he eats his eggs in the morning." This nun was known for her straightforward and frank talk and her answer was consistent with her reputation. She leaned toward the questioner and replied with a great deal of emphasis, "Well, my dear, you could change your mind about the situation!"

The response drew a big laugh from the audience, but it went right to the heart of the matter. It is an unavoidable part of the human experience to confront situations that are initially uncomfortable for us. In fact, this happens frequently to all of us. How much discomfort we feel, how much suffering, depends to a very large extent on our state of mind. We can become contracted and dominated by that aspect of the situation that we don't like, or we can learn to work with our mind so that our balance, our happiness, is not totally overwhelmed.

As we continue our journey together, we will see how mindfulness enables us to be patient with whatever arises and not "lose it" in the face of uncomfortable conditions. By working with the mind, we will discover our surprising capacities for enduring and keeping open, instead of contracting and closing off to the possibilities of our experience. As a result, we will strengthen the foundation for a happiness that is not so vulnerable to the uncontrollable ebb and flow of the conditions and circumstances we confront.

OBSTACLE THREE:

THE HYPERACTIVITY OF THE BRAIN

The human brain is truly magical. Neuroscientists refer to it as the most complex thing on earth. Within the small space of the upper part of our head, our brains contain approximately 100 billion neurons and each neuron has as many as 10,000 connections with other neurons, resulting in as many neural connections "as there are stars in the sky." It is no wonder that the neuroscientists speak of our brain with awe and reverence.

From the complexity of the human brain arises the beauty and creativity of the human experience. From it emerges art, music and literature, discoveries of all kinds and the precious opportunity to learn in ways that no other living thing can. Having said all that, and without losing any respect for this magical organ that serves us well in so many respects, we must also honestly confront a problem. The brain, at least as we experience it in the modern world, is hyperactive in important respects. We don't have to rely on detailed scientific analysis or explanations to know this. We experience it daily. Put simply, the brain has a great deal of automatic energy that often dominates our consciousness and controls our experience.

I am sure you can think of your own examples of this, but here are just a few: the spinning mind that will not stop playing out its repeating tape loops, the automatic negative messages of self-blame, guilt or shame that hold our attention hostage, the powerful anxious thoughts about possible disasters big and small that capture our attention, the disturbing memories that plunge us back into painful experiences of earlier times, or just the rapid-fire, often somewhat meaningless thoughts that prevent us from keeping our attention where we want it or need it to be.

Needless to say, the hyperactivity of our brain does not serve us well. To be blunt, it is a major obstacle to lasting happiness. It distorts our experience, undermines our ability to make positive choices, separates us from our loved ones and disconnects us from our true selves. If we don't confront it, we will be repeatedly entrapped in the brain's automatic (and often, negative) energies.

Scientists tell us that our species emerged roughly two million years ago. The human brain has continued to evolve from the primitive start of our ancestors, but some brain functions that were so important to the safety of pre-modern human beings have not kept pace with the rapid changes in the human experience over the last several centuries. In a sense, we need to accelerate the evolution of our brains by working more skillfully and conscientiously with the automatic energies of the mind. By doing this, we will solve the problem of the brain's hyperactivity, tap even more fully the capacities of our brain and manifest our best—and truly wonderful—potential as human beings.

OBSTACLE FOUR:

THE MYTHS OF OUR CONDITIONING

From the moment we emerge from the womb, our conditioning begins. (Some researchers believe that our conditioning actually starts earlier, as we are developing inside our mothers' bodies.) From the start, our young brains are absorbing information from our environment, evaluating it and storing substantial portions of it in the form of memory. Our brains are not only storing information; they are literally developing in response to all the information we constantly receive from our environment. As a result, neural connections emerge that "condition" how we see the world and ourselves.

We will explore the impact and operation of this conditioning in detail in later chapters; but suffice it to say here that some of this conditioning does not support our happiness. Not all conditioning is bad. Parts of our conditioning may enable us to be kind or respectful to others, to have a good work ethic, to be sensible about money or to appreciate the wonder of nature; but other aspects can lead to repeated negative messages, harmful emotions and, even for the most "normal" individuals, a distorted view of reality.

Keep in mind, this conditioning starts at the very beginning of our lives, before we are making conscious choices. We are not analytically sorting through all the information our brain is absorbing to determine what serves us well and what doesn't— or what is objectively true and what is not. We are just soaking it all in and storing it in the emerging neural connections we refer to as memory. At the heart of it, the neural connections forming in the brain create filters through which we view and interpret our on-going experience. These filters have a certain bias that has been shaped by the specific nature of our personal experience. In other words, the brain draws conclusions from our experience, gives it a certain meaning, and then has a tendency to react to future events in a way that confirms and strengthens the conclusions shaped by the earlier experience.

The young developing brain makes an effort to appraise the information it is receiving and storing. The trouble is that it often does not get it right. Mistakes are made, especially when it comes to conclusions about ourselves and our relationship to the world. As infants and children, we have this terribly unfortunate tendency to draw negative conclusions about ourselves. If Mommy is frequently irritable, depressed or on edge, if our family members repeatedly discount what we have to say or don't pay any attention to us at all, if Daddy often flies into unpredictable rages, if Mommy and Daddy bicker and fight a lot, we generally take it very personally. As young beings dependant on our parents and other caretakers, we don't have the ability to sort it all out, to analyze the situation and understand the family dynamics that produce such conditions. Instead of realizing the stress and conditions that drive the behaviors of our parents, we draw the instinctive conclusion that it must have something to do with us, that we have done something very wrong, that we're just not good enough or that there is something basically wrong with us.

These negative conclusions may have been a completely understandable reaction of the young brain to a given set of circumstances, but they are generally just plain wrong. Nevertheless, they are stored in our neural connections. They become our personal reality. To make matters worse, because of the tendency of the brain to react to present events according to the meaning given to previous experience, these negative messages are confirmed over and over again as we continue to see the world through the filter of the same old deeply-embedded conclusions and assumptions.

OBSTACLE FIVE:

THE STRESS OF LIFE IN THE 21ST CENTURY

This obstacle is both simple and complex. On one hand, it is self-evident that we live in very stressful times. At every level of our experience, recent trends and developments have added to the stresses we encounter. Even a brief list is impressive indeed. On the international level, there is the spread of terrorism and the proliferation of both nuclear and conventional weapons with devastating destruction potential. Nationally, we see the emergence of a more and more divisive political climate and the increasing imbalance in the distribution of wealth in our country. In our individual states and communities, there is ever-greater difficulty financing and delivering basic services such as quality education and health care, and on the family level, so many of us are intensely stressed by the challenging task of balancing demanding jobs in the fast-paced technology-driven workplace with the responsibilities of our households, children, relationships, elderly parents, finances, etc., etc., etc. Each of us could give our own account of how these and other stressors play out in our lives, but the overwhelming commonality is that our energies, our emotions and our minds often feel overburdened by the pace and complexity of the lives we lead.

Although the nature of this obstacle may be self-evident, how we arrived here is very complex. Trying to make sense of it all would require exhaustive (and exhausting) study of history, politics, economics, religion, psychology and on and on and on. There are, of course, academics and researchers of all types who are pursuing the complexities of our current situation so that we can both learn from our mistakes and make the best decisions possible at all levels of the world community to move in healthy, peaceful and life-sustaining directions. Although we may want to stay interested and involved with this exploration, most of us do not have the time or energy to sort through all these complexities. In the pursuit of a lasting happiness, our task is to accept that, like it or not, the stresses and anxieties of life in the early part of the 21st century are the conditions we face. They are the reality of the moment. Without giving up our hope that they will evolve in a positive direction, we must work with the present conditions in an honest and realistic way.

OBSTACLE SIX:

THE UNAVOIDABLE CHALLENGES OF THE HUMAN CONDITION

E ven if we could wave a magic wand and make all the obstacles mentioned above disappear, we would still confront the unavoidable challenges of being human. In the cardiac rehabilitation classes I taught for a number of years, I always did a brainstorming exercise with the participants. They made lists of what had been stressful in their lives and the same core issues emerged virtually every time: raising children, other family issues, finances, sickness, aging and loss of loved ones. (Fear of one's own death should be on such a list, but we have such a difficult time actually confronting the thought of it that it was not often mentioned.)

Several years ago, a gentleman in one of my classes had the initial impression that stress management meant avoiding our stressors. "We can't avoid our problems by hiding away in a cave somewhere," he said. Even if we tried the cave approach, we would be taking these core issues with us—or most of them, anyway. The simple truth is that this process of being human presents us with significant challenges, some of which are unavoidable. No one is going to escape sickness, aging and death. This sounds like bad news, but it really doesn't have to be. The amount of suffering that we experience as a result of these core issues depends, in large part, on our attitude about them—and we generally have very bad attitudes in the face of them. I am not saying that these challenges will ever rank as our favorite experiences; but we can, slowly, slowly, begin to change our minds about them. In doing so, we can reduce the amount of suffering they cause. Sickness can be a time of slowing down, resting and supporting the magical healing processes of our body. Aging can be graceful and beautiful as we more fully appreciate the blessings of our life and deepen our personal wisdom and spiritual dimension. Even death can be seen more clearly as a natural part of the life cycle that does not have to be feared as it so often is. In many traditions, the dying process and death are seen as great opportunities for learning and liberation.

Here is the basic truth: these core challenges are unavoidable aspects of our human experience, whether we like it or not. If we are truly interested in a durable, lasting happiness, we might spend less effort hoping that they won't happen to us (a futile exercise, of course, because they will) and devote more attention to working with them in a skillful way. In the process, we have the possibility of reducing our discomfort and maintaining our balance through these experiences.

If we bring sustained effort over time, we may even find ourselves in a state of mind that is surprisingly accepting and serene in the middle of even the most dramatic of these core challenges. I know this sounds like a tall order, but it is truly possible. Besides, what is the alternative? By not confronting these challenges directly, by not bringing some effort to changing our minds about them, by not working with them more skillfully, we will be defenseless to the understandable fear they provoke and our happiness will be very fragile indeed.

CONCLUSION:

THE NECESSITY OF TAKING INITIATIVE, OF REALIZING OUR POWER AS CREATORS

We could develop a more extensive accounting of the basic obstacles we face in creating the happiness we deserve. You could probably come up with your own list. Even the brief discussion above, however, leads us to a basic conclusion. If we are serious about experiencing a more stable happiness and lasting joy, if we yearn to live lives consistently energized by love and connection to others, if we aspire to be able to look back at our lives with contentment and satisfaction, if we truly want to maximize this profoundly precious experience of being human, we have to take initiative in ways that we may just be beginning to realize.

This is a hard reality for some. "How can I do more than I already am? I am just getting by now. How can I possibly find more time or energy to do anything else?" Those are fair questions and we will deal with them in detail as we explore this journey together; but the reality is that we must choose: continue the old cycles and patterns that leave us feeling disappointed, disillusioned, depleted and dissatisfied or honestly face the reality of the challenge and begin to move—gently, patiently and with great kindness for ourselves—in a new direction.

This reality, this necessity of taking initiative, doesn't need to be depressing because here is the good news: *It's possible.* It is do-able within the ordinary contexts of our lives. We do not have to abandon our families and jobs and run off to a monastery tucked away somewhere in the Himalayas. We do not even have to go back to school or get another degree. We can begin right where we are now, in this moment, and build on a few modest first steps.

I am not in the business of giving guarantees about what will happen in other people's lives; but I can confidently give you these strong assurances: This process of taking initiative is possible, no matter what your current circumstances are. If you bring whatever conscientious effort is available to you in the context of your life right now, your initiative will move you toward creating the happiness you deserve. I have seen this happen over and over with many individuals just like you and me who are seeking to balance all the ordinary and extraordinary challenges of leading a happy and healthy life.

I'll be even more direct. The question is not whether it can happen in your life. I am confident that it can. The real question is whether you will choose to take the first steps to make it happen. With great respect for the complexities of your life, with a profound belief in your possibilities, I urge you to suspend your disbelief, your fear of disappointment or failure, and just take the first modest steps with me.

As we begin to take initiative, to move in a new direction, it is important that we make small investments in thinking of ourselves as creators. So often, we are blind to our creative power. We are much more apt to see ourselves as helpless, as powerless, or as stressed-out beings who are barely keeping our heads above the water. The truth is that we are creating all the time, moment to moment, with our thoughts, our emotions, our words and our actions. The problem is that much of our creation happens unintentionally, or without awareness, and leads to the same old unsatisfying or even destructive results. We generally do not realize our true creative power—and we find it very difficult to believe in the magnificent possibilities our creativity offers. *A Course in Miracles* succinctly puts it this way:

> Somehow we must develop faith
> And trust in our Self.
> Anything the mind can conceive
> And believe, the mind can achieve.

We are often fearful of thinking of ourselves as creators. It seems like such an awesome responsibility. It is a responsibility, but it is one that we cannot avoid. Whether we realize it or not, we are creators. The issue is whether we can more and more consistently create intentionally, rather than blindly, and thereby give ourselves the chance to make what we create as positive and beautiful as possible. Nelson Mandela spoke so eloquently about this challenge in his 1994 inaugural speech:

> Our deepest fear is not that we are inadequate. Our deepest fear is that we are powerful beyond measure. It is our light, not our darkness, that frightens us.
>
> We ask ourselves, who am I to be brilliant, gorgeous, talented and fabulous. Actually, who are you not to be. You are a child of God. Your playing small doesn't serve the world. There is nothing enlightened about shrinking so that other people won't feel insecure around you.[7]

It is difficult to believe in our true power as creators, but philosophers, teachers and highly realized beings in all the wisdom traditions throughout the centuries have consistently sought to remind us of this power. Even the latest neuroscience research is confirming our power as creators when it comes to our happiness. Richard Davidson, a professor at the University of Wisconsin and a leading researcher on the impact of meditation and mindfulness practices on the brain, acknowledges that there are varying trait levels of happiness. He emphasizes, however, that happiness—and other valued qualities such as compassion—can be regarded as the product of skills that are nurtured and enhanced by mental training. In other words, happiness is not just an inherent trait in a particular individual; it is also the result of strengthening specific skills and cultivating positive qualities through such practices as mindfulness.[8]

I am not asking you take anyone else's word for it. I am simply asking you to open up your imagination to the possibility that wise beings throughout the ages—and, increasingly, leading neuroscientists—are on to something, that they speak the truth and that the truth applies to each of us.

If the concept of your creative power is too challenging, or seems too removed from your life right now, that's O.K. Just tuck it away somewhere in the back of your mind and let it rest there for the time being. It may become much more meaningful to you as we share this journey. The immediate task is to begin to define our strategy, our plan, for creating the lasting happiness we all deserve.

This brings us directly to the central theme of this book: the path of mindfulness. In the next chapter, we will explore mindfulness in detail. Suffice it to say here, it is not something that only a few special or talented individuals can experience. It is available to us all. We don't have to create it; it already exists. We simply have to open our hearts and our minds to its spacious qualities. This takes understanding and practice, of course; but it is truly possible for all of us to experience a quality of mindfulness that manifests our creative power. No matter what your life is like at the present moment, no matter what your circumstances, mindfulness can bring increased clarity and insight into your life. It is like a brilliant gem hidden in our consciousness by layers of conditioning, habits and old patterns. As we begin to rediscover its shining quality, it lights up our lives and illuminates the lasting happiness we so desperately seek.

CHAPTER 2

Mindfulness: A Path and a Practice

BEGINNING TO BUILD A VISION OF MINDFULNESS

The concept of mindfulness has entered broadly into the mainstream of our culture. It is taught in hospitals all over the country as a part of cardiac rehabilitation, wellness and other programs. In the areas of psychology and counseling, it has been integrated into a number of treatment modalities, such as dialectical behavioral therapy, mindfulness-based cognitive therapy for depression, and acceptance and commitment therapy. Mindfulness-based stress reduction has been taught to thousands of individuals at the pioneering program founded by Jon Kabat-Zinn almost thirty years ago at the University of Massachusetts Medical Center in Worcester. Numerous universities, colleges, continuing education programs, retreat centers and other organizations offer courses and workshops that explore aspects of mindfulness.

As you might expect, with all this activity by so many diverse organizations and individuals related to mindfulness, many definitions and concepts about it have emerged. It is important to remember that all these ideas about mindfulness are not mindfulness itself. They are not the state of consciousness, the quality of being, that we are seeking to rediscover. Nevertheless, descriptions or ways of thinking about mindfulness are useful signposts, guides to accessing an awareness that is our birthright, so let's explore various ideas about mindfulness and begin to build a vision that we can refine as we continue our journey.

Although there are meditative and contemplative traditions in the West,[9] the wave of mindfulness teachings that has washed over Western countries the past several decades originated in Eastern cultures. Mindfulness is at the heart of Buddhist practices that have been taught for more than 2,500 years in many areas of Asia. The term mindfulness is a translation of *sati*, a word in the Pali language used by early Buddhist teachers. Sati refers generally to awareness, attention and remembering. Clinical psychologist Christopher Germer writes that "mindful moments" are, among other things:

- **Non-conceptual.** Mindfulness is awareness without absorption in our thought process.
- **Present-centered.** Mindfulness is always in the present moment. Thoughts about our experience are one step removed from the present moment.
- **Nonjudgmental.** Awareness cannot occur freely if we would like our experience to be other than it is.
- **Intentional.** Mindfulness always includes an intention to direct attention somewhere. Returning attention to the present moment gives mindfulness continuity over time.[10]

Germer's descriptions of mindful moments are helpful and will be a useful reference as we explore mindfulness, but they are a lot to take in at one time. Jon Kabat-Zinn, who has made such a significant contribution to the understanding of mindfulness in the West, has a short definition. He describes mindfulness simply as "moment-to-moment awareness."[11] The highly respected Vietnamese teacher Thich Nhat Hanh says that mindfulness is "the miracle which can call back in a flash our dispersed mind and restore it to wholeness so that we can live each minute of life."[12]

Even these shorter descriptions may seem too abstract. One practical way to think about mindfulness is to consider an opposite state of being, what I will call "automatic pilot." In our car, we can sometimes drive for miles on automatic pilot, without really being aware of what we are doing. In the same way, with many activities, we may not really be "present", moment-to-moment, for much of our lives. We can often be miles away, drifting aimlessly or largely caught up in the automatic energies of our distracted brain without really being aware of our state of mind, body or emotions. On automatic pilot, we are much more likely to act reflexively and without much true awareness, driven by old patterns or habits. Events around us, thoughts, feelings and old memories of past experiences (many of which are lurking just below the surface of our normal consciousness and are therefore not obvious to us) can trigger old habits of negative thinking, as well as ineffective, unskillful and unloving speech and behavior.

As we shall see, mindfulness techniques enable us to switch out of automatic pilot mode and into a state of consciousness that is more aware of the whole spectrum of our state of being and the circumstances around us. By conscientiously practicing mindfulness techniques, we gradually become more able to respond to situations with choice, rather that just repeating old patterns and habits. We become more intentional, and less habitual, beings. We do that, in part, by switching off the automatic pilot and becoming more aware of what is going on in our thoughts and emotions. As we become more skillful, we find that we can identify the old patterns of the automatic pilot mode and intentionally make a different choice that better serves our happiness.

Making healthier and more skillful choices for ourselves supports our goal of creating a lasting happiness, but there is another aspect of switching out of the automatic pilot mode that profoundly enriches us. By being more present to our moment-to-moment experience, we connect more deeply with it. How many times have we all driven through a beautiful landscape but only barely noticed it because our minds were distracted by planning or worrying, or we may have sat with the intention of watching the sunset but have missed its true majesty because we were distracted by idle conversation. To draw on an old cliché, do we really stop and smell the roses? If we did, if we were more aware of the rose's subtle colors, shapes and smells, our experience of it would be much different than if we only half-noticed the flower in passing.

By switching out of the automatic pilot mode and into a more mindful state of awareness, we connect more deeply to this precious experience of being human. As we become more mindful, slowly and with practice, we discover beauty and magic that simply was not apparent to us before. In the process, we find inspiration about our lives that was missing as we drifted through so many of our days on autopilot.

Teacher and writer Jack Kornfield playfully refers to another aspect of more fully connecting with our present experience. He says that anyone interested in love should be interested in being more fully aware in the present moment, because we can love only in the present. Thoughts about love in the past are nostalgia and anticipation of love in the future is fantasy.[13] To put this another way, we cannot love fully—or be truly filled up with the magnificent feeling of love we all yearn for—if our minds are distracted from the present moment by thoughts of the past or future.

It is sometimes said that whenever we switch out of the automatic pilot mode and open to more awareness, we are tapping into our higher state of consciousness. It sounds a little grandiose at first, but think about it. When we are operating largely on automatic pilot, we are often caught up in a distracted or spinning mind and driven by old patterns and habits, whether they serve us well or not. If we are able to notice that we are caught in autopilot and open our awareness to a more full recognition of our state of being in the present moment, it makes real sense that we have, in that simple act, elevated our state of consciousness.

There are many shorthand references to mindfulness by teachers and writers. Gurdieff referred to it as "self-remembering". Krishnamurti spoke of mindfulness as "bare attention". As we begin to practice mindfulness in the practical aspects of our every day lives, we can think of mindfulness as *taking a second look at our first thought, emotion or impulse.* Our thoughts, emotions and impulses have a way of really grabbing our attention, narrowing our focus and often producing the same old behavior that undermines our happiness. By recognizing the momentary grip that first thought, emotion or impulse has on our attention and by opening to a larger, more spacious awareness in that second look, we dramatically increase our chances of seeing the situation more clearly and making choices that serve us well. Again, we are bringing more intentionality into our lives and connecting more deeply with our experience—we are acting from a higher state of consciousness. When we are able to do this more consistently, love, the sunset, the rose all become more incredible, more magical.

All of these ideas and concepts about mindfulness are just words on a page until we begin to discover mindfulness for ourselves. Nevertheless, as I said earlier, they are important guides. They open up our imagination to a different way of being and our imagination is an important door to the experience of precious new realities. In addition to the concepts about mindfulness, there are two overarching themes that are useful as we begin to explore the area. We turn to those next.

MINDFULNESS AS A PATH OF HEALING

In addition to our desire for happiness, we all, each and every human being, share another grand commonality. We each enter this world with a radiance that is profoundly beautiful. As newborns, we are beings intensely present to our moment-to-moment experience. We are new lives full of potential and possibilities. Despite these marvelous qualities and the wonderful state of openness we bring into this world, we begin to encounter the startling and sometimes harsh conditions of our environment. Even in the most loving households, our parents or other caretakers are not perfect. They are reacting to their own stressors and making moment-to-moment decisions about our care when often there are no clear answers about the right thing to do under the circumstances at hand. Furthermore, as we all know, home environments often are not consistently loving or affirming. The stress of the moment, or the conditioning of a lifetime, can be overwhelming, causing parents to say and do hurtful things to their children that, in their better moments, they never intended.

These gaps, both large and small, in being nurtured, in being affirmed and valued, are painful and difficult to bear, especially as a defenseless infant or small child. As a result, in a basic reaction to protect herself, the child begins to contract. You can see that in our everyday experience as adults. When we are afraid or startled, when someone is unkind to us, we contract or tighten. When a baby or young child isn't nurtured, she is in a very fearful and painful place. In fact, unlike most adult situations, it is a life-and-death matter. If the caretaker doesn't nurture the child, she could actually die—and there is an instinctive knowing of that. With the fear and resulting contraction, the child begins to close herself off to aspects of her true, radiant nature.

Psychologist and writer John Welwood describes the process as follows:

> . . . The child is like an open hand that gradually starts to contract and close.
>
> Although clenching the hand into a fist may be a fitting response to immediate threat, it would obviously be inappropriate to walk around that way for the rest of our life. Yet this is exactly what happens in our psyche! Our first response to emotional pain is to flinch, which is not a problem in and of itself. But then we start to take refuge in this contraction, and identify with it. It feels safer to be a closed fist than a vulnerable open hand. This protective tightening becomes installed in our body/mind as a set of chronic, rigid defenses that cut us off from our feelings and thus shut down our capacity to respond to life freely and openly. In our attempt to say no to the pain, we wind up saying no to ourselves instead. In this way, *we inflict on ourselves the core wound*

*that will haunt us the rest of our lives: We start to
separate from our own being.* (Emphasis in the
original.)[14]

Welwood goes on to say that this separation from our true
nature leads to distorted ideas and images about who we are,
false identities that we increasingly believe in as we get older. He
refers to this false self as "a soul-cage, which prevents us from
knowing who we really are or living freely and expansively."[15]

The teachings and literature of many psychological and
spiritual traditions discuss at great length this separation from
our true nature and the pain and suffering of believing in false
identities. Although it might be interesting, we don't have to delve
into long discussions or do exhaustive research of the writings.
Simply stop for a moment, take a deep breath and think about
a baby you have watched, maybe your own child or someone
else's. Imagine that she is seven to eight months old, rested, fed
and is crawling around the safe environment of her bedroom.
She is fascinated by a bit of fuzz on the floor or her favorite
toy as she explores her space with such great enthusiasm and
curiosity. She takes delight in the simplest things. Allow your
imagination to open to those qualities that are so obvious: the
radiance, the joy and the full presence to moment-to-moment
experience. These qualities cannot be faked at that age. She
doesn't wake up in the morning and say to herself, "I am really
going to put on a good face for Mommy and Daddy today!" The
qualities are a reflection of her true nature before the inevitable
conditioning results in a separation from the essence of who she
is.

How much do you experience those qualities—delight,
radiance, joy, full presence—in your own life on a daily basis?
If the answer is not much, or not as much as you would like,
you can bet that is the result of the process Welwood and many
other writers describe: the separation from our true nature as
a defense against the fear and pain we have all experienced in
growing into our lives.

Many years ago, I heard that the Catholic theologian Thomas Merton had this to say about the separation from self:

> Of what avail is it that we can travel to the moon if we can't cross the abyss that separates us from ourselves. This is the most important journey. Without it, all the rest is useless.

Mindfulness offers us a path to "cross the abyss that separates us from ourselves," to heal the wounds of past experiences and to break the persistent and painful grip of false identities. As we develop mindfulness and open to a more full awareness of our present-moment experience, old myths that have housed and protected our false identities begin to dissolve. We see them more clearly and are not fooled. By recognizing them for what they actually are, we begin the process of weakening their hold on our awareness. Over time, the mere notice of these false identities renders them powerless. In a very real sense, by identifying the myths we carry about ourselves and our place in the world, we begin the liberating process of re-connecting with the radiance of our true nature.

Once again, I know this can all sound grandiose and a bit overwhelming. I know what I thought when I began this work years ago and I can almost hear what you are thinking as you read this. "I am not sure I believe in my personal radiance. I don't really know what 'my true nature' is and I have a great deal of anxiety about facing 'my identities,' false or otherwise. Even if I did have the energy for that, I wouldn't have a clue as to where to begin."

If those thoughts, or something like them, are rambling around in your head, take a deep breath, relax—and don't worry about it! Just know that the path of mindfulness, as a path of healing, offers nothing short of liberation from false identities and false messages about who we are, as well as from the pain and confusion that inevitably comes with them. But no one achieves this liberation all at once. We can begin slowly, paying attention to what we can do right here and now. If we dare to contemplate this grand aspiration of deep healing, we can take comfort in the realization that we don't have to know what the whole journey will look or feel like when we begin. All we have to do is to take the first modest steps. As a friend of mine once said, all we have to do is keep picking up our feet and putting them down. Each step will lead to the next and, before we know it, we will have traveled quite a distance. Along the way, we will gradually accumulate amazing experiences that will illuminate the path yet to be traveled.

MINDFULNESS AS A PRACTICE

As I have said earlier, mindfulness is a state of awareness that is our birthright. We don't have to create it because it already exists. Yet throughout the teachings on mindfulness, the word "practice" repeatedly arises. In fact, in the meditation traditions from which mindfulness emerges, references are consistently made to "meditation practice" and the importance of bringing dedication to "the practice".

Throughout this book, I will emphasize the necessity of practice. This can be very confusing. If mindfulness already exists and it is my birthright, why do I have to devote so much energy to practicing something? Years ago, I heard Thich Nhat Hanh's straightforward answer to this question. He said we have spent so much time over the years of our lifetime falling asleep that we have to practice, over and over again, "falling awake".

Mindfulness can be thought of as awakened awareness. Jack Kornfield reminds us of this by referring to the first encounters with the Buddha:

> A story is told of the Buddha when he was wandering in India shortly after his enlightenment. He was encountered by several men who recognized something quite extraordinary about this handsome prince now robed as a monk. Stopping to inquire, they asked, 'Are you a god?' 'No,' he answered. 'Well, are you a deva or an angel?' 'No.' he replied. 'Well, are you some kind of wizard or magician?' 'No.' 'Are you a man?' 'No.' They were perplexed.

Finally, they asked, 'Then what are you?' He replied
simply, 'I am awake.' The word Buddha means to
awaken. How to awaken is all he taught.[16]

Why have we so consistently fallen asleep? Why does so
much of the human condition reflect behavior that is driven by
old patterns and habits that are ineffective, unhealthy and even
destructive to self and others? Why do we operate so frequently
on the automatic pilot mode instead of from a consciousness that
is more spacious and truly aware? There is no short answer, and
we are not going to delve deeply into those questions here; but we
have already touched on some of the factors. The conditioning
we experience as we grow into our lives, the contractions that
occur as we are confronted with the unavoidable fears and
anxieties of being human, the false identities that emerge in our
best effort to adapt to the challenges of this life, all are a part of
falling asleep to the spaciousness and openness of our awakened
consciousness.

Moreover, we know from neuroscience that our brain
develops in response to the anxieties and fears that cause us to
contract from the spaciousness of our basic nature. In a very
real sense, the contractions are recorded and stored in neural
firing patterns in our brains. As the contractions are repeated
over the course of years, those neural firing patterns become
stronger and stronger. The stronger they become, the more
likely they are to activate in the future, causing the patterns of
contraction to happen more and more frequently so that they
dominate our experience in important ways. If you think of each
such contraction, each activation of stronger and stronger neural
firing patterns, as a kind of "falling asleep" to the spaciousness
of our awakened consciousness, you begin to get the idea of why
it takes so much practice to once again "fall awake".

Fortunately, we don't have to understand the complex
"why's" of our condition. If we can honestly acknowledge that
we are frequently not operating at our full potential, that we are
often on automatic pilot mode, that we don't always behave in
a way that is consistent with out best intention or our personal

wisdom, then we can start from there and begin to practice "falling awake" through the path of mindfulness.

Like any practice, an important part of mindfulness practice involves skill building. There are many distinct skills we will explore as we proceed further, but we might think of them generally as skills that create supportive conditions for opening up to our innate spacious awareness. For example, our awakened awareness is sometimes described as having the clarity of pure, still water. The difficulty is that the sand and mud at the bottom of the water is constantly being stirred up by the on-going chatter of our minds, chatter that is often contracting, distracted and out of our conscious control.

The nature of the water—like the nature of our awakened awareness—is still, pure and clear; but we can't experience that because the constant swirl of the sand and mud is making it look cloudy and opaque. Once the swirling sand and mud settle, it is absolutely obvious, once again, that the nature of the water is clear. Following this metaphor, the skill of quieting the mind stops (or at least lessens) the constant mental activity, making the clarity of natural awareness more obvious—and more accessible. This skill creates supportive conditions for experiencing a state of awareness that already exists. But guess what (and I am sure you have already guessed), quieting the mind is a skill that takes practice.

If you stop and think about it, skill building through practice is familiar in one way or another to most of us. We practice learning new tasks in our jobs, or a sport, a musical instrument, a hobby, a craft, an art or a game. Mindfulness practice, like any new practice, requires the balance of two important qualities: patience and conscientiousness. We are anxious and insecure when we are first learning the skills of a new job or profession. We are clumsy and awkward on the tennis court initially (and from my experience as a tennis player, maybe for years). We don't immediately sound very musical when we begin to learn an instrument. So we have to nurture patience, patience with ourselves and with the process of learning. That's not easy, is it? We can so easily get frustrated with the process. The progress just isn't happening fast enough. The skills seem so difficult to master. Worse yet, we have this nagging fear that we are just not smart, talented or capable enough to do it anyway. Patience helps us endure through all of that, to keep plugging away despite our frustrations, fears and insecurities.

Conscientiousness is the other half of the equation. Although we need to be patient with the process and with ourselves, conscientiousness is the salve that soothes the frustrations we often experience with building any new skill. When we conscientiously apply ourselves, we more readily see the progress that can be made. We are motivated, and even excited, by the results of our consistent effort; and this, in turn, makes it easier to be patient and bear the challenges of the whole new foundation we are building.

I am blessed to be married to a very talented pianist. My wife can sit down at the piano and play the most wonderful music without any sheet of music in front of her. People hearing her do this will frequently ask, "Where did you learn that piece? It was so beautiful!" The truth is that she didn't learn it anywhere. She improvised it on the spot; it just flowed out of her. Needless to say, she didn't just sit down in front of those eighty-eight keys one day and have that magically happen. She began with basic exercises, learning simple scales, and then chords, and finally progressing to songs and compositions. Over the years of practice, she developed a vast array of musical skills that involve physical dexterity, memory and deep understanding of music so that it all became a part of who she is. The result: music flows out of her in a way that is spontaneous and effortless (and almost inconceivable to those of us who are not practiced musicians).

The point is this. Not all of us have the innate talent to be the kind of musician my wife is; but we all have the ability, each at our own pace and in our own way, to build the skills leading to greater mindfulness in our lives. If we bring some conscientious attention to the process, whatever that might be within the context of our lives right now, and are patient with ourselves and the results, we will develop the skills we need. Over time, they will not take so much effort. Like my wife and her ability to create music, they will just be part of how we are in the world.

There is one other quality we need to bring to this skill-building process: kindness for ourselves. In the Buddhist tradition of mindfulness, it is said that there are two essential wings supporting a meaningful mindfulness practice. The first is the more obvious: the wing of attention or presence. The equally essential other wing is usually translated as "heart." By heart is meant kindness for ourselves. This second wing is so important in our culture. We are blessed to have been born in the United States. Although our country certainly does not get everything right, we have so many freedoms and opportunities. We are known for being a very productive country; but this has a shadow side to it. Our productivity rests, in part, on our competitiveness and our competitiveness leads to a pervasive tendency to judge others and to judge ourselves. It starts so early, doesn't it? When did you get potty-trained? When did you start walking? When did you learn to talk? What kind of grades did you get? Are you as smart as everyone else? Are you a good athlete? Do you have the right body shape? Do you drive the right car? Do you have a prestigious job? Do you have as nice a house as your neighbors?

The comparisons (that is, judgments) go on and on and on. We can't avoid them and we can't insulate ourselves from them. Others' judgments of us—and often, our anticipation of others' judgments of us—become our self-judgments. The wing of kindness is so essential because, without it, we will not be able to look inside and face directly all the harsh judgments about ourselves. Without being able to confront these negative self-judgments, we will simply continue to play out their harmful effects and never be in a position to truly experience the happiness we deserve.

There are many other reasons why kindness for ourselves is so important, but here is just one more. As we begin with the first baby steps to a more mindful way of being, we will stumble and fall over and over again. We will start off the day intending to be more mindful, to take a second look at our first impulses, and somewhere along the way, often at the end of the day, we will suddenly realize that we have been operating on automatic pilot all day and have not been at all aware of our practice. It frequently takes much longer than just a day to once again "fall awake." Years ago I owned a small business. I distinctly remember sitting at my desk one morning, paperwork scattered everywhere and lots of people wanting my attention, and realizing that I had been operating fully on automatic pilot mode for weeks. The thought loudly bursting into my head at that moment was simply "Where have I been?" The sudden realization was that I had been so caught up in the press of day-to-day affairs that I had not really been aware of what I was doing—or how I was doing it. I had not been very aware of my own experience.

Put very bluntly, as we begin our mindfulness practice, we will forget or slip over and over again! It's not a crime. It is not because we are not capable, or smart or conscientious. It is simply inevitable! It is exactly at those moments, when we realize that we have once again fallen asleep, that we need to practice kindness for ourselves. Without kindness, we too easily fall into old negative messages about ourselves that drain away our courage, our patience and our conscientiousness. Without kindness, these old negative messages start becoming a self-fulfilling prophecy. We get down on ourselves and think we will not be able to make any progress. This undermines our energy and, before you know it, the old messages have dominated our experience and we are not making any progress because we are exerting very little effort.

Kindness for ourselves is a very different choice. Kindness allows us to see forgetting as an inevitable part of being human. Kindness offers the possibility of seeing that we have fallen asleep once again not as a failure, but as an opportunity for "falling awake." Making the choice for kindness to ourselves enables us to see more clearly one of the grand commonalties we share with all human beings, our imperfection. There is a wonderful quote from an ancient teacher referred to as the Third Zen Patriarch. He supposedly said that "living in balance, in harmony, requires a freedom from anxiety about our own imperfections."[17] I love his advice because it so succinctly reminds us that to experience a lasting happiness in our lives, we need to drop all the self-judgments, loosen from our anxiety, and with a full heart realize more deeply that our imperfections, our differences from others, are a universal and unavoidable part of the human experience.

Over time, we can even greet the forgettings, the giving-in to old patterns and habits, the arisings of negative thoughts and emotions, with a smile—a big friendly smile that simply recognizes the imperfection we share with all other humans on the planet. As the Sufi poet Rumi wrote centuries ago:

> The dark thought, the shame, the malice,
> Meet them at the door laughing,
> And invite them in.
>
> Be grateful for whoever comes,
> Because each has been sent
> As a guide from beyond. [18]

With kindness for ourselves, we will be much more likely to maintain the patience and conscientiousness necessary for the beginning stages of our mindfulness practice. Still, we need to be clear about what fuels our practice, what motivates us. The motivation in other types of practice is often instinctual. With our jobs and professions, we work through the mistakes and inevitable challenges of the learning curve, at least in part, because we need to earn a living and support ourselves or our families. With sports, musical instruments and games, we hang in there with the awkwardness and the less-than-outstanding performances because of a passion for the activity itself. Here, we have a much grander aspiration, an aspiration that enhances the effectiveness of every other practice or endeavor in our lives: the return to the spacious awareness that is our birthright and the creation of the lasting, durable happiness we deserve.

Please, don't for a moment think that this aspiration is selfish. Although it may be seen as initially self-oriented, it is by no means selfish. In fact, we may be able to intensify our motivation to practice mindfulness if we realize its broader implications. The Buddhist teacher Sakyong Mipham Rinpoche reminds us that our personal work to create a stronger foundation for a lasting happiness directly contributes to the benefit of others.

> The best thing for society, even in an everyday situation, is the complete fulfillment and happiness of the individual. If we want a world that generates love and happiness, we need to start watering the seeds of peace and stability in our own mind.[19]

THE SEVEN STEPS TO MINDFULNESS

I have had the wonderful blessing of introducing mindfulness to thousands of individuals in cardiac rehabilitation classes, in wellness and stress management programs, in groups of cancer patients and to my clients in counseling sessions. In addition, I have had the opportunity to lead workshops for several thousand more counselors, social workers, psychologists, nurses and other health professionals all over the country who are devoted to refining the quality of mindfulness in their lives and clarifying how they can support others' practice of mindfulness. Through these experiences I have learned so much from both the lay individuals and the health professionals. I have seen the pure delight on people's faces as they realize, often for the first time, that there are alternatives to repeating the same old patterns that don't feel good and that undermine their happiness and well-being. I have heard about the joys of treating themselves and others better through the practice of mindfulness. I have experienced the truly beautiful shifts in individuals' presence as they literally change their minds about how they bring themselves to their lives. But I also have witnessed, from individuals as diverse as you could imagine in age, background, education and situation, the significant challenges in integrating mindfulness into one's life.

Despite my faith in mindfulness as a path of healing, as a vehicle for creating lasting happiness, I am not at all naïve about the rigors of this journey. In fact, as a result of my experience with thousands of individuals, I have become more and more convinced that we must continue to clarify and refine what it is we are trying to do. All the nice definitions and concepts discussed above are useful guides or signposts, as I have said. They often describe a state of being, but they don't really help us understand what we might do to access and cultivate that quality of being, or they are a shorthand description of a technique that doesn't leave us with a full picture of the process.

The seven steps to mindfulness that we will explore in this book have emerged from the experiences I have had sitting with and teaching all the wonderful people referred to above. The steps also reflect, of course, my own practice over almost thirty years, and the blessings of guidance and wisdom I have received from my own teachers during that time.

The seven steps to mindfulness are designed to help you discover your own practice and to nurture mindfulness in your own life. They consider both the skills that support a mindful way of being and the obstacles that undermine it. There are many writers and teachers in the area of mindfulness. If they have authentically explored this area and integrated mindfulness into their lives, they all have useful guidance to offer. Without detracting from the insights of others, my intent in developing the seven steps is to provide a clear, down-to-earth outline for exploring your own path, right now, in the context of your own full and often very busy life.

The seven steps are interdependent. What I mean by that is that they all support each other. The development of each of the steps strengthens the development of all the others. To put that another way, your work on any of the individual steps both has value in its own right and brings you naturally to a deeper connection with all the other steps. In the best of worlds, the seven steps can be woven together in a fine and beautiful tapestry that reflects all your effort to bring more mindfulness into your life and create the lasting happiness you deserve.

If you find the seven steps interesting, my hope is that you don't race through them. This is not a novel with a fascinating plot line that carries you quickly from page one to the end. Although this might be classified as a self-help book, it is not intended to be another quick cure or a short-term diet. As I have said a number of times already, our aspiration is much bigger than that. We are opening up the possibility of re-connecting with our own spacious innate awareness, with our own radiant true nature. We are exploring the possibility of creating a truly durable happiness. We are seeking to create meaningful change for the rest of our lives, change that will enhance in profound ways the preciousness of this incredible human experience.

If all of this is what you really want, I hope that you will move slowly through the seven steps. Spend time with each one of them. Think about them in the in-between spaces of your day, on the drive home or the walk to your office or job site. Talk about them with others. In short, practice and try to strengthen your connection with each step. In doing so, be assured that you are building a foundation that is increasingly solid and strong, not only for the remaining steps, but for whatever arises in the rest of your life.

Finally, before you go any further, I want to say how much respect I have for the fact that you even have this book in front of you—that you, in your own way, are committed to your growth, that you have the courage to face your imperfections and that you have the wisdom to realize that there may be something still to learn about your mind, your emotions and your life. What a magnificent being you already are!

CHAPTER 3

Step One: Nurturing the Witness...
Opening to Spaciousness

THE AUTOMATIC ENERGY OF THE MIND

I don't get sick that often; but this past winter I caught a nasty flu bug that brought with it the usual lovely symptoms: fever, chills, headaches, body aches, etc. One afternoon in the middle of it all, I was lying down, trying to take a nap. As I settled into bed and closed my eyes, thoughts of a retirement party for a colleague I hoped to attend over the weekend popped into my head. A stream of thoughts followed. "Oh, the party is potluck. I'm not going to feel like making anything the way I feel now. Well, maybe I can pick up a pie at that pie place at the Public Market in Portland. Wait a minute . . . I don't think that pie place is there anymore. I wonder what happened to it? It seems like there are a lot of shops that come and go at the Public Market. I sure hope they are doing O.K. It would be a real shame if that wonderful facility can't make it financially."

I was trying to take a nap, for heaven's sake, and all of the sudden I am analyzing the financial stability of the Portland Public Market! I didn't intend any of this mind chatter. In fact, my intention was exactly the opposite. I lay down for the purpose of drifting off into a nap and getting some rest. The point is the obvious one: there is often a constant stream of thoughts flowing through our minds that we are not consciously directing. This stream arises from the automatic energy of the mind. My first meditation teacher compared this automatic energy to having two monkeys residing in the back of your head, relentlessly fidgeting and chattering away. The monkeys have a mind of their own that isn't easily controlled by our intention.

In the Buddhist tradition, the mind is sometimes compared to a wild horse that is very hard to tame. It is always going its own way. Sometimes the mind starts running so fast that we have a hard time slowing it down. Other times, when we want it to move swiftly, it walks slowly. Or it gallops in exactly the opposite direction from the way we want it to go.

Neuroscientists refer to the brain as "an anticipation machine," always scanning our environment, referring to the past and looking to what might happen in the future. In fact, on a more technical level, there is actually a level of noise that is constantly being generated by our brains. Harvard Medical School Professor John Ratey describes it this way:

> During both waking and sleeping, there is an ongoing din in the cortex (of the brain). Neurons are constantly interacting with each other, even if they are not currently being called upon to perform a specific duty. This 'noise' is not random, however. Rodolfo Llinas at New York University made the remarkable discovery that all areas of the cortex emit a steady level of noise, or oscillation, at a frequency of 40 cycles per second (40 Hz).[20]

In an article entitled "The Benefits of Mindfulness," the Harvard Women's Health Watch referred to this automatic energy of mind by asking the following questions:

> If a high-tech device could tune into your mind occasionally throughout the day, would it receive a smooth signal of your mind fully engaged in what you're doing? Or would it likely pick up static? Perhaps your attention jumping from one thing to another? Fretting over the future or second-guessing

the past? Half-listening while silently remarking on another's words?[21]

I am sure you could identify your own example of the automatic energy of the mind. Possibly it is the spinning mind that just keeps jumping from one thought to another, or the specific tape loop of an old message that plays over and over again, or the anxious thought that will not stop repeating itself, or the details of a plan that are repeatedly spelled out and on and on and on. The stream of thoughts that often flows through our minds, without our intent and seemingly beyond much of our control, has as many variations as there are moments in the day. Much of this automatic activity is not useful or terribly interesting. As a friend of mine once said, "If my automatic thoughts were a movie, I would get up and walk out!"

If we stop and think about it, we usually know when we are not fully connecting with our present experience because our mind is distracted by, or caught in, the automatic energy of our mind and emotion. Those moments might include eating without much awareness of what we are putting in our mouths (and without really tasting the food), rushing by beautiful scenery without noticing it, only partially listening to someone because the mind is distracted by other thoughts, or ignoring signals of stress, discomfort or tension in the body.

It is important to recognize that this automatic energy generated by our brains is "pre-intentional." Because the brain is hard-wired to always be scanning our environment for possible dangers or risks, it is constantly taking in information from our senses, evaluating the information by comparing it with memories of earlier experience, alerting the rest of the body and often motivating behavior. The truth is that this process goes on whether we are paying any attention to it or not—and generally we are not consciously aware of it. As a result of this scanning, alerting and motivating process, the brain gets ahead of our intention.

We recognize that when we "get triggered" and act in a way that is not consciously thought out or chosen. We don't wake up in the morning and *intend* to feel dread or anxiety about the busy day we have ahead of us. We don't intend to spark the brushfire of aggravation that sweeps through us because our spouse or partner has done something around that house that doesn't meet our expectations. We don't intend to yell at the kids because they're just being kids and not paying much attention to the adult timetable for getting to work or school. We don't intend to fly off the handle or even slip into road rage if another driver cuts us off at an intersection. These internal processes literally happen to us and the reactions that follow happen to us; we don't plan them out. Of course, that doesn't mean that we aren't responsible for our behavior. We are; but it is important to know that these pre-intentional reactions are a result of the brain's automatic energy getting ahead of the more thoughtful, reflective and logical processes of the brain.

In order to live in a more mindful way and cultivate the happiness we deserve, we need to nurture the ability to pull ourselves out of the stream of automatic thoughts flowing through our minds. We need to be able to catch up with the pre-intentional reactions that sweep away our best intentions, undermine our experience in the moment and often result in ineffective, unskillful and even harmful behavior. In a very real sense, we need to begin reclaiming control of our minds.

THE WITNESS AND THE CIRCLE OF LIBERATION

Working more skillfully with the automatic energies generated by our brains begins with a notion that at first seems revolutionary, namely, that we can have a thought and notice it at the same time (or, at least very close to the same time). Often our thoughts fill up our whole consciousness, leaving no room for seeing the thoughts from a larger, more spacious awareness. In this first step to mindfulness, we are going to nurture what I will refer to as "the witness." We are going to practice switching out of the automatic pilot mode, loosening the grip the endless stream of thoughts has on our awareness and watching what is going on in our mind from a larger perspective. We could talk about the witness by giving lengthy descriptions, but it is much more useful to begin immediately creating an experience. So let's turn to the Circle of Liberation.

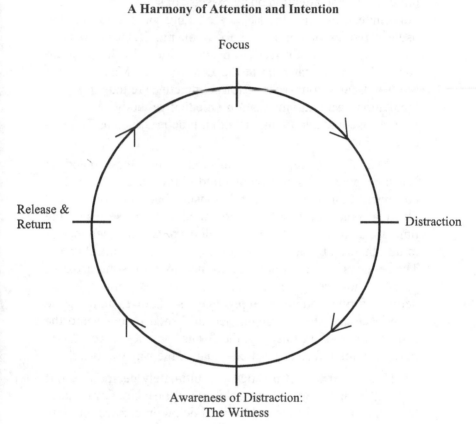

The Circle of Liberation
A Harmony of Attention and Intention

Focus

Release &
Return

Distraction

Awareness of Distraction:
The Witness

Focus – on a task, your surroundings, the breath

Distraction – by a thought, worry, emotion or sensation

Awareness of Distraction – noticing the mind has drifted

Release & Return – letting go of distraction with patience and kindness for self and simply returning to focus

The Circle of Liberation is a template my wife and I designed when we first started teaching mindfulness and meditation practices many years ago. It is useful as a guide for both formal and informal mindfulness practice. What do I mean by formal practice? In formal practice, we are concentrating all our energies and attention on an exercise of some sort to nurture mindfulness. In other words, we are taking some time from the usual activities of our life to focus on mindfulness practice. Formal practice is not just sitting meditation. In the program started by Jon Kabat-Zinn at the University of Massachusetts Medical Center, four types of formal practice are taught: sitting meditation, walking meditation, meditative body scans and yoga. One could add to that list other practices such as T'ai Chi and Qi Gong.

What do you suppose is informal mindfulness practice? Informal practice is nurturing mindfulness in all the rest of our lives. Can you see the relationship between formal and informal practice? If we are motivated and can set aside the time, we do formal practices to develop a personal experience of mindfulness and, in a sense, to develop the skills of mindfulness. The sessions of formal practice are not done for some isolated purpose, however. They are done so that we build a bridge between formal and informal practice—so that we can bring the experience and skills strengthened in formal practice into the rest of our lives. In this way, the formal practice is constantly informing the informal practice—that is, the way we live.

How much formal practice you ultimately decide to do, if any, will be up to you; but I am asking that you take a few minutes to do the simple exercises described below in connection with the Circle of Liberation. Actually, I am *urging* you to take just a few minutes to try the exercises after you have read through them. Otherwise, the practice will just be words on the page and you will have missed the most important part, the creation of an experience you can begin to nurture in your life. Without the experience, the words will be relatively meaningless.

The Circle of Liberation reflects an ancient practice of meditation that is sometimes called one-pointedness or concentration practice. In order to create the best conditions for doing the practice, it is useful to relax the body and soften the mind. To do this we will begin with a relaxation exercise and then move on to the Circle of Liberation. As we will discuss in greater detail later on, the relaxation exercise is very useful in itself to strengthen our awareness of what is going on in our bodies and to be able to release the inevitable tension and contraction that is a by-product of living such busy, fast-moving and often stressful lives. Just as with all aspects of formal practice, in doing the relaxation exercise, we are nurturing important skills that will serve us so well in the challenging process of keeping our balance.

RELAXATION EXERCISE

INTRODUCTION

A primary purpose of this relaxation exercise, and many others like it, is to nurture the ability to self-regulate our states of mind, emotion and body. Self-regulation is one of the keys to living a balanced, skillful and satisfying life.

Although the benefits of self-regulation extend far beyond the management of stress, the negative impact of stress on our bodies, our minds and on our experience of day-to-day life offers a strong source of motivation for continuing to build our self-regulation skills. It is unquestionably established in the medical and scientific communities that the stress response (often experienced as anxiety, fear, anger, aggravation, etc.) takes a tremendous toll on our health over time.

This exercise is designed to minimize the negative effects of the stress response by learning to stimulate what Dr. Herbert Benson of Harvard Medical School has labeled "the relaxation response."[22] The relaxation response not only helps to return our stress level to baseline, it also enhances a state of balance that is the foundation for living in a mindful way.

The following instructions look long and complicated at first, but the exercise is actually quite simple. Remember that it is a practice that is designed to build new skills. Like any skill building, it takes some effort. With a little conscientiousness, though, the skills become second nature. Even when you do not have the time to sit and do the whole exercise, the skills drawing on the resources of the natural softening quality of your exhale, the power of your body-mind communication and the power of your imagination can be used throughout your day to relax and balance your body, mind and emotions.

Try reading through the instructions before beginning the exercise. When you are just beginning, it is perfectly fine to read one part of the instructions, practice that part and then read the next part, and so on. Very soon, it will just flow nicely for you.

INSTRUCTIONS

Find a comfortable sitting posture, spine upright, hands held comfortably in your lap or on your knees.

Lightly close your eyes. If closing your eyes is not comfortable for you, look down at the floor with a relaxed, unfocused gaze.

Begin by bringing your attention to your exhale and taking a few relaxing breaths. The relaxing quality of the exhale can be enhanced by drawing together three resources: (1) the natural softening quality of the exhale, the quality we experience spontaneously in a sigh, (2) the body-mind communication and (3) your imagination. The power of the body-mind communication is utilized by giving the body direction on the exhale—simply say silently to yourself on the exhale "relax, release, let go," or just one of those words. The power of imagination is utilized by imagining the muscles and tissues of the body relaxing, softening and letting go. Although it may seem a little complicated at first to think of all three of these resources on each exhale, with a little practice it begins to feel very natural to use the three resources at the same time.

Breathing normally, continue with the relaxing breaths until you feel you have settled in a bit. If you become distracted at any time by a thought or emotion (and you undoubtedly will), simply notice that your mind has wondered off and bring your attention gently back to the exhale. A very important part of the practice, even at this early stage, is to watch the temptation to judge yourself. This can happen in many ways: "Oh, I'm distracted; I can't do this right." Or: "I don't like that thought—or that feeling." Here the practice has a simple and repetitious aspect to it: just notice the temptation to judge yourself, your performance in the practice or the process itself, let go of the temptation as well as you can and gently return your attention to the exhale.

When you have settled into the relaxing breaths, bring your attention to the top of your head, your fore-head and around your eyes and ears. Again you are going to use a combination of the natural softening quality of the exhale, the body-mind communication and your imagination. Pretend you are bringing the inhale in right through the middle of your forehead. Keeping your attention on that area, on the exhale, send the silent message of "relax, release, let go" and imagine all the tissue, skin and small muscles in that area releasing and softening.

If there is no big change, try not to judge the result. This takes a little practice, but check in with the small muscles around the eyes, eyelids, mouth and jaw and see if you can intentionally relax them.

Let any relaxing energy you might have felt spread throughout your face on the exhale. Reinforce the practice by saying silently to yourself: "My face is relaxed and at rest."

Let any relaxing energy you have experienced flow down through your neck and bring your attention to your shoulders. If your shoulders feel stiff or tight, rotate them backwards a few times and then forward. Bring your shoulders up toward your ears as far as you can on an inhale, hold them there for a brief moment and then let them drop down to a natural and relaxed position on the exhale.

Continue by bringing your attention, at your own pace, down through the arms and to the hands, noticing along the way any tightness, discomfort, fatigue or other sensations. When you reach the hands, make fists. On the inhale, tighten your fists and arms as tight as you can. Hold them tight for just a few seconds and then, on the exhale, release your hands and arms as fully as possible. Really tap into the sensation of release as you intentionally let go of the muscles in your hands and arms. Repeat the tightening and release exercise several times to become even more familiar with the contrast between muscle tension and the sensation of release. After the final time, check in with your hands to make sure you are holding them softly and say silently: "My arms and hands are relaxed and at rest."

Bring your attention to your chest area and continue your slow scan down the body. If you notice areas of tightness, discomfort or fatigue, stop in that area and repeat the exercise you did with the forehead. Pretend you are bringing the inhale in right through that area and, on the exhale, say silently "relax, release, let go" while imagining all the skin, tissue and muscles in that area softening.

When you reach the feet, experiment with reinforcing the relaxation process by trying one or more of the following techniques.

1. *Imagine all remaining tension or tightness draining out the bottom of your feet and into the floor.*

2. *Go back up to the top of your head. On one long exhale or a couple of exhales, imagine a soothing liquid draining all the way down through your body to the feet, leaving your body even more settled and relaxed.*

3. *Go back up to the top of your head. On one long exhale or a couple of exhales, imagine that a warm, comforting white light is moving down through your body, leaving it even more settled and relaxed.*

4. *Go back up to the top of your head. On one long exhale or a couple of exhales, imagine that a wave of relaxing energy, a "body sigh," is moving down through your body, leaving it more settled and relaxed.*

Finally, let go of any technique and just notice what it feels like to intentionally relax and let go of tightness or tension. Open to the experience of release and relaxation as fully as possible and just *enjoy it!* Rest in the experience until you are ready to move on to the Circle of Liberation.

CIRCLE OF LIBERATION

Maintaining this relaxed presence as well as you can, bring your attention back to the exhale. Remembering that this practice is designed, in part, to strengthen our ability to hold our attention where we choose to place it, bring a sense of determination to holding your attention lightly on the exhale.

Despite your determination, I can guarantee you that, sooner or later, the automatic energy of the mind will take your attention away from the breath and off in a different direction. Maybe a thought will arise (something like "Oh, I forgot to write that check!" or "I wonder what I should have for lunch?" or "I can't believe she said that to me this morning!"); or you will notice an ache or pain somewhere in your body; or you will be drawn away by some emotion, a little nervousness or anxiety, perhaps; or you simply will become impatient or restless. Please know that this will happen. It is not some personal failing or a defect of your brain. It is the unavoidable automatic energy of the mind that *everyone* experiences.

The circle itself reminds us that it is not possible to stay focused all the time. The practice here is not about stopping thoughts; it is about nurturing the witness, the ability to see directly what is going on in the mind, the emotions and the body.

Keeping the circle in mind, the distraction that takes your attention away from the breath is at three o'clock. When you notice that you are no longer paying attention to the exhale, you have moved down to six o'clock on the circle. In noticing the distraction, you have accomplished something very important: you have switched from the automatic pilot mode to mindfulness. You have loosened from whatever distraction gripped your attention and have opened up to a more spacious awareness.

Now the practice is very straightforward. As you move from nine o'clock of the circle back to twelve o'clock, you simply return your attention to the exhale, completing the circle with an energy of gentleness and kindness for yourself.

You might also think of this returning as releasing, or letting go of, the distracting thought, body sensation or emotion. That is not to say that the distraction will instantly disappear (although it might); but as you return your attention to the exhale and once again make the breath the center of your attention, the distraction will move more to the edge of your awareness and generally become softer or quieter, if not disappear altogether.

If it is more useful to you, you can also just think of just letting the distraction be as it is, as you return your attention to the breathe.

You might experiment with labeling the distraction, saying softly in your mind something like, "Oh, thinking!" or "Oh, restlessness!" and then gently returning your attention to the exhale. The key is to keep the practice very simple:

— *attend to the exhale*
— *notice the distractions*
— *return to the breath*

There will be a strong temptation to judge what distractions arise ("I don't like that thought.") or to judge whether you are doing the practice right ("I can't do this!!! My mind just won't stop!"). This judgment is just another distraction. When it arises, and it probably will at some point, the practice remains the same. Notice the judgment and with great kindness for yourself and for your active mind, and simply return your attention to the breath—relax back into the exhale.

REACTIONS TO THE PRACTICE

Most people who do this exercise notice that their mind is very busy with thoughts and chatter. That's O.K. It's natural. The point at this stage is not to stop thinking. It is much more about noticing directly what arises in the mind, loosening from those automatic arisings and returning attention back to the point of focus you have chosen. In beginning the practice, we all have to go fully around the circle many times, returning our attention to the breath over and over again in a short period of time. I would be surprised if that is not your experience, too. As one famous meditation teacher has said, the process is like training an energetic young puppy.[23] The puppy runs off, not paying any attention to what you want him to do. Over and over, you gently bring him back, only to have him run off again. So it is with our minds.

It is interesting to note that, although the wave of mindfulness that has swept over our culture is relatively recent, recognition of the importance of bringing the wandering mind back to intentional focus is not. In 1890, William James, often referred as the "father of Western psychology," wrote:

> The faculty of voluntarily bringing back a wandering attention over and over again, is the very root of judgment, character, and will. No one is 'compos sui' if he have it not. An education which should

> improve this faculty would be the education 'par
> excellence.' But it is easier to define this ideal than
> to give practical instructions for bringing it about.[24]

James was apparently at a loss about how to nurture this important "faculty of voluntarily bringing back a wandering attention." We now are blessed to have very practical instructions, techniques and practices for engaging in this "education 'par excellence'."

I am going to be a bit of a nag. Now that you have read through the descriptions of the relaxation and Circle of Liberation exercises, please do not read any further until you have tried them. It is a little difficult to do them on your own for the first time, without having someone lead you through them; but give it a try. If you have to go back to the instructions part way through to remind yourself of what you are doing, that's perfectly all right. If you can muster the patience to stumble through the exercises several times, they will quickly become more natural to you. I am not saying they will be easy to do necessarily; but with just a few sessions of practice, you will know what you are doing without looking at the book.

Take whatever time feels comfortable for you to do the relaxation practice. When you get to the Circle of Liberation, start with just five minutes or so. Yes, it is perfectly fine to use a timer or to look (mindfully) at your watch. As you get more accustomed to the practice, you will have a natural sense of the time you want to spend. When you are familiar with both the relaxation and the circle parts of the practice, experiment with shortening the relaxation phase and increasing the time spent in stabilizing the mind with the Circle of Liberation practice.

There is always a balance between extending yourself a bit, hanging in there with the practice even when you become impatient or restless, and not creating too much discomfort for yourself. If you do the practice with some amount of regularity, it would be useful to gradually increase your sitting time to at least twenty minutes.

STRENGTHENING MOTIVATION: REALIZING THE MA
BENEFITS OF PRACTICE

The Circle of Liberation is useful because it gives us a clear, straightforward way of working with our minds. As I emphasized above, it is important to keep the practice simple: focus attention, notice the distractions arising from the automatic energy of the brain, loosen around distraction and return the focus to the object of attention. Even though the practice is simple, there is a lot going on when we do it. Put more positively, we are nurturing a whole range of skills, abilities and qualities as we do the practice. Even a partial list is impressive:

- attention and concentration
- presence in the moment
- patience
- endurance
- acceptance
- gentleness/kindness
- compassion
- letting go
- equanimity
- a more insightful understanding of the mind

It is worth spending a little time considering how all this arises out of the simple practice you have tried.

Attention and concentration

These two are pretty obvious. In bringing our attention to the breath, we are choosing the focal point for our mind. We are willfully directing our attention. To put this another way, rather than letting the automatic energy of mind control where our attention is directed, we are consciously making the choice. Having made the choice, we are bringing determination to holding our attention there. We are nurturing the ability to hold our attention where we want it. We are strengthening our power of concentration.

Have you ever had the experience of reading through a paragraph three or four times and still not being sure what it says? Obviously, it's not that you can't read or understand most, if not all, of the words. The difficulty is that, at that moment, your power of concentration is weak. You are trying to read through the paragraph, but you are not really absorbing the meaning of it because the automatic energy of the mind is distracting you with other thoughts. Or maybe you are at work, trying to finish a project to meet a deadline; but you keep thinking about that disagreement you had with your partner before you left for work that morning—or you are repeatedly distracted by your anxiety about the possibility of not meeting the deadline. Again, there is a problem with choosing the focal point of your attention and holding your mind there.

With the Circle of Liberation, we are working with all of that. We are choosing a focus, noticing the automatic energy of the mind that is so effective at distracting us and bringing our attention back—over and over again. In doing so, we are training the mind to be more stable, to be able to keep our attention where we want it. How extremely useful—whether we are just trying to read a simple paragraph, work effectively at our jobs or concentrate on anything else that is important to us.

Presence in the moment

In strengthening our powers of attention and concentration, we are nurturing our ability to be present in the moment, to connect with the preciousness and lushness of this incredible experience of being human. I have the good fortune of living in a beautiful country setting. Many of my mornings begin with a walk around the large pond on our property. I have walked these paths hundreds of times in the years we have lived here. On many occasions, I feel like I am greeting an old friend who has new stories to tell. With so much time spent together, we have an intimate relationship and no detail is too small or insignificant for my friend to reveal to me. The height of the clover beneath my feet, the subtle changes in the color of the reeds, grasses and leaves, and the newest web creations of the resident spiders all tell me the story of the landscape's last few days.

When I am able to make the walk mindfully, and connect fully with my experience in the moment, the display of life and light, of movement and color and change, is such a blessing. But you know how it goes. If my mind is distracted, if I am immersed in thoughts of the tasks and challenges of just being alive on the earth at this time, or if I can't stop thinking about all the things I "should" be doing to take care of our property, I miss the magical display of beauty I am walking through.

There is grace in every moment if we can only focus our gaze sharply enough to see it. So the challenge becomes precisely that: seeing through all the unavoidable distractions of our busy lives and minds to experience this pervasive grace. We cannot always maintain our focus in this way, of course. We will always be pulled away by one distraction or another; but with practice, with energy conscientiously devoted to nurturing our mindfulness, we can become more consistently aware of our distractions and return our focus to the preciousness accessible in every moment.

Patience and endurance

When we sit in formal practice, even for five minutes, we are strengthening patience. We are nurturing our ability to be present with whatever arises. In my edition of Webster's New World Dictionary, the definition of patience and patient includes such phrases as "the will or ability to wait without complaint," steadfastness or perseverance," "bearing pain, trouble, etc., without complaining or losing control," "calmly tolerating delay, confusion, inefficiency, etc.; able to wait calmly."

When we sit, we just sit. For the minutes involved with our practice on any given day, we are not going anywhere. We may think we would like to do something else, and we may not initially think we like what arises, but we are just sitting. We are nurturing our ability to be present with whatever arises "without complaining or losing control." We may get restless, we may wish our mind were not so active; but we just continue sitting, bringing as much stability and calm to the practice as we can. We are developing greater patience—and what a valuable skill that is as we continue to build the bridge between our formal practice and the rest of lives.

Along with patience comes endurance. It naturally arises out of patience. As we bring our commitment to just sit and notice the active energy in our minds and bodies, we also increasingly realize that we can endure whatever arises. The lack of this quality can get us into so much trouble. We think we can't endure the behavior of our child or partner, so we lash out in ways that are not effective or loving—and regret it later. We cannot endure the pain of old experiences or the negative messages that keep whispering (or shouting) to us about ourselves or about the state of our lives, so we abuse substances or turn into workaholics to numb out or escape the pain. In many ways, the thought that we cannot endure a situation often results in creating more of a mess for ourselves. By sitting with the simple Circle of Liberation practice, we are slowly, slowly realizing that we can endure much more than we thought. Whatever arises, whatever we are dealing with, may be initially unpleasant; but we begin to learn that we don't have to be so afraid of it. We can endure it.

Years ago I attended a workshop given by a famous psychologist. Truthfully, I don't remember much of what he said during the day-long course; but I do recall one small part. He emphasized that, in his opinion, a primary task of the counselor or therapist is to help the client make the transition from viewing her experience as *un*bearable to bearable. That is not to say that the previously unbearable experience will somehow magically become pleasant. It may still be very unpleasant, but at least the client will be able to endure it without shrinking in fear or escaping into destructive behaviors. By doing the Circle of Liberation practice, we become our own therapists. We learn that we can bear more than we might have thought. In doing so, we strengthen our confidence that we can confront whatever challenges arise in our lives.

There is a wonderful instruction in Eastern meditative traditions to "sit with the majesty of a mountain." For many reasons, I love to sit with that aspiration in mind. It encourages a sense of grandeur and stability in my sitting. As I imagine the steadfastness of a mountain, its enduring presence, I am reminded of my own ability to endure, to just be present with whatever arises in my meditation—and with whatever I encounter in my daily life.

Acceptance, kindness and compassion

Most definitions of mindfulness practice include the concept of non-judgmental attention. We aspire to witness, to be present with, whatever arises in our mind or body without judging it. If we notice that judgment spontaneously arises, we make our best effort to loosen around that judgment, to not be so strongly hooked by it. It is natural, given our deeply embedded inclination to judge, that we will often judge what arises. Frequently, it is a negative judgment. "Oh, I don't like that thought!" And then we pile judgment on top of judgment. "I can't believe that I am still thinking that way! What is wrong with me?!?" This tendency to harshly judge the automatic energies of our minds and emotions alienates us from ourselves and this alienation is a great wound that dramatically undermines our happiness.

So we start healing the great wound by simply noticing the tendency to judge the arisings in our minds, loosening around that judgment and creating the intention to accept whatever arises. There is no magical potion or dazzling surgical procedure that can quickly remove the tendency to judge ourselves. This is slow, step-by-step work; but what is the alternative? If we don't start to replace judgment with acceptance, we only deepen the wound and create an even more painful separation from our true and wondrous nature. Over time, the intention to accept what arises in our minds and emotions will lead to an actual experience of acceptance. But acceptance is only the start. From acceptance emerges kindness and kindness gives birth to compassion.

Imagine what it would be like to move through your day with an unshakable kindness for yourself, a friendliness toward your imperfections and imperfect acts. Imagine how it would feel to experience a deep-seated compassion for yourself and your state of being in every moment. Close your eyes for a few moments and really allow yourself to imagine this.

What a foundation for happiness! This is the foundation we are building, one brick at a time, as we bring even a modest initial energy of acceptance to the automatic arisings of mind in the Circle of Liberation practice. It would be terrific if, from this minute on, from the moment you read this, you could just stop judging yourself; but that really is a "mission impossible." You can begin making a transition right now, however, by being clear about your new mindfulness approach. By setting the intention to notice when you fall into self-judgment, you will be able to identify it more often. Each time you become aware of it, you will have more of an opportunity to loosen from its entrapping energy and resolve to generate more of an attitude of acceptance for whatever it was about yourself that you were judging. With repetition over time, the practice will invariably lead to the warm energy of kindness for yourself.

Equanimity

In all my years of practice, I have found equanimity to be one of the most challenging concepts or qualities to truly understand, let alone to integrate into my life. For a very long time, I have reflected on it, contemplated it and sought to explore its nature—and I am still a long way from the end of this process. Despite its complexity, there are some short descriptions that help us open our imagination to the idea of equanimity:

— keeping our balance under any circumstances

— never really losing our seat or groundedness

— moving calmly and skillfully with the entire flow of our lives

— maintaining an accepting openness to whatever arises both inside and around us

It doesn't sound simple, does it? In my mind, equanimity is a very grand aspiration. It is a huge challenge to react with stable balance to life's small and large challenges. It is one thing to bring greater equanimity to waiting in line at the grocery store or to the inevitable traffic snarls; it is quite another thing to truly keep our balance in the face of a serious illness or any of the other major calamities we all experience at some point in our lives.

At its essence, the attainment of full and complete equanimity is the same as being liberated from suffering. It may or may not be possible in this lifetime. Each of us will have to discover that for ourselves. Still, the aspiration is important. Although we may never totally integrate equanimity into our lives, any practice that deepens our understanding of it, that builds skills supporting it, moves us in the direction of liberation.

Mindfulness practice definitely nurtures equanimity. Think about it. Think of the aspects of the Circle of Liberation practice we have discussed above: presence in the moment, patience, endurance, acceptance of whatever arises, kindness and even compassion for ourselves. All these elements of the practice move us along the path toward equanimity—and therefore along the path to a true and lasting happiness. In a way, we don't have to bring too much specific attention to equanimity as we start mindfulness practice. We can simply have confidence in the basic elements of the practice and know that as we conscientiously bring attention to them, we are, in the process, constructing the infrastructure of equanimity.

A more insightful understanding of the mind

In the Circle of Liberation practice we are looking directly at the mind. We are noticing how its automatic energies distract us, how our "mindstream" flows without our intending it. In the Tibetan language, the word for meditate means to familiarize or become more familiar with. By engaging in the practice, we are becoming more familiar with how our minds actually work. We are literally becoming better students of our minds. This, in turn, enables us to work more skillfully with our minds—to be less vulnerable to the automatic energies of the mind that can so undermine our happiness and to be more intentional in making affirmative choices that support our happiness.

This more insightful understanding of the mind will deepen as we proceed with the seven steps to mindfulness; but it starts right here in the beginning with the simple Circle of Liberation practice.

All the qualities that we have just briefly explored sound like a great deal to work on; but I don't want to leave you with the impression that we have to take them all on and laboriously plow through them. Instead, my message here is that by bringing some amount of effort to the straightforward practice of the Circle of Liberation, they begin to spontaneously flow out of the practice. Sometimes they emerge effortlessly as we move from automatic pilot to mindfulness.

Several years ago I was leading a course on mindfulness for psychologists, social workers and counselors. In the break right after we had discussed the Circle of Liberation and the qualities we are strengthening as we engage in that practice, a counselor shared the following story with me. She and a colleague were on an expressway heading to the course early that morning when all of a sudden the busy flow of traffic ground to a halt. There was a little movement, but it was the stop-and-go pattern we are all too familiar with—the kind of situation in which the expressway begins to feel more like a long, endless parking lot. She and her colleague initially reacted with strong aggravation and impatience, as the anxiety about being late to the course flowed through them.

Suddenly, they turned to each other and one of them said, "We are going to a course on mindfulness, for heaven's sake! Maybe we can change our minds about this." In an instant, their whole bodies softened, their aggravated energies released and they sat back to mindfully watch the experience. From that moment on, they were able to enjoy the little break in the otherwise rushed part of the early morning, chat with each other and even bring compassion to the obviously "worked up" drivers around them. All the qualities we explored in connection with the Circle of Liberation were there for them by the simply awakening to mindfulness. We are not always able to flip the mindfulness switch like that, but it is so wonderful when we can. Instantly, some unpleasant energy that has grabbed us (such as aggravation, impatience or anxiety) eases and we wake up to a whole range of more satisfying possibilities.

CONNECTING FORMAL AND INFORMAL PRACTICE

As we have just seen, there is a lot going on as we engage in formal mindfulness practice. How wonderful it is to sit and begin to truly change our relationship to our mind, to our emotions and to something essential in ourselves. How courageous it is to stop moving for a few minutes, to take a break from our task-oriented activities and nurture the qualities of presence, patience, endurance, kindness and equanimity. Think of how much time we spend in relatively meaningless activities, of how many minutes, or even hours, are "frittered away" mindlessly each day. By engaging in even just a few minutes of formal practice on a regular basis, we are tilting the balance toward truly meaningful effort. We are investing in our best human qualities, in our true radiant nature.

Formal practice is also an investment of our time and energy. For that investment to really pay off, we need to continually build a bridge between formal and informal practice. As I mentioned earlier, formal practice is the time we take to stop our regular activities and bring attention to some aspect of mediation, such as the Circle of Liberation practice. Informal practice is everything else in our lives. I have often heard people say, "I am so stressed out; I should meditate." Or: "I really need to meditate so I can relax." I appreciate the sentiment, but it is missing the point in a way. Formal practice may be relaxing—or it may not be if our minds don't settle down on a given day.

Whether any specific meditation session is relaxing or not, pleasant or not, is not terribly important. The larger aspiration of formal practice is to build a stronger, more stable foundation for the rest of our lives, for how we experience everything else in our day. In other words, we are engaging in formal meditation practice not just to settle down for ten or fifteen minutes, but to change the way we live.

So we are constantly seeking to build the bridge between formal and informal practice. To do this, we ask how the experience of the formal practice informs and affects our "post-meditation" experience. What is it that we are trying to do or remember when we get up from the cushion or chair and once again immerse ourselves in our daily routines? There are many ways to approach this, of course; but let's just begin with an easy-to-remember technique that we can begin to incorporate into our lives right now. The technique draws on the skill, nurtured in the formal practice, of mindfully paying attention to the automatic energies arising in our mind, body and emotions. I especially like this technique because it basically involves remembering just four words: **Stop, Breathe, Reflect** and **Choose**.[25]

It all starts with the **Stop** piece, paying attention as soon as possible to a negative emotion (irritation, frustration, anger, anxiety, to name just a few), a spinning mind or a troubling sensation in the body. It is by paying attention to these mind/emotional/body states that you give yourself the chance to switch out of the automatic pilot mode and into a more mindful way of being.

Having awakened to some reaction, some challenging emotion, you just **Breathe**, bringing as much attention as possible to your breathing and the effect it has on the challenging energy in the body and the activity in the mind. Taking a couple of conscious breaths helps you to settle down (think of the natural settling quality of a sigh) and often slows down the process of reacting to whatever is arising.

Just as you did in the relaxation exercise earlier in this chapter, it is helpful to reinforce the natural settling quality of the breath with the two other resources available to you: the body/mind communication and your imagination. Send the silent message to "relax, release and let go" as the attention goes to the breath and imagine the body and the mind settling. I suggest to my clients that they take a big audible sigh if they are by themselves when engaging in the Stop-Breathe-Reflect-Choose practice. This really enhances the Breathe part of the technique. If you are with others or are otherwise unable to take a big sigh, the practice is simply to bring attention to the exhale and utilize the body/mind communication and imagination resources as much as possible. You are always breathing, so no one will even notice that anything different or out of the ordinary is happening.

The **Reflect** part is checking in with your insight about the situation. What do you need to remember about this reaction in your mind, emotions or body to be able to speak or act skillfully—or to be able to make a good decision? You will often need to have a little silent conversation with yourself about your best insight, about what you need to remember. Having paid attention, settled yourself and had this little inner dialogue, you are ready to **Choose**. What is the best action to take or decision to make under the circumstances?

The Stop-Breathe-Reflect-Choose practice is applicable to so much of the automatic energies arising in our mind and bodies that I am sure you can think of a few circumstances in your own lives where it might be helpful. Here's one example that often comes up in my classes. Let's say that you sometimes fall prey to "road rage." Well, maybe it's not actually rage, but you do experience some amount of aggravation or anger when someone cuts you off or commits one of any number of discourteous driving misdemeanors. If you had been in one of my stress management or cardiac rehabilitation classes, I would have tried to persuade you that this old pattern, *although totally understandable*, is contributing to your stress load, impairing your immune system and just generally impacting negatively on your health and experience in life.

You listened sincerely to my little sermon and decided to work on this reaction. Keep in mind that this reaction has an automatic quality to it; it is pre-intentional. It is not as though you decided that the next time someone cuts you off, you are really going to fly off the handle. In a real sense, the reaction happens to you—and unless you begin to intervene, the neural connections in your brain that activate the reaction will continue to strengthen and the reaction will just keep happening, over and over again.

Since the reaction has an automatic, pre-intentional quality, you will notice it only after it has begun. Despite your intention to change the pattern, it already has a head start. That's O.K.; we start right where we are. Having committed yourself to the Stop-Breathe-Reflect-Choose practice, you notice the next time the reaction begins. Rather than just being carried along with the reaction, you **Stop** and pay attention to what is happening in your body, mind and emotions. Next, you remember to **Breathe** and reinforce the natural settling quality of the breath by saying to yourself, "relax, release, let go"—and by imagining muscle tension releasing and energy settling.

Then you move to the **Reflect** part. In the beginning phases of the practice, it is best to keep this stage simple by focusing on the core reminders regarding your emotional reactivity. Here are a couple of examples of core reminders with several types of old patterns. One of my clients was applying the practice to his anger that had caused so many messes in his relationships. When he sensed that the anger was already flushing through him, his core reminders were, "Don't speak, don't text, don't send e-mails. Just go inside." It was great that his witnessing awareness was beginning to recognize the anger, but he knew that he was not settled enough to be able to act towards others.

Another client was working with pervasive anxiety that so often made her feel unsafe. As the Witness began to develop, enabling her to notice that the anxiety had already grabbed her, her core reminder was: "Take another look. Am I really unsafe?"

One of my old patterns was to be irritated and defensive if my wife made some suggestive comment about some household task I was doing. When I first started bringing mindfulness to the pattern (after years of just repeating it on the automatic pilot mode), my core reminder was: "This is my wife whom I love very much."

As you become more experienced with the Stop-Breathe-Reflect-Choose practice, the Reflect part can be expanded to more thorough self-talk that reminds you what is really happening, why you are intervening in the pattern and what you are investing in as you act more mindfully. In a real way, you are becoming your own counselor, talking yourself through the situation. If you were working with road rage, the more extensive self-talk in the Reflect part of the practice might go something like the following:

> You know, I've reacted this way for so long and it just doesn't feel good. Besides, I've learned that getting angry adds to my stress load and undermines my health. What am I accomplishing, anyway? That driver isn't paying any attention to me and certainly isn't going to change his behavior because of my reaction. On top of everything else, I guess I am just wasting my energy. I need that energy for all the other things I have to do today.

I feel that this practice is so helpful with all the varieties of negative or challenging energies that arise in our body, mind and emotions that I give these hand-outs to every client and every class member that I work with. If the subheadings are not helpful or are too much to take in when you first start the practice, don't worry about it. Just focus your attention on the key reminders: **Stop, Breathe, Reflect, Choose.** As you become more experienced with the practice, go back and read the details under each stage and see if you can expand and refine your practice by being more reflective at each stage.

MINDFULNESS IN DAILY PRACTICE

Mindfulness can be a powerful tool for changing habitual emotional reactions that hijack our ability to think clearly, act skillfully and live meaningfully. Each time you encounter a negative emotion that threatens to dominate your awareness (for example, irritation, impatience, anxiety, anger, etc.), practice applying the four-step model set forth below.

STOP

– Bring your awareness to the negative emotion as soon as possible.

– Begin to recognize the early warning signals of the emotional reaction.

– Remind yourself: "I need to pay attention to this – now."

BREATHE

– Relaxing into the exhale, allow the negative emotion to soften.

– Use the power of body-mind communication: send a mental message to release and let go.

REFLECT

– Appraise the situation. What is my old pattern here?

– Is my reaction supported by old myths or messages?

– What resources and options do I have right here in the present moment?

– Can I change my mind about how I see myself in this situation?

– What is my best insight about this situation? What do I want to remember?

CHOOSE

– Having become more aware of my reaction, settled myself a bit and tapped into my insight, what is effective or skillful

– Can I shift my old pattern and make a creative choice?

MINDFULNESS IN RELATIONSHIPS

Mindfulness can be a powerful tool for changing habitual emotional reactions that interrupt our experience of love and undermine our relationships. Each time you encounter a negative emotion in your relationship (for example, irritation, impatience, anger, a feeling of lack of respect, etc.), practice applying the four-step model set forth below.

STOP

– Bring your awareness to the negative emotion as soon as possible.

– Begin to recognize the early warning signals of the emotional reaction.

– Remind yourself: "I need to pay attention to this – now."

BREATHE

– Relaxing into the exhale, allow the negative emotion to soften.

– Use the power of body-mind communication: send a mental message to release and let go.

REFLECT

– Appraise the situation. What is my old pattern here?

– What is my reaction calling me to work on?

– Can I change my mind about how I see myself in this situation?

– Can I be patient or understanding of my loved one's struggle?

– Can I change my mind about how I see my loved one in this situation?

– What is my best insight about this situation? What do I want to remember?

CHOOSE

– What is effective, skillful, respectful or even loving?

– Can I shift my old pattern and make a creative choice?

– What is my best choice under all the circumstances?

CHAPTER 4

Step Two: Becoming Brain Savvy...
Making Sense of Old Patterns

SUE'S STORY

Years ago Sue appeared in my office with a request for help with a very specific pattern. (The names, and certain details of their circumstances, of all clients referred to in this book have been changed to protect their confidentiality.) Sue was an energetic, bright thirty-seven year-old woman who had been divorced for about five years. She had been dating for the last few years and frequently acted in ways that bothered her. If any man whom she had been dating withdrew attention from her, she would become rather hysterical and often found herself begging or being uncharacteristically manipulative in an effort to once again attract the man's attention. As she said to me in our first session, "I don't like the way I've become and I don't understand it."

Like many old reaction patterns we all have in one way or another, Sue's pattern caused her a great deal of turmoil, kept her stuck in a negative emotional state and undermined her sense of self. Worse yet, it didn't help her get what she wanted. In fact, as you can imagine, it had the exact opposite effect. Rather than attracting the man's attention, her reaction inevitably pushed him farther away. We will return to Sue's story later in the chapter after we have looked at some basic brain functions that will enable us to make sense of it.

No one is totally immune to old reaction patterns that can overwhelm our best intentions, get us stuck for some period of time in challenging negative emotions and lead to speech and behavior that is unskillful, disrespectful or worse. I like to think of it this way. There are many ways to classify human beings, but here is one way I have found especially useful. There is a very small class of individuals who are fully enlightened. By that, I mean that they have attained such a state of realization and integration that they are able to remain consistently in enlightened awareness and all their actions flow from that unbroken state of consciousness. In the Buddhist tradition, this is sometimes referred to as "Diamond Knowledge," a state of awareness that is indestructible and immune from penetration by the countless inner and outer stimuli that so often cause the rest of us to lose our balance.

Eager to talk to one of these rare beings, I always ask the many groups I lead if there is anyone present from this small class. Guess what? I have yet to encounter anyone who is fully enlightened. Even the Dalai Lama says that he is not. If we are not in that very small class of human beings, *then we are all in the same boat!* Put another way, if we are not in that class, then we all have some old conditioning that does not serve us well, that undermines our happiness and often leads to unfortunate behavior. Not all conditioning from our background is negative, of course. It's the so-called negative conditioning that produces patterns like Sue's. Although such patterns can be both confusing and disturbing, they point us in the direction of very useful work, work that peels back the layers of "old stuff" that separates us from our beautiful and radiant basic nature.

As I mentioned in Chapter One in connection with the obstacles to a lasting happiness, this conditioning starts at the very beginning of our lives, before we are making conscious choices. We do not analytically sort through all the information our young brain is absorbing to determine what serves us well and what doesn't. We just soak it all in and store it in our brain.

If we are going to understand this negative conditioning, and the challenging patterns it produces, it is important to understand a little about how the brain works. We are not seeking to become neuroscientists by any means; but a basic understanding of brain function as it relates to our negative reaction patterns is extremely useful. We do not have to become experts on the brain to be experts about our own negative conditioning, the conditioning that so frequently undermines our happiness.

In presenting this material to thousands of individuals over the years, I have found that there are major advantages in understanding a few basic aspects of what is happening in the brain when one experiences challenging negative emotions. First, becoming a little "brain savvy" enables us to make sense of patterns of reaction that often are confusing and/or misunderstood. As we begin to understand that the reactions are a natural result of the way experience is stored, processed and triggered in the brain, our insight reduces self-judgment. Our tendency to see our negative patterns as some personal defect, as something basically wrong with us, is gradually reduced as we strengthen our ability to see the pattern in terms of the understandable functioning of the brain. Since harsh self-judgment is often such an important factor in intensifying the suffering of negative emotional patterns, this gradual transformation of self-judgment is helpful in working skillfully with the challenging pattern.

Second, becoming brain savvy provides a strong foundation for practicing mindfulness with regard to our negative emotional reactivity. Understanding basic brain functioning involved with our challenging patterns enables us to identify the triggering of an old pattern more quickly and to see it with perspective. It makes it possible for us to have the "ah ha" experience of realizing what is really going on when a strong emotional reaction arises. In practicing the Stop-Breathe-Reflect-Choose technique introduced in the last chapter, our insight about the brain makes it easier to step back and say to ourselves, "Oh, I know what is going on here!"

Third, as we see our old patterns as an understandable result of basic brain function and learn that the brain is capable of great change over our entire life span, our belief in the possibilities available to us is strengthened. The ability of the brain to continue to build new circuits, and to let older ones weaken, offers a sense of hope that we are not be inextricably stuck in the old pattern. This insight is a strong motivating force for working with the process of change through our mindfulness practice.

For all these reasons, we are going to spend a little time with basic brain functioning as the next step in building a foundation for mindfulness and the lasting happiness we deserve.

The Magical Brain

The neuroscientists who devote their careers to studying the human brain describe it as the most complex thing ever discovered on earth. Even though there have been wonderful and exciting advances in neuroscience over the past several decades, our brains are so complex that there is still a great deal that the experts do not understand. The complexity and continuing mysteries of the brain give it a rather magical quality. Just a few basic facts illustrate this. The neuron is the basic cell of the brain. In the small space it occupies in our heads, our brains have over one hundred billion neurons and each neuron may have as many as ten thousand connections with other neurons, resulting in trillions of neural connections. Moreover, there is more than two million miles of "neural wiring" in the brain.

It's hard to imagine the physical reality of such numbers, I know. One way I try to get some vague sense of it is by looking up at the sky on a moonless night. I live in the country, away from the lights of town; and when the conditions are right, I can see lots of stars. The neuroscientists tell us that there are more neurons in our brains than there are stars in the night sky, so when I look up I can begin to picture the beautiful web of connections inside my head. To add to the picture, I imagine all the stars being connected, with bolts of lightning flashing along the connections. This brings me a little closer to being able to visualize the magnificent web of connectivity that is the human brain.

One more little fact: by the fourth week of pregnancy, the fetal brain is developing 500,000 new neurons every minute. I have no idea how the neuroscientists figure out such things, but I am sure they have a reliable system. What I do know is that it is quite a miracle!

THE TRIUNE OR THREE-PART BRAIN

We are not going to try to probe all the complexity of the human brain. In fact, we are only going to look at one aspect of its functioning. To do that, we need to be aware of the most general anatomy of the brain. The brain has many components, but its basic structure can be thought of as the triune or three-part brain. Evolutionary science isn't the only way to look at things, of course; but from an evolutionary viewpoint, the human species has been around for about two million years. During that time, the human brain evolved from the bottom up. To get a feel for the structure of the brain as you read this, bring one of your arms up and make a fist with your fingers folded over your thumb. Hold the palm of your hand in front of your face. Your fist then becomes a funny little model of the brain.[26] Since the human brain is about the size of a medium head of cauliflower and weighs about three pounds (or maybe three and a half pounds if you have a really heavy brain), your model is definitely smaller and lighter than the real thing. Your wrist represents the brainstem, the oldest and most primitive part of the brain. The brainstem connects with the spinal chord extending down through your body to form an important part of the body's amazing communication system.

The top of your fist, where your fingers are, represents the cortex. Of course, the cortex is actually much bigger. It has a number of layers and fills the major portion of the top of your head, extending down to the area behind your forehead. It is the size and complexity of the cortex that distinguishes the human brain from the brains of other mammals. I am sure that some of you are cat lovers. My wife and I have a cat we love dearly. No matter how smart you think your cat is, I can tell you that her cortex is quite small, especially in comparison to ours.

An important part of the cortex is the prefrontal lobes behind the forehead. On your fist model, the prefrontal cortex is located in the area from the last knuckles on your fingers down to the fingernails. Among many other functions, the prefrontal lobes regulate emotion and emotionally attuned communications. This region is also involved with "response flexibility," the ability to take in information, think about it, consider various options for responding and then produce an adaptive response. In other words, the prefrontal lobes are intimately involved with our ability to be mindful and to make intentional choices.

If you look under the cortex, by lifting your fingers in your fist model and locating your thumb, you will have found the third part of the brain called the limbic region. As you will notice, the limbic region is surrounded by the cortex. If you look more closely, the place on your thumb between the knuckle and the fingernail represents a very important part of the limbic region called the amygdala. It's an odd word that has the same root as the word almond because the two parts of the amygdala have roughly the same shape as an almond. The amygdala has an important role in the processing of emotions, especially such challenging emotions as anxiety, fear and anger. "Processing" in this sense means generating the internal emotional state and the external expression of such emotions. Although the amygdala is not the only part of the brain involved with emotions, it is certainly an important role-player in the experience of emotions.

THE BRAIN'S ALARM SYSTEM

The brainstem and the limbic region work together as the brain's alarm system. There are strong neural connections between our eyes, ears and nose and the limbic region. There are, of course, neural connections from our senses to the cortex; but the neural route to the limbic system is sometimes referred to as the fast track. In other words, although the differences are very small in relation to our sense of time, the flow of information constantly taken in by our senses gets to the limbic region before it reaches the cortex. It is the hard-wired job of the alarm system to appraise or evaluate all the in-coming sensory information to determine whether we are in danger or at risk. It is sometimes said that the amygdala acts as "a smoke detector"—always on the alert for potential dangers that may be confronting us.

If the alarm system appraises the in-coming information as indicating that we are at risk, it triggers a whole cascade of events geared to meet the perceived danger. Among other things, our heart rate and blood pressure go up; our muscle tension increases; and various hormones, such as adrenaline and cortisol, are secreted into the bloodstream. At the same time, our digestive, immune, reproductive systems, and other processes that support our vitality and health, are suppressed. Essentially, the alarm system puts us into a protection mode, gearing us up to meet the perceived danger.[27] When the triggering of the alarm system is sufficiently strong, we end up in a fight-flight-or-freeze state. This is very useful when the danger is real, when we don't stay in this state too long and when the triggering only happens every once in awhile. You sometimes read of someone who, with an unusual burst of strength, has freed a person from being trapped or who has met some danger in a powerful way. These examples demonstrate how the alarm system is able to trigger and direct the energies of the entire body to effectively respond to a difficult or dangerous situation.

This alarm system was very important to pre-modern human beings in responding to wild animals, dangerous weather, hostile neighboring tribes or any number of other threats. As you can imagine, those pre-modern human beings who had the most effective alarm and response systems tended to survive, further strengthening the hard-wiring of the alarm system in the human brain during the approximately two million years our species has been evolving.

As essential as this alarm system is in responding to dangers, in modern culture, it also poses significant problems. Whereas the body can handle and recover from a big burst of energy expended in the fight-flight-or-freeze reaction if it only happens every once in awhile, the reaction takes a real toll on us if it is triggered frequently or if we stay in the protection mode too long. It is fair to say that in modern cultures, the fight-flight-or-freeze response has evolved into the stress response that we experience all too frequently. It is no secret that humans now experience long-term stress with significant harmful effects. The various possible consequences of chronic stress include fatigue, stress-induced hypertension, ulceration, colitis, loss of vitality, inhibited cell growth, impotency, loss of libido, greater disease risk and neuron cell death, to name just a few. Years of research have generally established that chronic stress is a risk factor for a number of illnesses we all would like to avoid, such as gastrointestinal problems, cardiac disease and various forms of cancer.

It is also important to realize that the challenging emotions that can sweep away our best intentions, such as anxiety, fear and anger, most often indicate that our alarm system has been activated with the resulting cascade of events discussed above happening in our body/mind/emotional complex. In other words, there is generally a hard-wired link between the brain's alarm system and our experience of these challenging emotions. You can see this most clearly with anger. Anger is a strong trigger of the alarm system, resulting in a full fight-flight-or-freeze reaction. With anger, the changes in heart rate, blood pressure, muscle tension, for example, are unmistakable. The signs with other negative emotions may be more subtle, but the connection with a triggering of the alarm system is generally there nevertheless.

THE ALARM SYSTEM AND MEMORY

In order to understand the relationship between the brain's alarm system and our challenging reaction patterns, we need to think a little bit about memory. There are many ways one could talk about memory, but one general description is useful for our purposes. Memory is the way the brain records and stores present experience so that future experience is affected. What is meant by that will become clear as we think about memory in terms of the function of the alarm system. As we have already said, the alarm system of the brain is hard-wired to evaluate in-coming sensory information, determine if we are at risk and, if we are, trigger changes in the body/mind/emotional complex that enable the individual to respond to the perceived danger. Its job doesn't stop there however. The brain is constantly learning from experience. What it learns is then stored in memory so that, in the future, it can better do its job of trying to anticipate dangers and keep us safe.

The young brain of the newborn is an especially rapid learner. As the neuroscientists say, the new baby has a fresh neural network in her brain that is constantly taking in information from her environment for future reference. Let's take a simple example of this to see the connection with the alarm system. Imagine that a toddler is now able to walk and she is exploring her house with great curiosity. She sees this beautiful glowing thing and is immediately attracted to it. As she moves closer and reaches out her hand to touch it, she pulls her hand back quickly and starts to cry. The beautiful thing that attracted her attention just happened to be on top of the stove. The alarm system alerted her to danger. In addition, it learned and stored important information about the experience in her brain so that the alarm system could be on alert and avoid a similar danger in the future.

Let's take another example that more specifically illustrates the relationship between the hard-wired functions of the alarm system and our challenging emotional reactions. Imagine that a young couple is on vacation with their three-year-old daughter. They are having a nice afternoon together walking near the Washington Monument. All of sudden, a large dog comes running toward them from behind. The daughter, being surprised by this fast moving animal, reacts in fear and starts crying hysterically. Why shouldn't she? The dog is bigger than she is and, at her age, she has no way of telling whether it is friendly or not. At first glance, it sure looked threatening.

The young girl's reaction tells us that the brain's alarm system has gone off: "danger . . danger . . danger." The brain then stores the experience in neural firing patterns for future reference and the storage can be thought of generally as an energetic or emotional component, as well as an informational one. Here, we can see that the information would include dog and danger and the emotional component could certainly be described as fear. In fact, the brain might even go further and make what is referred to as an associational link between the danger and the Washington Monument because that is where the danger was experienced.

Before we continue with this example, there is one more piece of information you should have about the alarm system: it values speed over accuracy. This makes sense when you think about it. If you were hiking in the desert of Arizona and caught a quick glimpse out of your peripheral vision of something long and curly on the ground about two feet off to the side, it would not serve you well to delay your response until your had carefully determined whether the object is a branch, a piece of old hose or a deadly rattlesnake. The alarm system doesn't make this mistake. It makes quick decisions and triggers responses rapidly to err on the side of caution. This has certainly served human beings well over thousands of years, but it also means that the alarm system frequently makes mistakes. In other words, it may react quickly to the *possibility* of a risk and trigger a full fight-flight-or-freeze reaction when there is actually no danger. It was only an old hose on the ground after all.

Now let's go back to our example of the little girl and the dog and flash forward thirty years. The girl is now a grown woman walking in the safety of her neighborhood when a little dog scampers up from behind and startles her. As we know, the alarm system is constantly taking in information from our senses and evaluating it for potential dangers. The little dog is a trigger for the alarm system. We might think of the alarm system taking that trigger and doing a very rapid and sloppy computer scan of all the information stored from previous experience (that is, memory).

If a link is made with an earlier time when the individual felt at risk, the neural firing pattern storing the information and energy/emotional components from the earlier event is activated and impacts on the present experience. This is obviously not a technically accurate description, but I find it useful anyway: If the alarm system makes a link with the earlier experience, it is like a pipeline opens and the information and emotional components from the previous situation flow into the present, influencing, often dramatically, the individual's reaction in the present.

In our example, the now-grown woman could have a very strong fear reaction to the little dog that startled her, even though the dog presented no danger to her at all. As I said, the alarm system values speed over accuracy. Consequently, it has reacted very quickly (pre-consciously, you might say) before the slower, more thorough processes of the cortex have had a chance to evaluate the situation more carefully and determine whether there is any real danger.

Remember those associational links I mentioned? The woman might even be looking through a magazine, come across a picture of the Washington Monument and have a flash of confusing anxiety. If we keep the hard-wired function of the alarm system in mind, it makes sense. The brain has made a sloppy link between the earlier fearful experience that happened by the Washington Monument. The neural firing pattern that stored the information and emotional components from that experience has been activated, causing the woman to feel a small part of the fear she experienced on the earlier occasion.

A couple of years ago, a counselor in one of my workshops shared an experience that so interestingly illustrates how the alarm system makes mistakes. Several years before the workshop, she had given birth to her first child. At about the same time, she suffered a trauma. She didn't say specifically what had happened, but apparently it was quite significant. In an effort to move through the after-effects of the trauma at the same time she was caring for her newborn, she frequently played a piece of music that helped her calm her anxious energy.

About a year and a half after she had recovered from her trauma, she was at a friend's house having a nice, relaxing afternoon. Unexpectedly, the music she had played frequently in the months after the trauma came on the radio and she had a powerful wave of anxiety. Even though she had previously used the music to calm her energies, her alarm system had made an associational link between the music and the trauma. When the piece came on the radio unexpectedly, her alarm system took the stimuli, did a quick and sloppy scan of her entire memory and found a loose link between the music and the trauma. This link was enough to trigger the neural firing patterns that housed some of the challenging energy from the trauma. To use our metaphor, the hypothetical pipeline opened up and some of the anxious energy from the time of the trauma flowed into the present, dramatically influencing the counselor's experience on the otherwise pleasant afternoon with her friend. Again, the alarm system was just trying to do the job it was hardwired to do, but it simply made a mistake in alerting her to danger when none was present.

EXPLICIT AND IMPLICIT MEMORY

The sometimes confusing nature of our emotional reaction patterns becomes more understandable when we add this next piece to the picture we are building. We can talk about two general types of memory. Explicit memory is when we are aware that we are remembering something. If we think about it right now, we could remember some part of what we did today and we would know that we were having a memory. Keep in mind that, for purposes of our discussion, we can think of memory as the activation of neural firing patterns that store information and energy/emotional components.

Implicit memory is when one of those neural firing patterns is activated, opening up that fictional pipeline for information and energy to flow into and impact on our present-moment experience; but (drum roll, please, because here's the key point) *we are not aware we are having a memory!* We think that our whole reaction is in response to something right here in front of us, when the truth is that our reaction is being heavily conditioned by a memory of an earlier experience. To repeat myself, the confusing aspect of the whole experience is that we're not aware that the alarm system, in responding to a trigger in our present-moment experience, has made a link with the previous situation.

Many times I have heard my clients say things that reflect this dynamic. I remember a client who was struggling with anger issues say something like, "I got so angry at that situation, but when I settled down, I couldn't believe that I had such a strong reaction. It just didn't seem that important." Another client said, "I got so upset that I was acting like a five-year-old child." Both clients were instinctively sensing the flooding that can occur from the activation of implicit memories, but they had no way of knowing what was going on in their brains. They had no way of realizing that the strength of their present-moment reaction was greatly intensified by the link the alarm system had made with an earlier experience when they had truly felt at risk or unsafe.

An anecdote from a therapist in another one of my workshops reflects the persistent, and often confusing, power of implicit memories. After I had talked about implicit memories in the workshop, she shared the following story with me at a break. She said that for as long as she could remember, she had had an intense fear of even the smallest flying insect in her house. Although she had done a lot of personal work and felt, in her mid-forties, a good deal of stability in her life, she had not been able to overcome this fear—or to understand it.

About a year earlier, she had been out to lunch with her mother and her older brother. For some reason, her mother asked her brother whether he remembered an incident that occurred in their home when the therapist was very young. Apparently, a bird had flown down the chimney and into their living room. Not finding an escape route, the bird was flying frantically around the room. When the therapist heard this story, she immediately felt goose bumps all over her body and asked where she had been and how her mother had reacted. Evidently, she was in her playpen in the living room when her mother became terribly frightened and began screaming hysterically.

As the therapist related it to me, when she heard her mother's reaction, she had a powerful realization and something softened and released inside her. It was suddenly clear to her that her intense fear of flying things in her house was a direct result of the incident her mother had just described. When an insect was flying inside her own home, it triggered the implicit memory with her mother more than forty years earlier and she was flooded with the same fear she experienced as a young child. However, after she became able to identify the fear reaction triggered by a flying bug and see it as an expression of an old memory (and not as a current danger), the whole reaction faded and disappeared in a short time.

This story is an excellent reminder of several important points about implicit memories. First, most of our memories in the first eighteen months to two years of our lives are, by their nature, implicit memories. As adults, we generally relate to our memories linguistically (that is, in words); but early on, we are not recording memory in that way because we do not yet have language skills. The memories are there, but they are very difficult to access consciously. Second, our early memories are heavily influenced by the reactions of our parents or other primary caretakers. In other words, we look to our parents for an interpretation of our experience and what is stored in our neural firing patterns is largely determined by what we learn, moment to moment, from our parents' reactions.

In the anecdote related above, the therapist's young brain interpreted the experience with the bird in the living room based on her mother's reaction. Her mother was screaming hysterically, so the child's brain modeled the mother's reaction and stored the incident as one of great danger resulting in intense fear. Interestingly, the child probably would have had a different reaction if she had been alone when the bird flew down the chimney. Without the strong reaction of her mother, she may very well have reacted to the bird as just another fascinating moving thing, similar to a mobile in her bedroom, and not have recorded any sense of danger at all. If that had been the case, the implicit memory would have been very different indeed and she would not have been plagued by her own fear reaction for the next forty-plus years.

EMOTIONAL HIJACKINGS

Some of our early memories have a great deal of intensity to them. This makes perfect sense when we consider the hard-wired job of the alarm system and the vulnerability of the child. When you think about it, children, up to a certain age, are in a life-and-death struggle for survival. If they don't receive the basic necessities from their caretakers (usually their parents), if they are not nurtured, they could die. As we all know, unfortunately some children do die as a result of insufficient care or, worse yet, abusive and harmful acts.

Young children do not have reflective abilities, but they instinctively know how vulnerable they are in this world where everyone is bigger and more powerful than they are. So fearful experiences are very intense for them. Think of the three-year-old who is crying hysterically because she is afraid of something; there is no real limit to her sense of fear. Now think of the job of the alarm system: to store important information about the fearful experience for future reference so that it can wake up the whole body/mind/emotional complex to protect itself if anything like that happens again.

In fact, the neuroscientists tell us that the imprinting of these early memories is state specific. In other words, the more intense the emotional arousal (of fear, for example), the more strongly the essential aspects of the experience will be recorded in the memory. This makes sense in terms of the alarm system's job, of course. If the early experience involved an intense sense of being at risk or in danger, the alarm system is going to react with something like, "This is really important. I need to make sure that I make a strong record of this so that if anything like this happens in the future, I can recognize it quickly and alert the whole system to protect itself."

As I mentioned earlier, when the warning system sounds the alarm and we shift into the protection mode, changes are triggered in the body/mind that enhance our ability to meet the perceived danger. At the same time, other systems inside us are inhibited. This was essential for pre-modern human beings who often needed all their energies directed to confronting real dangers. It continues to be important for us when we need to marshal all our focus and energies in times of dangers, but the same dynamic frequently doesn't serve us so well. Due to the hard-wired responsibility of the alarm system and the intensity of earlier emotional experiences, the sounding of the internal alarm can lead to an emotional hijacking.

Let's review how this happens. The alarm mechanism of the amygdala is often described as sloppy. When the amygdala receives information from our senses, it compares the present perception with all the past experiences stored in our memory. If a key element of the present situation is associated with a past experience that was fearful or hurtful, it makes a loose connection and finds a match. The amygdala, and other components of the brain working with it, then command our body/mind/emotional complex to react with the thoughts, emotions, and reactions that were learned in connection with the past events. The result is that we react with old, out-dated emotional responses that are not effective or appropriate under the present circumstances.

In an important sense, the amygdala and the cooperating components of the limbic region and brainstem have "hijacked" the more thorough and analytical processes of the most sophisticated part of our brain, the cortex. So, when someone says, "I was so angry I couldn't think straight," there is a neurological reason for that. The alarm system has gone off, the limbic region and the brainstem have taken over and the thinking processes of the cortex are temporarily overwhelmed. The neuroscientists even talk of "neural static" being given off that inhibits the functioning of the cortex. In the middle of an emotional hijacking, we are simply not able to be reflective, logical, analytical human beings. Simply put, we are not operating with all our resources and therefore our best intentions are often swept away.

The brain's damper switch for the amygdala's surges is in the prefrontal lobes. This more evolved area has the capacity to analyze our perceptions more thoroughly, sort out the details of the situation and moderate the alarm signals of the amygdala if we are not really at risk. The problem is that the prefrontal lobe circuits actually fire after the amygdala has already begun to send out alarm signals. The analytical process in the prefrontal lobes, although more complete than the amygdala's "quick and dirty" evaluation of sensory information, is simply slower.

Consequently, an emotional hijacking occurs because the amygdala's quick alarm system essentially short-circuits the prefrontal lobes' ability to more thoroughly process the situation. The mind and body then become locked into a recurring pattern of the anygdala's emotional arousal, flooding us with stress hormones and fear, anxiety or anger. These internal reactions often result in repeating old unhealthy and ineffective patterns of speech and action.[28] As I often say to my clients, when we get caught in an emotional hijacking, we are neurologically impaired. It is not a personal defect. It is simply how the brain is hard-wired to function.

RETURN TO SUE'S STORY

Let's return to Sue's story and see how all that we have learned about the brain helps to make sense of her reaction. As you recall, Sue sought counseling with me because she was upset and confused by her reaction if a man withdrew attention from her. To use the term now familiar to us, she often found herself in an emotional hijacking when this occurred and was not able to respond the way she would have liked. From our discussion above, we know that her reaction may have had its origins in earlier experiences where she felt at risk. In taking a look at the possible connections, she had a specific memory that so clearly illustrated how the alarm system and memory interact to dramatically impact on present-moment experience.

Sue had four older brothers and a father who struggled with alcohol. Her mother may have had some depression, but she wasn't sure about that. Upon reflection, it was clear that her mother was generally worn out by the five kids and a struggling marital relationship. Sue remembered one evening when she was six years old. Everyone was at the dinner table and Sue was trying to tell her family something, but no one was paying any attention to her. This had happened on so many occasions in so many ways that it was very upsetting to her. She recalled leaving the table, running out of the house into the woods across the street, lying down and sobbing for what seemed like a long time. The entire time, two sentences were running through her mind over and over again: "Nobody pays any attention to me! Nobody listens to me!"

Sue's alarm system clearly had been triggered. She felt very hurt and alone. We know that, since Sue felt at risk or unsafe, it is the hard-wired job of the alarm system to record the experience for future reference. The imprint in her neural firing patterns (that is, in her memory) would be something like the following:

Information	Energy/Emotion
"Nobody listens to me."	Fear
"Nobody pays attention to me."	Helplessness
	Lack of safety

Very frequently, there is another piece of information that comes along with this type of experience. Sue loved her family and thought that they loved her. Consequently, the fact that so frequently no one in the family gave her the attention she would have liked was very confusing. At age six, she didn't yet have the capacity to be reflective about the whole situation. Instead, like most children up to a certain age, she came to her own conclusion as to why no one in her family was paying attention to her. Can you guess what she instinctively concluded? It was something like "Nobody pays attention to me *because* I am not important"—or "*because* something is wrong with me," or "*because* I am not good enough!" When a child comes to such a negative conclusion about herself, it becomes totally bound up with the difficult emotional experience and plays a powerful part in the whole reaction. It's not just that no one pays attention to me and I feel afraid or helpless. Even worse, no one pays attention to me *"because* I am just not good enough!"

As you can imagine, the early experiences of not receiving attention from her family were very powerful for Sue and left her with a feeling of pain and helplessness. In a way, when the alarm system connects the present moment trigger with the childhood experience, it is distorting time and persuading her that she is just as helpless as she was as a child. Because all this is happening as an implicit memory and Sue is not aware that she is being flooded by information and energy from her childhood, the experience is all the more confusing.

You can probably see where all this is heading. Flip forward thirty-one years from age six to thirty-seven when Sue appeared in my office. Now the reaction that was so confusing to Sue makes clear sense in terms of the functioning of the brain's alarm system. Some guy she has been dating doesn't want to go out on a particular evening. This information is a surprise to her and makes her feel uneasy. The alarm system takes this trigger ("He's not paying attention to me"), does its quick "computer scan" of everything in Sue's memory and finds a loose link with the earlier experiences when she felt so unsafe and helpless ("Nobody pays any attention to me."). To use the analogy I mentioned above, it is as though a pipeline then opens up and all that information and emotion from the previous experiences flow into the present. The result: Sue would find herself in an emotional hijacking. In that condition, she acted more with the energy and reaction of a six-year-old than with the full resources of the bright, capable grown woman she was.

The power of this reaction pattern over Sue has undoubtedly been growing for many years. There is a principle in neuroscience called Hebb's axiom. Simply stated, it is that neurons that fire together, wire together. Looking at Sue's situation again, we can see how this works from the specific memory we have reviewed. The information and emotional components of the experience ("Nobody listens to me because I am not good enough," plus fear and helplessness) gets stored in connections of neurons that become a neural firing pattern. Every time the neural firing pattern is triggered (unleashing the information and emotional components), that neural firing pattern is strengthened. In other words, it increases the likelihood that the particular firing pattern will get triggered again in the future.

Over time, in a firing pattern like Sue's, it can become a filter or a bias that impacts on how her alarm system is interpreting in-coming information. More and more, her brain was likely to interpret not just withdrawal of attention but also other slights or insensitivities with the same helpless reaction that "I am just not good enough." This conclusion about herself, drawn at a very early age and reinforced many times over the years, had become a state of mind significantly affecting how she viewed herself in relation to others and to the world. Put another way, it became her truth. Whether it was really true, is a very different question we will consider in detail later.

This perceptual bias or state of mind about herself acquires a stability from the way the brain naturally processes information from Sue's on-going life experience. Psychotherapist Louis Cozolino describes it this way:

> Another phenomenon that reflects the functioning of the hidden layers [of brain processing] is referred to by social psychologists as 'belief perseverance.' Put simply, belief perseverance is our tendency to attend to facts that support our beliefs while we ignore those that contradict our beliefs (Lord, Ross, & Lepper, 1979). . . . This may, in part, explain why many people with negative beliefs about themselves hold onto those beliefs with such tenacity. . . .[29]

Sue's experience was unique to her; but the way the brain's alarm system reacts to and stores early fearful experiences impacts on all of us. Just like Sue, virtually all of us have recorded painful or fearful experiences, especially from our early years when we are so vulnerable, not just as dangers that need to be remembered for future reference but as messages that there is something basically wrong with us. This negative conditioning about ourselves then gets triggered over and over again, undermining our happiness and leading to behavior that frequently is unskillful, ineffective, unloving or worse.

As we discussed in the last chapter, mindfulness enables us to interrupt these old patterns and begin the process of transforming them. The Stop-Breathe-Reflect-Choose practice offers a specific technique to work skillfully with our deeply-imprinted emotional memories and the quick alarm mechanism of the amygdala. In Sue's case, she utilized this practice to learn how to switch from the automatic pilot mode to mindfulness. Her growing ability to witness her internal landscape enabled her to notice when she was getting triggered and moving toward an emotional hijacking—or at least to notice that she was already caught in a hijacking. Slowly, she became more able to bring sharp awareness to her strong emotional arisings before acting or speaking. In terms of brain operation, this literally gave her prefrontal lobes a chance to catch up with the alarm signals of the amygdala, make a more thorough analysis of the situation and avoid repeating old patterns from the past. The practice enabled her to ask more thoughtful questions when a man withdrew attention from her, questions like, "Do I even like this guy? Is he worth getting upset about? Does his behavior really have anything to say about me—or is it more a reflection of his own fears or limitations?"

In a later chapter, we will look beyond Sue's case and explore more thoroughly the many ways the brain's alarm system becomes conditioned to react with negative patterns that do not support our happiness. For now, however, I encourage you to begin to see your own negative emotional patterns as something that makes sense in terms of the alarm system's hard-wired job to try to keep you safe, not as an indication that there is something basically wrong with you.

THE GOOD NEWS

This whole chapter we have focused on the real challenges presented to us due to the way the brain stores and then re-activates information and emotions from fearful or hurtful experiences. There is, thankfully, good news to this story. To borrow a word from an old movie, the good news is "plastics." In *The Graduate*, a man at a party excitedly explained to the Dustin Hoffman character how the future was in plastics because plastics could be molded into so many forms for different uses. In similar fashion, the neuroscientists talk about the "plasticity" of the brain. By this they mean that the brain is very adaptable and that our neural firing patterns are dynamic and can be re-worked over the entire course of our lifetime. It may surprise you to learn that the brain's capacity to change throughout our life has only recently been accepted by the neuroscience community. This realization is the result of a major paradigm shift in this area of science.

For virtually the entire twentieth century, the accepted "truth" in neuroscience was that although the human brain is quite plastic in the early years, the situation is quite different once a person reaches adulthood. The dominant belief was expressed in 1913 by Spanish Nobel Laureate and neuroanatomist Santiago Ramon y Cajal: "In the adult centers the nerve paths are something fixed, ended and immutable."[30] In the 1980's and 1990's, exciting research by many creative neuroscientists substantially undermined this conventional wisdom, but the old paradigm did not die easily. By the start of our new century, however, the cumulative effect of the new research could no longer be dismissed. Jeffrey Schwartz, research professor of psychiatry at the UCLA School of Medicine, has stated the new paradigm this way:

> The existence, and importance, of brain plasticity are no longer in doubt. . . . Cortical representations are not immutable; they are, to the contrary, dynamic, continuously modified by the lives we lead.[31]

It is not an exaggeration to say that this shift opened a new era in neuroscience and researchers all over the world are devoting substantial resources to exploring the exciting possibilities implied by the expanded view of the brain's plasticity. In just the past decade, new modalities of treatment have been developed for such diverse conditions ranging from obsessive compulsive disorder, dyslexia and disabilities resulting from strokes (to name just a few), as researchers and clinicians draw on the expanded understanding of the brain's amazing capacity for change.

This paradigm shift reinforces the path of mindfulness we are exploring throughout this book. It is a strong voice supporting our premise that the old undermining messages embedded in our brains from the early years of our lives are not fixed. The brain can be re-wired. Another aspect of the new research reminds us specifically of the importance of mindfulness. Dr. Schwartz makes the point emphatically:

> Physical changes in the brain depend for their creation on a mental state in the mind—the state called attention. Paying attention matters. . . . It matters for the dynamic structure of the very circuits of the brain and for the brain's ability to remake itself.[32]

As the strength of our mindfulness increases, and we are more able to bring clear attention both to the automatic energies arising in us and to the way we respond to them, we are maximizing the brain's plasticity, its capacity for change. To say it again: Paying attention matters!

I have witnessed the reflections of the brain's marvelous capacity for change in the lives of my clients, participants in workshops, my friends and in my own life. There is no silver bullet, of course, no magic wand we can wave to instantly change old neural firing patterns and the unhealthy reactions they trigger; but change is always possible. Just as in Sue's case, the challenge for us all is to bring the courage to face these old patterns that undermine our happiness and the persistence to continue working with them.

New neural firing patterns are imbedded in a fresh neural network relatively quickly. Think of how fast a toddler learns new language skills. Because our neural firing patterns have been strengthened for years through repeated activation, it requires many repetitions to interrupt the old reactions and invest, over and over again, in new ways of reacting and thinking. In the process, we are literally changing our brain.

In a real sense, the practice of mindfulness allows the old brain circuits, conditioned by fear and impacted by negative messages about ourselves, to lose their power over us as we replace them with new neural firing patterns created by our best intentions. So far, we have considered two aspects of the path of mindfulness: (1) the witness quality of mind that enables us to see the automatic activity of the brain and (2) insight about how the functioning of the brain's alarm system results in patterns that are not healthy for us. As we continue our exploration, we will draw on these two aspects and add other resources to strengthen our mindfulness practice. We will be creating, one small step at a time, a foundation for the lasting happiness we deserve.

SUMMARY

Much of what we have considered in this chapter about the brain's alarm system, memory and negative conditioning is new to many people. Others may have heard of some pieces of the information, but have not had the overview that can enable us to make sense of old and sometimes confusing reaction patterns. To help you make practical use of the information, the basic concepts we have considered in this chapter are set forth in summary fashion below.

1. The basic anatomy of the human brain reflects three parts: the **brainstem**, the **limbic region** and the **cortex**.
2. The brainstem and the limbic region function together as the brain's **alarm system**.
3. The hard-wired job of the alarm system, evolved over millions of years, is to evaluate the constant stream of

information coming in from our senses to determine if we are at risk and to alert the entire body/mind/emotional complex to prepare to meet any perceived danger.

4. The **amygdala**, a component of the limbic region, serves as "the smoke detector" and is always on alert to determine from information received from our senses whether we are at risk. In this role, the amygdala is central to the emotions of fear, anxiety and anger that are activated when the alarm system is reacting to a perceived danger.

5. When the alarm is sounded, we go into a **protection mode**.

6. The **fight-flight-or-freeze reaction** is the result of the alarm system preparing the whole system to protect itself from the perceived danger.

7. The **stress response** is often an indication that the alarm system has been triggered and that our system has shifted into the protection mode. Although we might not experience a full-blown fight-flight-or-freeze response, emotions such as fear, anxiety or anger are activated.

8. **Memory** is the way the brain records present experience so that future experience is affected.

9. It is the hard-wired job of the alarm system to imprint in our memory (in connections of neurons that result in **neural firing patterns**) experiences in which we have felt at risk, so that it can be alert to similar experiences in the future and warn the system if any such danger is confronted again. In this way, the alarm system is learning from our experience and storing what it has learned for future reference.

10. Fearful childhood experiences are generally, by the nature of the child's vulnerability, very intense experiences. Consequently, they are embedded strongly in our memory for future reference by the alarm system.

11. The memory of the fearful experiences generally has an **information component** (such as "Nobody pays attention to me!") and an **energy/emotional component**

(such as fear, helplessness, confusion, etc.). There often is also some **negative conclusion or message about self** (such as "I am not good enough!") that is embedded with the other components.

12. In the process of doing its job, the alarm system is constantly evaluating information from our senses and comparing it with past experiences.

13. The alarm system values speed over accuracy in making determinations about potential dangers. In an effort to keep us safe, it makes quick and sometimes sloppy decisions about potential dangers. As a result, it often makes mistakes about the nature of the present situation.

14. The alarm system reacts to present-moment triggers by doing what might be thought as a very rapid computer scan of all the information stored from previous experiences.

15. If a link is made with an earlier time when the individual felt at risk, the neural firing pattern storing the information and energy/emotional components from the earlier event is activated and impacts on the present experience. In other words, **the memory of the earlier experience conditions how we react in the present**.

16. **Implicit memory** is a firing of neural connections (with the resulting activation of information and energy/ emotion) without our conscious awareness that something is being recalled.

17. Many of our challenging emotional reactions of fear, anxiety and anger are heavily conditioned by powerful energies and messages recorded from past experiences without our conscious awareness of this impact (that is to say, without awareness that we are having a memory).

18. Due to the intensity of past fearful experiences, an **emotional hijacking** can occur when the alarm system reacts to a present-moment trigger by associating it with a strong memory from the past and directs our whole system to react with the thoughts and emotions

imprinted much earlier. In the process, the alarm system inhibits the processes of the cortex that could otherwise more thoroughly analyze the present-moment trigger and keep our emotional response in balance. In essence, the alarm system temporarily "hijacks" the effective operation of the upper regions of the brain.

19. Emotional hijackings often lead to ineffective, unskillful or harmful behavior that complicates our lives and undermines our happiness.

Some years ago I had a very sweet couple in their seventies in my cardiac rehabilitation class. The week after I presented the material about the brain discussed in this chapter, the husband said he had something to share with the class. With his wife sitting beside him with a big smile on her face, he related the following experience. "We have been together for many years. We love each other very much, but I am sorry to say that we have a long history of bickering and getting triggered by each other over the smallest things. This past week, when we started to do that, we frequently just looked at each other and said, 'Oh, that's just Amy talking.' It really helped us to back away from our old habit, avoid silly bickering and stay connected to each other in a much better way."

They hadn't quite remembered the whole name of that crucial part of our alarm system (the **AMY**gdala), but the presentation about the frequent triggering of the brain's alarm system made sense to them and they immediately began putting their new knowledge to use by effectively shifting an old pattern and creating a new experience. According to both the husband and wife, the result was that they enjoyed each other much more during the week.

The clear lesson from this wonderful sharing is very simple. As I said earlier, you don't have to become a neuroscientist for this information to be helpful. Just being a bit more savvy about your own brain, taking the pieces of this information that appeal to you now, can help you make sense of the challenging emotional patterns that undermine your happiness and support your ability to make healthier decisions for yourself. In the process, you are—slowly, slowly, slowly—changing your brain.

Set forth below is an exercise designed to bring together the Stop-Breathe-Reflect-Choose practice with the information reviewed in this chapter. You might find it helpful in giving your growing mindfulness practice a boost.

Mindfulness Practice in Everyday Life

Mindfulness can be a powerful tool for changing emotional reactions and automatic thinking that undermine our health and happiness. Like many other healthy habits, mindfulness is a practice, which becomes stronger and more effective as we repeatedly apply it to our lives. In order to nurture mindfulness in your life, do the following exercise.

1. Identify a reaction pattern that you would like to begin changing. This could be largely an internal habit or a reaction to recurring situations. Examples of internal habits could be harshly judging yourself in certain circumstances or drawing anxious or negative conclusions even though objective information does not support them. Examples of reactions to recurring situations could be anger at a loved one, road rage or impatience in specific circumstances.

2. List some reasons why you think you might have this habitual reaction pattern. Does it seem to be connected to any earlier experiences from your past? Does it make sense in terms of the brain's alarm system and the way earlier experiences are recorded in memory for future reference and activation? Is an implicit memory being triggered, opening up information and energy/emotional components from a past experience?

3. List some reasons why you would like to change this reaction pattern.

_____

_____

_____

4. Set a personal reminder to apply the mindfulness technique to the reaction pattern you have identified: **STOP—BREATHE—REFLECT—CHOOSE**. Again, be patient and kind to yourself! Take delight in your growing mindfulness every time you notice your old pattern, no matter how infrequently you notice. Resist the temptation to judge or be harsh with yourself for the many times you may not have been mindful. Remember, every time you mindfully notice the old reaction pattern, it is your innate wisdom waking up. Invest in that moment, in your own wisdom!

5. Monitor your experiment with this mindfulness practice. Did you remember to use Stop—Breathe—Reflect—Choose? Was there any change in your reactions? How did the experiment feel? Did you notice any resources that became available to you in applying the mindfulness practice? Can you be patient and kind with yourself when you were not mindful of the pattern and got hooked? Can you take delight and appropriate pride in those times (however rare) when you were mindful and were able to apply some of the Stop-Breathe-Reflect-Choose practice?

_____

_____

_____

_____

6. Stay with the one reaction pattern you have chosen until you notice that you remember to apply the Stop-Breathe-Reflect-Choose practice more consistently (not every time or perfectly, of course). When the practice feels more accessible to you, something that occurs to you more naturally, expand the practice to another reaction pattern that no longer serves your best intentions or supports your happiness.

CHAPTER 5

Step Three:
Self-Regulation...
Nurturing the Ability to Settle
Negative Energies

The Impact of Emotional Hijackings

While I was writing the last chapter on the brain, a client called. I will refer to him as Bill. Bill was very upset. Over the previous several months, a number of circumstances had resulted in his experiencing an increasing amount of stress at work. Just prior to his call, his supervisor had been "nagging" him to redo a simple form for the fourth time. Part of Bill's stress resulted from a deteriorating relationship with his supervisor and this morning's events were just too much for him. He found himself speaking very loudly to his supervisor. He has a booming voice anyway and everyone in the office must have been startled by his response. Bill knew he was upset, on the verge of possibly exploding; but he had the mindfulness to go to his supervisor's supervisor to ask permission to leave the office so he could settle down.

Bill had fallen into an emotional hijacking and he knew it. In my telephone conversation with him, I listened to all the morning's events. Although he wasn't where he wanted to be yet, he had already calmed himself considerably. I commended him for realizing how escalated he was and pulling himself out of the situation—for maintaining a connection with his mindfulness even in the middle of an emotional hijacking. At the end of our talk, he decided to take the rest of the morning off to make sure he had fully settled himself and processed what had happened.

Emotional hijackings occur so frequently in today's world. Unfortunately, in many cases the person who has become escalated does not have the mindfulness to catch himself, as Bill did, and bring restraint to his behavior. The resulting actions are often unfortunate at the least and horrific at the worst. I don't think anyone gets up in the morning and says to himself, "This is the day I am going to yell and scream at my kids!" or "This is the day I am going to fly into road rage on the way to work!"— and yet it happens over and over again. In fact, it is part of being human. Each and every one of us gets caught in an emotional hijacking from time to time.

When this happens, our best intentions are swept away and we act in ways we never would have imagined if we were "in our right minds." I am sure you could think of many examples from your own life, starting with yelling at the children or a partner or responding to a work colleague harshly. It can get much worse, of course. It could be fairly said that the lack of control and judgment during an emotional hijacking results in much of the emotional and physical abuse we hear so much about these days.

We know from the neuroscience reviewed in the last chapter that emotional hijackings can occur when the alarm system is activated by a present-moment stimulus that links up in the brain with an intense emotional experience from the past, flooding the individual with the overwhelming information and emotional/energy components from earlier events. We also know that when this happens, the alarm system temporarily hijacks the more thorough, analytic and reflective processes of the cortex. Consequently, during an emotional hijacking, we are simply not operating with all our resources.

The neuroscientists have another way of talking about this phenomenon. As we have said, the human brain is an extremely complex entity with many differentiated parts that need to communicate and work well with each other for us to operate at our maximum capacities. When this is happening, we are experiencing neural integration. In an emotional hijacking, we are experiencing neural disintegration. In other words, the magnificent harmony that occurs when the differentiated components of the brain are in balance has fallen apart. As a result, our thoughts and actions are dominated by the fear-based reactions of the alarm system, unchecked by the more reflective processes of the cortex.

Yet another way of thinking about all this is in terms of emotional intelligence. In his exhaustively researched and persuasive 1994 book entitled *Emotional Intelligence*,[33] Daniel Goleman made a powerful argument about the impact of emotional hijackings on our society. In a nutshell, his thesis can be generally summarized as follows. There are multiple aspects to human intelligence, two of them being intellectual and emotional intelligence. The development of these two aspects of intelligence does not necessarily go hand in hand. In other words, just because someone has intellectual gifts and has nurtured those capacities, does not mean that person has much emotional intelligence.

We have all met individuals who are very bright, but who do not seem to have any sense of their big egos and the negative impact their egos and actions have on others. The German language even has a specific term for this type of individual. It is not a particularly kind term, but I will share it with you anyway. It is *Fachidiot*. I'll bet you can guess where this is headed. *Fach* refers to a specialist and *idiot* means, yes, an idiot. The term refers to someone who is gifted in his specialty area but is kind of "an idiot" outside that area. One could say that he has very little insight about himself or his behavior towards others—in other words, very little emotional intelligence.

The next part of Daniel Goleman's thesis is that we devote a great deal of time to the education and nurturing of our intellectual intelligence. This is important, of course. The problem is that we spend comparatively little energy and resources designed to nurture emotional intelligence. Since emotional intelligence does not emerge automatically as a by-product of intellectual intelligence education, as a society we suffer greatly from a lack of emotional intelligence. This lack of emotional intelligence is constantly undermining the full use of our intellectual intelligence. Let's consider just one example of this. Suppose you have studied conscientiously for an important exam, possibly as a part of an educational program or for a license you are trying to acquire. You are confident that you know the material very well. At the time of the exam, you look at the first question and, unfortunately, you have no idea about the answer. The alarm system goes off, you are flooded with anxiety and now you can't remember much of anything about all the material you spent so many hours studying and mastering. The emotional hijacking has temporarily undermined your intellectual intelligence by inhibiting your ability to recall all the information you stored in your memory.

This is a relatively benign example of intellectual intelligence being undermined by the lack of emotional intelligence. Goleman's thesis casts a far wider net. He suggests that our society's relatively underdeveloped emotional intelligence is a major reason that we often treat each other in such disrespectful, harmful and even violent ways. In fact, Goleman begins the chapter on "The Anatomy of an Emotional Hijacking" with the frightening story of a man named Richard Robles, who in 1963 brutally murdered two young women in their New York City apartment. As Goleman related it: "Looking back on that moment some twenty-five years later, Robles lamented, 'I just went bananas. My head just exploded.'"[34] Needless to say, Goleman's book is a powerful argument for devoting more energy to the education and nurturing of our capacity for emotional intelligence.[35]

THE ALARM SYSTEM AND RISKS TO PHYSICAL HEALTH

As we reviewed in the last chapter, the human brain, like the brains of all other mammals, is "hard-wired" to respond to perceived danger in an effort to protect the individual. In essence, the body/mind/emotions go into the so-called protection mode that shuts down or inhibits the growth mode of the system. When the response is short-term (acute), it serves an important function in protecting the individual. In many instances, however, human beings often experience long-term stress (chronic) with significant harmful events.

If we were in a hospital setting, such as in the cardiac rehabilitation or wellness programs where I have taught, we would spend significant time talking about the risks to our health of the frequent triggering of the alarm system and the failure to effectively manage the fight-flight-or-freeze and the stress responses. We won't go into any great detail here; but the effects of the adaptive stress response (short-term or acute stress response) and some of the disorders resulting from long-term stress are summarized below.[36] The stress-related disorders in the right-hand column can result when the adaptive, short-term response in the left-hand column becomes chronic and we stay in the stress mode too long.

Adaptive Stress Response	**Stress-Related Disorders**
• Mobilization of energy	• Myopathy, fatigue
• Increase of heart rate & cardiovascular tone	• Stress-induced hypertension
• Suppression of digestion	• Ulceration, colitis
• Suppression of growth mode	• Loss of vitality, inhibited cell growth
• Suppression of reproduction	• Impotency, loss of libido, amenorrhea
• Suppression of immune system	• Greater disease risk
• Sharpening of cognition	• Neuron death

SELF-REGULATION AND EMOTIONAL INTELLIGENCE

In exploring mindfulness and working on our happiness project in the first several chapters of this book, we have already taken important steps toward nurturing our emotional intelligence. We have begun to develop more of a witnessing quality that enables us to see more clearly our inner landscape of thoughts and emotions, and we have become more "brain savvy" so that we can more readily identify when our alarm system is getting triggered. The next step is self-regulation.

Self-regulation is a key component to mental and emotional well-being. What exactly is meant by self-regulation? Simply put, it means settling ourselves down. It is human nature to get triggered, to have challenging emotions such as fear, anxiety or anger grab us by the throat (or by the heart) and threaten to overwhelm us. No matter how mindful, or how long we have worked on our own growth, we are still going to have these reactions. The task is not eliminating them altogether, but recognizing and managing them when they occur, as they inevitably will for all of us.

From all that we have learned about the alarm system of the human brain, we know that settling the powerful energies resulting from emotional hijackings is so important because, if we don't, we will not be operating at our full capacities. As I often say to my clients, we are "neurologically impaired" when we are in an emotional hijacking. It's not a personal defect. It is simply how the brain is hard-wired. Unless we settle down, we will not remember all the information we have studied for that important exam, or we may speak to our children or partners in a disrespectful or unskillful way, or we may do all sorts of silly or harmful things. Our happiness has already been undermined by the negative emotion. If we don't settle down, self-regulate ourselves, the likelihood is that our happiness will be further undermined by the repercussions of the actions and speech that flow from the initial emotional reaction. Moreover, settling the energies arising with stress enables us to minimize the significant health risks resulting from chronic stress.

Paul Ekman is one of the most highly regarded American scientists in the area of emotions, having devoted more that forty years to studying the area in cultures all over the world. In his 2008 book, *Emotional Awareness: Overcoming the Obstacles to Psychological Balance and Compassion*, Ekman offers a very pithy reminder of the dangers of acting when in an emotional hijacking, more technically known as "a refractory period:"

> When an emotion is triggered, a set of impulses arise that are translated into thoughts, actions, words and bodily movement. Once the emotional behavior is set off, a refractory period begins in which we are not only not monitoring, we cannot reconsider. We cannot perceive anything in the external world that is inconsistent with the emotion we are feeling. We cannot access the knowledge we have that would disconfirm the emotion. [37]

Let's apply Ekman's insight to a real life situation. Imagine that your boss, who is generally very kind and caring and who has consistently given you very good reviews, is having a bad day and makes a critical comment about your performance on a current project. If you were not having a particularly good day either, it is quite possible that you could feel a surge of emotion coursing through your body/mind, stimulating an inner dialogue that goes something like this:

> I can't believe he said that. It was so mean. He doesn't value my work at all. He doesn't even like me or care about me. I am not sure I am safe here. Maybe I should start looking for another job.

Ekman's research reminds us that when we fall into such an emotional hijacking (to use his term, a refractory period), our brain will only allow information that confirms our first emotional interpretation and we will not have access to information that would enable us to see the bigger and more accurate view. In the example above, your worst fears about your boss and your job will keep swirling around in your body/

mind, strongly reinforcing themselves. Until you settle down, you will not be able to remember that your boss is, in fact, a caring man who has valued your work for years.

In his 2009 book, *How God Changes Your Brain,* doctor and neuroscientist Andrew Newberg offers another useful reminder of the dangers of an emotional hijacking:

> Anger interrupts the functioning of the frontal lobes.
> Not only do you lose the ability to be rational, you lose
> the awareness that you're acting in an irrational way. [38]

What a dangerous double-whammy from an emotional hijacking! Not only do we lose the ability to be rational, logical and clear-seeing; we think we are acting with the very qualities that we have temporarily lost. We all know, from our personal experiences of acting when upset, how much of a mess this can repeatedly create in our lives.

Self-regulation begins, once again, with mindfulness— switching from the automatic pilot mode of being totally caught in our negative emotional reaction to identifying that we are getting triggered. We need to be able to recognize that we are headed toward, or caught in, an emotional hijacking. Sometimes it is very clear. We are getting upset, captured by some emotional energy, and we can see it. Often we recognize this, however, when we are well down the road to an emotional hijacking and the energies are so big that they are difficult to manage. We need to be more aware of our early warning signals.

This brings us to the wisdom of the body. Remember what happens when the brain's alarm system is triggered? Whether it is a dramatic fight-flight-or-freeze response or a more subtle stress response, a cascade of physical events is triggered. Among other things, our blood pressure, heart rate and muscle tension all increase and certain hormones are generated that make us feel "keyed up." Our body offers us signals that we are becoming escalated and need to pay attention. This is different for each of us. Maybe our stomach is churning nervously, or we are feeling heat in the body, or our muscles are tightening, or our heart or mind is racing, or the tone of our voice is changing. Mindful awareness of these signals helps us to wake up and pay attention. These changes or sensations in the body are warning bells that bring us to wakefulness in the middle of the challenging emotional reaction.

The earlier in the reaction we can pay attention, the better. Many of our negative emotions have a way of building and intensifying if we do not attend to them. A little anxiety can build to much bigger anxiety and lapse into panic. Irritation can grow to aggravation and then to hostility. Fear can start small and then gain an overwhelming hold on us. Paying attention to the wisdom of the body offers us the opportunity to recognize these challenging energies at an early stage when they are more manageable.

All this brings us back to the Stop-Breathe-Reflect-Choose practice. The **Stop** piece is the process of recognizing the early warning signals and switching into a mindfulness mode: "Stop! I need to pay attention to what is happening in my body and emotions—and I need to do it now!"

The **Breathe** aspect of the practice begins to work actively with the challenge of backing away from the threat of an emotional hijacking by settling the energies and emotions experienced in the body. As I mentioned earlier, I suggest that you take a big, loud sigh if you are by yourself and bring as much awareness as possible to feeling the effect in the body. This will enable you to tap into the natural settling and relaxing quality of the exhale.

Take a moment to remind yourself of this right now. After finishing this paragraph, put the book down and direct all your attention to taking several long sighs. After each one, just pause a moment, before you begin the next inhalation, and relax into the settling quality stimulated by the sigh. Notice how it softens your body or releases holding. What a wonderful feeling! Experiment with feeling the releasing quality of the exhale sweeping all the way from the top of your head down through the body to your feet. If you don't experience a settling quality in the first few breaths, take a few more conscious exhales and continue to notice what happens.

If you are with other people when you mindfully notice that you are getting triggered, the Breathe part is accomplished by simply bringing your attention consciously to your breath and settling in as much as possible to the relaxing quality of the exhale. We are always breathing and no one needs to know that you are applying your mindfulness practice.

You can strengthen the impact of your self-regulation by adding the additional resources referred to in the relaxation exercise described in Chapter Three. As you may recall, the first added resource is the body-mind communication. Simply say silently to yourself, as you bring your attention to the exhale, "Relax, settle down, let go!"—or any other such words that are useful to you. The body will follow the mind with a little practice. Finally, add the power of imagination and imagine that your muscles are relaxing, that your heart is slowing down and that your body is softening generally. Putting all three of these resources together—the natural softening quality of the exhale, the body-mind communication and your imagination—will make the simple process of mindfully bringing your attention to your breath a powerful self-regulation practice.

It is wonderful if we can catch the arising of strong negative energy before it has overwhelmed us (that is to say, before we have fallen fully into an emotional hijacking); but we're human and that is not always possible. Consequently, it is important to be clear about mindfulness practice when we recognize that we are already caught in an emotional hijacking. This came up in a retreat I attended several years ago with my meditation teacher. A very intellectually gifted man at the retreat posed the following situation. "I get so upset and angry. It catches me by surprise and I don't know what to do about it." My teacher's response was straightforward: *Just stop! Just stop!"*

This answer was coming from the basic position of doing no harm. When we get angry, there is a possibility that someone could get hurt by our actions or our words. Anger is like a brushfire. It is a powerful energy that can spread through our whole system and literally overwhelm our senses in an instant. We may not be able to prevent the brushfire from starting, but we can limit the damage that could result from its intensity.

From a neurological point of view, my teacher's response was just as appropriate, whether the strong negative emotion is anger, fear, anxiety, hostility or a similar arising. Unless we stop and do our best to settle the emotion (self-regulate), we now know that we will continue to be in a state of neural disintegration and will not be speaking or acting with our full resources available to us. One of my friends shared with me the following good advice about this situation:

> If you can't think straight
> And you don't know who to call,
> It's never too late
> To do nothing at all.

When we are angry or caught in some other emotional hijacking, we would also do well to remember the police warning we all have seen on TV shows or read about in the newspaper: "You have a right to remain silent. Anything you say may be used against you." We should even change that a bit to relate realistically to our lives. Anything you say to a partner, a child or a work colleague while caught in an emotional hijacking almost certainly will be used against you, or otherwise come back to haunt you, at some later time.

All these reminders point us to a key concept in the practice of self-regulation: *restraint*. The emotions activated by the triggering of the alarm system can be very powerful. Despite our best mindfulness practices, they do not always settle down easily. Consequently, even though we may be doing our best to settle the energies and pull back from an emotional hijacking, we need to bring restraint to our behavior. Many times, the best approach is simply to continue working with the self-regulation process until we have truly relaxed the energies and regained the neural integration that enables us to see the whole situation clearly and make wise choices about our speech and action.

An internal dialogue can be very useful in restraining our speech and behavior until we have settled down. Simply give yourself good sense reminders such as "I don't have to do anything right now. I don't have to argue or fight or defend myself. I can just be silent for a few moments and relax."

A participant in one of my workshops shared a cute reminder about restraint. She suggested that when we are in an emotional hijacking, or heading in that direction, we should think of the word "wait," which is a good reminder in itself and also an acronym for:

"Why am I talking?"

Just as my client Bill recognized in the example at the beginning of this chapter, sometimes we need to remove ourselves from the situation that triggered us so that we can devote all our energies to the continuing process of settling down. By doing this, we are also giving ourselves the best opportunity to bring restraint to our behavior and avoid doing harm that will only further undermine our happiness.

Even when we are successful in restraining harmful or unhealthy behavior, we often still face the challenge of settling churning thoughts. We can get so caught up in ruminating about the incident that triggered us. Many times, we go over and over it, trying to convince ourselves that we were right or worrying about some aspect of the situation. Thinking about our experience and learning from it is always important; but we cannot really draw meaningful lessons until we quiet this inner turmoil. Only then will we have all our resources available so that we can see the situation clearly. Consequently, it is important to continue with the conscious breathing (or other self-regulation techniques discussed below) until we have settled the powerful inner energies and churning thoughts.

THE POWER OF IMAGERY

Utilizing the breath to self-regulate, especially when combined with the reinforcing resource of our body-mind communication, is very useful; but it is not the only way to approach this big challenge. The power of imagery is also an important resource. Imagery has been used for thousands of years to touch us, to shift something in us in positive ways. More than thirty thousand years ago, pre-modern human beings crawled deep into dark caves to paint or scratch images that meant so much to them. Throughout the Middle Ages, most Western art was spiritual or religious art that was crafted to inspire us, to shift our mind, emotions and spirit in a positive way. In Eastern traditions, there are many practices using images to overcome negative tendencies and nurture positive qualities. Viewed from our perspective, it could be said that using positive imagery to self-regulate has always been a part of the human experience.

Our understanding of how imagery supports the self-regulation process has been reinforced by discoveries in neuroscience. When you bring your attention to a positive image, it stimulates the left prefrontal cortex part of the brain, the area that is roughly just behind the left part of your forehead. The left prefrontal cortex has strong neural connections to the limbic region and one of its many functions is to moderate the alarm signals that originate in the amygdala. When you focus on a positive image, you are stimulating neural activity that is wired to settle the challenging negative emotions experienced when the brain's alarm system has been triggered.

There is another reason to use an image that is powerful for you. As we all know, the negative emotional reactions we are working with, along with the old messages that usually are deeply embedded in them, have a strong hold on us. Once they grab us and get us stuck, they are not easy to let go of. To settle ourselves and bring our attention to something else, we need something that has power of its own, that has a chance to hold our attention in the face of these other strong mind-grabbing arisings.

One teacher describes it like this: The four-year-old boy has a toy fire truck that he has had for as long as he can remember. He loves it; he even likes to sleep with it. In other words, it has the capacity to really hold his attention. He is not going to give it up easily; but if you present him with a shiny new bike (all outfitted with training wheels for the four-year-old), he is much more easily distracted from the fire truck that so stubbornly held his attention just a minute before. Moreover, he can hold his attention on the bike, because it is so powerfully attractive to him. In searching out and utilizing an image that evokes an unconditionally positive reaction, you are giving your mind and heart something that can hold their attention in the face of the strong negative energies that would otherwise dominate your awareness.

Here are several examples of this. A number of years ago, I had two similar clients who were doing individual counseling with me at the same time. Neither knew the other—or that the other was seeing me. Both clients were men in their early fifties who were experiencing a great deal of anxiety, anxiety that was having an increasing tendency to lapse into overwhelming panic. After doing some initial work with both of the men and explaining the use of imagery in working with self-regulation, I asked each man if he would be interested in trying to use imagery in connection with his anxiety. Both were open to the experiment, so I asked each to think about it during the coming week and see if he could discover an image that had an unconditionally positive impact on him.

Keep in mind that they did not know each other and did not know that the other was doing work with me. Nevertheless, they came back with the same image. Both men decided to use their pet dog as their image. It made total sense. They experienced unconditional love with their pets and, because of that, just thinking about their dogs had the power to shift something in them. In addition, their pets' unconditional love was a strong energy for them. As a result, their minds were able to keep their focus on it in the face of other nagging negative energies. Over the following several weeks, whenever the men began to experience anxiety, they focused their mind on their dogs and reinforced the settling technique with internal reminders to relax. The practice was very helpful in preventing their anxiety from overwhelming them.

Another simple example is from my own practice. Have you ever awakened in the morning only to realize that your mind is already churning with anxious anticipation or dread? I think most of us have experienced this at one time or another, maybe all too frequently. It's amazing, is it? We are barely awake, yet our minds are already triggered and heading in a negative direction. The Dalai Lama has been a primary teacher for me for almost three decades. I don't have an "up close and personal" relationship with him, of course; but in the good company of thousands of other individuals, I have attended many of his teachings over the years, have read many of his books and have listened to recordings of talks I did not attend. He has been a great inspiration to me.

Photographs of the Dalai Lama's kind, smiling face are unconditionally positive for me. I have one of those lovely photos on the cabinet right next to my bed. Many mornings, the first thing I do upon beginning to wake up is to roll over and focus my sleepy eyes on the photo of the Dalai Lama's smiling face. Whether you want to look at the result from a neurological or a spiritual perspective, the result is the same. When I look at his face, the dread or anxious anticipation is stopped dead in its tracks as something very different, and very positive, is stimulated in me. It is a simple practice that takes no more than twenty or thirty seconds, but it is a powerful self-regulator that gets my mind and energies going in a direction that serves me well as I begin my day. What a relief it is to quiet that energy of waking dread!

There are so many advantages to using imagery as a technique for the essential task of self-regulation that I encourage you to experiment with it. Think of it: you will be doing important practice just by bringing your attention to something that you like thinking about! Don't worry if you think you are not good at visualizing, that you can't actually see a visual image in your mind. Actually, I'll bet you are better at it than you think. Can you see the face of a loved one in your mind's eye? Can you imagine walking into your kitchen, opening a cabinet and seeing what is in that cabinet that you go to every day? If the answer is yes to either of these questions, you are better at visualizing than you thought. In any event, even if you can't actually see an internal visual representation of your positive image, just bringing your attention to it and focusing on a memory or thought about it will have the same effect.

Here are a few guidelines for exploring the use of positive imagery to self-regulate:

Be patient until you have discovered an image that is unconditionally positive for you. Some individuals' first instinct is to use the face of their child. Be careful! That image may not be unconditionally positive; it may be tinged with anxiety, uneasiness or even guilt.

Explore a wide variety of possible images. Your image could be a favorite pet, as it was in the example I shared with you, or it could be a place in nature where you had a very positive experience. For you, maybe it is the face of a loved one or an image that has a spiritual connection. A good test is this: does the image you have selected make you smile, or warm your heart, or soften your body or energy when you think of it. If it does, you probably have found something just right for you.

If you have discovered an image that is really good for you, but not quite perfect, feel free to change or modify it in any way that does make it perfect. Add or delete something. For example, if it is a place in nature where you had a wonderful experience, but there was one aspect of the setting that was distracting, just remove that aspect or change it in some way as you begin to work with the image.

Experiment with creating a visual picture of your image in your mind's eye. If this is easy for you, practice sharpening your image, adding as much detail and making it as clear as possible.

More than twenty years ago, I was travelling alone in Ladakh, the most northern part of India. The area around Leh, the capital of Ladakh, is a high river valley above 11,000 feet. Since Ladakh is just on the other side of the Himalayan mountain ridges from Tibet, the area has been heavily influenced by Tibetan culture for centuries and there are many Buddhist monasteries there. One day I was visiting a monastery on top of a large hill overlooking this magnificently beautiful valley, and I discovered a forty-foot statute of "The Future Buddha" that filled an entire temple. Walking into the third floor of the temple, I came face-to-face with the eight-foot head of this incredible work of art. The face was so beautiful, the expression so serene and compassionate, that I spontaneously wept. After spending quite some time just sitting in front of the statute, I took lots of photos and it is an image I have used in my practice ever since.

I am telling you this story, because at the time, I didn't feel I was good at visualizing. Consequently, I spent time at home, sitting in front of my image, looking at a part of it (the eyes, for example), and then closing my eyes and sharpening my view inside of what I had just seen outside of me. In no time at all, despite my lack of natural skill, I had a clear mental image of the beautiful face that was so moving for me.

Energize your relationship with your image. This is easy and fun. All you have to do is spend some time with your image—that is, bring your mind to it— when you don't really need it for self-regulation. The purpose of this is to exercise your self-regulation muscle. By energizing your relationship with your image at times when you are not being challenged by negative emotional energies, you are strengthening your neurological and emotional response to the image. Then, when you really need to settle yourself, to self-regulate and regain all the resources of that wonderful brain of yours, the use of your image will be as effective as possible.

This easily can be worked into the flow of your day. For example, while driving to work or on errands, you can shut off the radio for a few minutes, close all those mental files that are active in your head, and just bring your attention to your image. You are still fully aware of the traffic, of course; but with a little practice, you will be able to easily handle your driving responsibilities and keep your image clearly in mind. Think of all the little spaces in your day when you could spend a few minutes, or even a few seconds, allowing yourself to delight in the memory and energy of your image: walking to the car, waiting in line, riding up an elevator, waiting for a red light to change, and on and on and on.

Naturally, it is useful to spend a little time here and there, devoting all your attention to your positive image and the reaction it stimulates in you. This, too, can be very simple. Just sit quietly anywhere, take a few relaxing breaths to soften your body and quiet your mind a bit and bring a focused attention to your image. Allow yourself to really open to the warmth and positive energy it evokes in you. There is a four-word reminder that will help you get the maximum benefit from this exercise:

Identify	—	your image and the positive qualities it stimulates.
Connect	—	with those positive qualities.
Intensify	—	your connection with those qualities by opening your heart and mind to them as fully as possible.
Rest	—	allow yourself to rest in the felt sense of what has been evoked in you.

When you need to self-regulate (that is, when you need to settle any challenging energies or emotions), bring your attention to your image with some determination to hold it there. If you can visualize a mental picture of your image, you may find it helpful to focus on a specific part of your body (for example, your heart area or the middle of your forehead) and visualize your image there. Allow yourself to open to the qualities your image evokes for you. If you have prepared for this practice by working through the steps I have outlined above, I am confident that your image will work for you in those situations that are emotionally or energetically throwing you off balance. It may not get you all the way to a full settling; but, with a little practice, it will definitely move you in the right direction.

After you have utilized your image for awhile, you might experiment with adding the resource of your body-mind communication. When you bring your attention to your image, try adding the silent message used in the other relaxation techniques: "relax, release, let go," or any other such words that work for you. For some, this increases the effectiveness of the settling process. For others, it is too distracting and it is better to just keep all your attention on the image and the qualities it evokes.

Something quite magical can happen if you utilize a positive image to soothe and self-regulate consistently. Naturally, the use of the image requires intention. You have to intend to bring your attention to your image to stimulate the neurological response that moderates challenging energies. After you have energized your relationship with the image for some period of time, you may find that it works for you without intentionally bringing your attention to it. In other words, you may find that in the middle of a stressful day, your image suddenly appears in your mind and, without trying to do anything, the energies swirling in your mind, emotions or body soften. I have had this happen many times with the two positive images I have used the most over the years. It not only softens my energy, it always makes me smile when my image unexpectedly gives me this little gift.

I had another surprising occurrence of a positive image spontaneously arising many years ago. Back in the early 1990s, I had a melanoma on my back. As you probably know, they can be quite nasty, even lethal. Fortunately, mine was discovered at an early stage and the prognosis was optimistic. Nevertheless, I supplemented my medical treatment with the use of imagery. I would frequently visualize a positive image on the site of the melanoma as a way of sending love and support to that struggling part of my body. One morning, after engaging in this practice for some period of time, an image of a big happy face, like those simple yellow ones that are so popular, appeared in my mind totally on its own, smiling at me from the site on my back where the melanoma had been. I had never used the happy face in my practice; but there it was, smiling so beautifully. It has been many years ago now, but I still vividly remember what a heart-warming experience it was. I always felt that my body, in its own magical and compassionate way, was thanking me for supporting it with the healing power of my positive image.

COMBINING TECHNIQUES

The task of self-regulation is so important, and so difficult at times, that is useful to experiment with combining techniques to increase the effectiveness of your practice. There are many more approaches than the basic ones I have discussed in this chapter. Although we will not have an opportunity to explore them exhaustively here, there are a couple of other techniques I would like to mention.

A combination technique that builds on the use of imagery involves the following two-step process:

a. Shift your attention to your heart and hold it there for a few seconds, and

b. Recall a positive image or setting, a person you love or a joyful event in your life and hold the positive feeling of the recollection without shifting your attention from your heart area.[39]

Another technique is referred to as anchoring and it is very simple. My opinion is that it is best used in combination with one of the techniques already discussed. It utilizes the grounding of the body by simply touching a place on the body as you bring your attention to the relaxing quality of the exhale. Even touching two fingers on the same hand together as you do conscious breathing will strengthen the self-soothing impact. My favorite approach is to put your hand over your heart as you tap into the breath or bring your attention to your positive image.

If you are alone when the need to self-regulate arises, a more comprehensive version of the anchoring approach is to literally wrap both arms around your body as you bring your attention to the inhale and then really settle into both the hug and the releasing quality of the breathe as you exhale. You might want to continue with the hug for several rounds of breath to further enhance the impact of the technique. When you let go of the hug, pay special attention to the sense of release that flows through your body. Whether you need to self-regulate or not, what a wonderful gift it is to give yourself a soothing hug!

GETTING STARTED

Self-regulation is so essential to our happiness. We could state this in a number of ways. We know from our review of the brain's alarm system functioning that automatic, pre-intentional arisings of negative energies, such as fear, anxiety and anger, are an unavoidable aspect of the human condition. Without effective self-regulation, we can so easily get stuck in these energies. We also know that when the alarm system gets triggered, we can fall into a state of neural disintegration—an emotional hijacking—and not have access to all our resources of logic, reflection, analysis or even memory. Stated yet another way, without being able to self-regulate, we are lacking emotional intelligence. For all these reasons, it is often said that self-regulation is a key component to mental health and well-being generally.

You may well have your own ways of settling down. If you do and they work for you, that's terrific. I don't want to interrupt what is already working. What we are doing from a mindfulness standpoint, however, is to create a cohesive practice that increases both the consistency and the effectiveness of the self-regulation. With that in mind, let's review the steps we have taken so far. Briefly stated, with Step One we are working to strengthen the witness quality of the mind, to see more clearly what is happening in our whole body/mind/emotional complex. With Step Two, we have become more brain savvy so that we can clearly identify what is happening when challenging energies arise, threatening to undermine our happiness and limit our capacities. Step Three now builds on the first two steps by increasing our ability to skillfully manage or regulate these unavoidable automatic arisings.

As the witnessing quality of the mind becomes more stable (and that certainly takes some patience), we are able to see our stuckness more promptly—and actually remember to use our self-regulation techniques. The remembering part also takes patience to strengthen, of course; but when we do remember to apply our practice, the self-regulation techniques I have discussed in this chapter are immediately accessible to us—and so simple. Think about it. We are basically returning over and over again to the natural settling quality of the breath and/or to a positive image that we love. We don't have to go out and buy any equipment, take a pill or turn to something outside us. We are relying on resources that are always available, are a part of our own natural capacities and are free. How wonderful!

As with all mindfulness, the trick is to be specific about what you are doing. By that, I mean you need to answer this basic question: *What is my self-regulation practice?* When you are clear about that, you can apply your practice consistently when you get in trouble with challenging emotions—and each time you return to your practice, you are exercising your self-regulation muscles. Like anything else, with consistent practice repeated over time, the muscles get stronger and you become more skillful.

So here is my recommendation. Choose the self-regulation technique that appeals to you and start exercising your muscles. If your practice is the simple process of bringing your attention to your breath and consciously relaxing into the natural softening quality of the exhale, terrific! If you decide to work with a positive image, take some time to review and work through the guidelines set forth above to lay the foundation for effective practice. Whatever you decide, the key is to bring as much intention and consistency to it as possible.

You may find that you don't remember to apply your practice as much or as often as you think you should. That's O.K. Forget the "shoulds". When you feel like you are not remembering enough or are not doing it well enough, be kind to yourself and just let those thoughts go. We are all in the same boat with this. It takes practice over time to strengthen our muscles and build consistency. When you remember to apply your practice, take delight in the fact that you have remembered and give yourself a pat on the back, even if it has been a long time since you returned intentionally to your practice.

There is a four-word reminder that might help you build the consistency of your self-regulation practice. It's the following "Four Rs":

Recognize — that you are stuck or caught in an unhealthy or unproductive mental or emotional arising.

Refrain — from speech or action until you have settled yourself with your self-regulation practice.

Relax — into your practice and into yourself.

Resolve — to recognize your stuckness and practice again in the future.

Set forth below is an exercise called the Safe Place Visualization and Meditation. If you are attracted to using imagery in your self-regulation practice, it is just one way to get started. Please do not be intimidated by the length of the instructions. A good approach is to read them through once or twice before trying the practice. As with all the meditative exercises in this book, it is perfectly fine to do one part, read the next part of the instructions and go back to the exercise until you have worked your way to the end. Very soon, the practice will become second nature to you.

Safe Place Visualization and Meditation

Instructions

Find a comfortable sitting posture, spine upright, hands held comfortably in your lap or on your knees.

Lightly close your eyes. If closing your eyes is not comfortable for you, look down at the floor with a relaxed, unfocused gaze.

Begin by bringing your attention to your exhale and taking a few relaxing breaths. The relaxing quality of the exhale can be enhanced by drawing together three resources: (1) the natural relaxing quality of the exhale, the quality we experience spontaneously in a sigh, (2) the body-mind communication and (3) your imagination. The power of the body-mind communication is utilized by giving the body direction—simply say silently to yourself on the exhale "relax, release, let go," or just one of those words. The power of imagination is utilized by imagining the muscles and tissues of the body relaxing, softening and letting go. Although it may seem a little complicated at first to think of all three of these resources on each exhale, with a little practice it begins to feel very natural to use the three resources at the same time.

Stay with the relaxing breaths until you feel you have settled in a bit. If you become distracted at any time by a thought or emotion (and it is almost certain that you will), simply notice that your mind has wondered off and bring your attention gently back to the exhale.

A very important part of the practice, even at this early stage, is to watch the temptation to judge yourself. This can happen in many ways:"Oh, I'm distracted; I can't do this right." Or:"I don't like that thought—or that feeling." Here the practice has a simple and repetitious aspect to it: just notice the temptation to judge yourself, your performance in the practice or the process itself, let go of the temptation as well as you can and gently return your attention to the exhale.

When you feel that you have settled into the relaxing breaths, open your imagination and see if you can remember a place or setting where you have experienced a special feeling of wholeness, safety, awe, inspiration or well-being. For some people this is a place in nature; for others, it might be a special place in their home or the home of a loved one. It might be a place experienced recently or long ago. In short, scan your imagination for a place or setting where you had a very positive feeling or response. If nothing comes up right away, be patient and allow your mind to work in a relaxed and spacious way.

Some people are not able to identify such a special place from their actual experience. If this is true for you, if you never have experienced a sense of safety or wholeness anywhere, you can create your special place from your imagination. If you spend some time with this creative process, the body will react with the same softening, the same positive reaction, as though you had actually experienced it.

You might create a beautiful garden, for example. If you do, pay attention to the colors, sounds, aromas and sensations that you want to be a part of your garden. What flowers and other plants do you want there? What would the light and sky be like? Your garden, or other environment, born of your imagination and creativity, can become a very special place for you, a place of safety and wholeness.

If you have discovered your special place, notice any colors that are a part of this place and sharpen them in your mind's eye. Even if you have difficulty actually "seeing" the colors, imagine how they looked when you were in this place.

Notice any smells or aromas that are a part of your special place and open your imagination to them.

Notice any sounds that are a part of your special place and sharpen your awareness of them.

Notice any physical sensations you experienced in your special place, perhaps the wind against your skin or something you touched, and open your imagination to the sensations.

If there is anything in this image that you would like to change or modify in any way to make the image even more positive for you, feel free to do it. If it is just perfect the way it is, that is fine, too.

Once you have connected with all the sights, sounds, smells and sensations of your special place, see if you can open your heart and mind more fully to the positive feelings and emotions you had there. In a relaxed manner, without straining, experiment with getting in touch with the felt sense of what you experienced in your special place. Possibly you can even intensify your sense of wholeness or well-being as you open to your experience. Relax into what has opened for you, the memories, the images, the feelings and sensations—all of it.

Now just rest! There's nothing more to do, nowhere to go—just rest in whatever experience has opened up for you.

When you are ready, conclude the exercise by setting a reminder that this special place—and the positive physical, mental and emotional reaction it stimulates—is always available to you. As you become more familiar with the image or setting, you can bring it up in just a second or two to help you settle a negative emotion, to relax your body and to return to a condition of balance and wholeness.

In addition to falling into dramatic emotional hijackings, we are hard-wired to get caught in somewhat lesser emotional states such as stress, physical tension, low-grade anxiety, and rushing or hectic energies. They are almost daily occurrences that we often barely consciously recognize. They are, however, very depleting, take a toll on our health and simply don't feel good. As a part of our self-regulation practice, we can begin to bring conscious awareness to the state of our body/mind during the course of our day and return to balance. Acting from a more balanced state of body/mind, not only will our brain be more able to draw on all our resources; but we will feel much better both during and at the end of the day.

Set forth below is a simple exercise that enables us to strengthen our self-regulation practice during even the busiest days. At the beginning, the most difficult part of the practice is remembering to do it. I suggest to my clients that they associate the practice with something they do several times a day and set the intention to do the practice each and every time this repeating part of their day occurs. One of my favorites is to associate it with walking to the bathroom. We do this several times a day and it is a great time to take 60 seconds to do the practice. Other times might be every time you get in the car if your work requires you to frequently drive or after every difficult phone call. After awhile, the practice will become more of a habit and speak to you spontaneously during the course of your day.

Mindful Transitions

The simple practice of mindful transitions set forth below is a wonderful strategy for settling stressful, hectic or anxious energies during the course of the day so that you remain more balanced and effective. Try to take a few seconds several times a day (or as many times as you like) to make a mindful transition. To start, it is helpful to link the mindful transition practice with a repeating activity you do during the day, like walking to the car, walking to the bathroom, etc.

1. *Bring your attention to and connect with the softening quality of the exhale.*

2. *Check in briefly with the state of your mind/ emotions/body.*

3. *Using the exhale, relax/soften your body and settle any negative energies.*

4. *Be accepting and gentle with yourself, even if you wish the state of your being were different.*

CHAPTER 6

Step Four: Life Story...
Discovering and Realizing Connections

A PERSONAL STORY

When I was in my twenties, I had this unfortunate reaction of being instantly triggered into irritation anytime my first wife made a directive or suggestive comment about something I was doing around the house. I am probably not the only American male to have this reaction, but I certainly had it in big way. When I got triggered—and we now know that my alarm system had gone off, producing a very noticeable energy in my body—I usually spoke to my wife from that energy of irritation. I am glad I don't specifically remember how many years I repeated this pattern, but it was quite a few.

At some point in my late twenties, or maybe even my early thirties, something like the following inner dialogue arose in me: "This is the person I love more than anyone in the world. Is she being rude or disrespectful?" I was trying to be ruthlessly honest with myself at that point and had to answer that ninety percent of the time . . . or at least eighty percent of the time, she was not in any way being disrespectful. She was just trying to express her opinion—to which she was totally entitled, by the way.

If she was not being rude, I realized that I had to look more closely at my own inner landscape and try to figure out what was going on with me. Why was I so sensitive to her comments? What fear in me was producing such a defensive, and sometimes offensive, reaction? This led me to look at my life experience to see if I could make a connection between some patterning earlier in my life and my reaction to my wife's comments. We will return to my personal story and see where my inquiry led me in just a moment, but I want to briefly review our insight about the brain's alarm system to emphasize the value in looking at the overview of our life story.

We know now from Step Two in Chapter Four that the "hardware" of the brain's alarm system, reinforced over millions of years of evolution, has the heavy responsibility of trying to keep us safe. It does this by constantly evaluating the steady stream of information from our eyes, ears and nose to determine whether we are facing some risk or danger. If, from the appraisal of this continuous flow of stimuli, it perceives a danger, it sets off the alarm and triggers a cascade of events in the body designed to gear us up to meet the perceived danger. It is this triggering that shifts us into the protection mode and can end up in a fight/flight/or freeze response.

The alarm system is hard-wired to learn from every experience in which we feel helpless or unsafe. It stores the circumstances of being threatened in our memory so that if anything similar happens again, it can once again be alert to the perceived danger. From that point forward, the alarm system will be sensitive to any signals that loosely link up with the earlier set of experiences. If even a sloppy connection is made between a person's on-going life experience and the earlier memory of being at risk, the alarm system will do its job to react to the present-moment trigger with a great sense of alarm—and quite possibly initiate a shift to the protection mode with all the messages and emotions experienced on the earlier occasions.

Once we realize the hardwired job of the alarm system, it is clear that looking at our history can reveal to us important healing information. Put another way, developing our life story with both courage and kindness for ourselves creates a context for the relationship between brain function and the negative emotional patterns that so often undermine our happiness. Creating our life story enables us to see our experiences and patterns in a holistic way. The experts in this area talk about creating a "coherent autobiographical narrative." In essence, this means that we are making sense of how our whole history is intimately connected to our present-moment experience. It's not a matter of re-living every horrible experience in our lives; rather, it is simply a process of creating an overview that may be detailed in some areas and more general in others. We will explore how we do that, but let's return to my story for the moment.

At the time that I began my inquiry about my aggravated reaction to my first wife's comments, I didn't have all the wonderful information we now have about the processes of the brain's alarm system, but I instinctively felt that I should explore the dynamics of my home environment when I was a child. Even in my early thirties, I did not remember many of the day-to-day details and nuances of my family's interactions; but I discovered that I did not have to look that far back to get important clues. All I had to do was to look at the patterns I could see in my parents now that I was an adult.

Here's what I have found to be true in reviewing my own life and the lives of my clients for many years now: if you look closely (and with as much compassion as you can muster) at the patterns and reactivity of your parents, you can bet that the reactions you now notice were also there when you were growing up. You can then imagine how you might have reacted to your parents' patterns.

I was very fortunate to have the parents I had. They weren't fully enlightened individuals or perfect parents (who is, really!); but they had a good relationship and were together fifty-nine years until my Dad died. As far back as I can remember and right up until they each passed away, they were very loving and affirming to me. All that was an amazing blessing, but it does not mean that I avoided developing my own challenging conditioning from my home environment.

My father was a very smart man, but my mother's mind tended to work a little faster than my Dad's. Mom was a wonderful woman, an inspiration to me and many others; but—bless her heart—she had a bit of a controlling nature and she tended to correct my father a lot, or be directive to him. (To her great credit, in the last ten years of my Dad's life, she worked very hard at not doing this.) My father loved my mother with all his heart; but he wasn't perfect either. Sometimes, because of his love and respect for her, he could take in my mother's corrective or directive comments without too much disturbance; but often he could not. My mother's comments would frequently undermine his confidence, confuse him or be heard as personal judgments on his capabilities; and he would react with some combination of irritation, defensiveness or aggravation.

I heard a teacher jokingly say once, "Yea, I inherited my father's eye color, hair color, height and all his aggravating habits!" We don't actually inherit habits, but we do often learn them from the modeling of our primary caretakers, usually our parents. More technically, our neural firing patterns have a tendency to develop in relationship to the neural firing patterns of our caretakers. Daniel Siegel, psychiatrist and professor at the U.C.L.A., describes this "interpersonal neurobiology" generally as follows:

> . . . I am proposing that the mind develops at the interface of neurophysiological processes and interpersonal relationships. Relationship experiences have a dominant influence on the brain because the circuits responsible for social perception are the same as or tightly linked to those that integrate the important functions controlling the creation of meaning, the regulation of bodily states, the modulation of emotion, the organization of memory, and the capacity for interpersonal communication. Interpersonal experience thus plays a special organizing role in determining the

development of brain structure early in life and the ongoing emergence of brain function throughout the lifespan.[40]

Siegel and colleague Mary Hartzell have a direct message for parents about the impact of interpersonal neurobiology:

> In fact, experience shapes brain structure. Experience is biology. How we treat our children changes who they are and how they will develop.
> . . . Parents are the active sculptors of their children's brains. The immature brain of the child is so sensitive to social experience that adoptive parents should in fact also be called the biological parents because the family experiences they create shape the biological structure of their child's brain.[41]

Seeing my Dad's reaction to my Mom's corrective comments was like having a light bulb switched on in my head. Although I didn't have the terminology at the time, there was interpersonal neurobiology at work. As a child, either I identified with my Dad or just internalized the tension between my mother and father at those moments. At any rate, my reaction directly paralleled my father's. In fact, when I looked at my reaction, I discovered a whole internal subtext, just slightly below the surface and previously out of my sight, that went along with my reaction: "What! You don't think I am capable! You don't think I am smart! You don't think I know what I am doing!" Looking at my Dad's reaction, once I could see it more clearly as an adult, I could see all those messages firing off in him when he reacted to Mom in an irritated or defensive way.

In earlier chapters, I introduced the concept of the plasticity of the brain, the brain's amazing capacity to change throughout our entire lifespan. We also reviewed how mindfulness practice enables us to witness the triggering of the alarm system just trying to do its job to keep us safe. As we begin to see the specific connections between our life stories and the triggering of our alarm systems, our mindfulness practice becomes even more effective. When we have developed a more holistic overview of what is happening with the triggering of our negative emotional patterns, we are able to identify them more clearly—and to see them with a deepened insight. This enables us to work more skillfully with the stuckness and contractedness that often result from being triggered. We then have a better foundation for managing the triggering, settling ourselves to regain our balance and making choices that better serve our well-being. In the process—slowly, slowly, slowly—we are literally changing our brains. We are creating the conditions for a more durable happiness.

I didn't have the exact language of the Stop-Breathe-Reflect-Choose practice when I first consciously realized the connection between my reaction to my first wife and the earlier experiences from my life story; but I instinctively did what that practice encourages us to do. I paid attention to the warning signals that I was triggered. I did the best I could to settle myself by paying attention to my breath and sending a mental message to relax and let go. On those occasions when I could even get to the next stage, I tried to remember my most helpful and healthy insights about the whole reaction. My inner dialogue would go something like this: "I know this old process. I have seen it before and it has a long history that began with very early influences. This is the woman I love more than anyone else. Since she is not being rude or disrespectful, I should just keep trying to settle myself and really check in on what she is saying to me without drawing all sorts of conclusions about myself or her intent that are not supported by the reality of the present moment."

Of course, I am like everyone else in these situations. Once the alarm system has gone off and the resulting energy has moved all through me like fast-moving brushfire, it is not so easy to fully settle the emotions and truly return to balance. Consequently, when I first started working with my pattern, the best choice I could make was often *restraint*. I tried not to respond until I could really settle down and speak in a way that was consistent with my best intentions.

With just a few decades of practice, I can honestly say that those old neural firing patterns have withered and lost their power over me. They may not be totally gone; but now I can respond to my second wife, with whom I have shared my life for more than twenty years, with a reaction that serves us both so much better when she makes a suggestion about something I am doing around the house. I don't have the same brushfire of aggravated energy and can ask for feedback or clarification about her suggestion. My reaction might even be the good-natured response of "That sounds like a terrific idea, Sweetie! Why don't you take care of it."

I want to emphasize something very important here. This change in my reactivity, and the literal change in my brain, is not something special about me. The change is a result of all the mindfulness practice we have discussed so far. With practice, practice, practice, such changes are available to us all.

EXAMPLES FROM CLIENTS' LIFE STORIES AND THE GUIDES REVEALED

As I said earlier in the book, I have yet to meet anyone who is fully and totally enlightened. If we are not in that very small class of human beings, we are all in the same boat—we just have our own unique and special berths on that boat. We all have some conditioning producing repeated patterns of reactivity that undermine our happiness and do not serve us well. Once we see our present moment reactivity holistically, within the context of our life story and with insight about the processes of the brain's alarm system, our reactivity makes a great deal more sense. In my counseling practice and teaching experience, I have had so many examples of how exploring the life story of the individual revealed connections that were meaningful. Sharing a few of these examples may help you to discover your own themes and messages hidden in the holistic view of your life story.

Jane was a woman in her late thirties who had a good job and a successful track record of employment. She came to me because she was getting into difficulty at work for being over-reactive to even the slightest criticism. Whenever I sense that it may be useful to look for connections between the present-moment reactivity and the individual's life story, I always ask whether the person feels comfortable creating an overview of her or his autobiographical narrative. I asked Jane if she felt ready to do this and she said she was.

The themes and messages emerging from our life stories can arise in many ways from creating a narrative overview. There are often a number of themes that may emerge, but single memories or one pattern from childhood experience can be a powerful aid in making sense of the unhealthy conditioning. When these are discovered, they serve as a clear guide for action.

Jane reported having a decent relationship with her mother, with the usual ups and downs that generally occur between mother and daughter; but she realized that her mother never gave her a compliment that wasn't followed by the three-letter word (can you guess it?) . . . "*but*." "Boy, that B on your report card was pretty good, *but* if you had just worked a little harder, you could have gotten an A." "That skirt looks nice, *but* if it were just a little longer." "It was nice that you cleaned out the sink, *but* I wish you would have wiped down the counter, too." . . . and on and on.

No one would say that this pattern in the relationship looks like a big trauma. It certainly does not have the acute intensity of being slapped or hit; but if it is repeated frequently, over time it can become very disturbing to the child. Furthermore, what is the message the young girl's alarm system is likely to store from such a repeated pattern? For Jane, it was clearly something like, "I can never get anything right!" Many times, as we have seen before, there will be another conclusion that goes along with the primary message: "I can never get anything right, *because* I am just not smart enough . . . or not capable enough . . . or *because* there is just something basically wrong with me!"

For Jane, her alarm system would go off in response to criticism at work as her brain made a loose connection with the old pattern with her mother. Without her realizing it (remember, *implicit memories*: no conscious awareness that we are remembering something), all those old messages and the upsetting energy of the young child would flood into her present experience and trigger an emotional hijacking. Once in an emotional hijacking, logic and reason were not available to her and her reaction to her work colleague would be dominated by the upsetting energy and helplessness of the whole line of earlier experiences.

Paul was in a class I taught. After we had spent a class on the dynamics of the brain's alarm system, he realized for the first time that his young brain had stored some very specific messages and that these messages had heavily impacted on him all his life. Paul shared with the class that he relentlessly beat up on himself every time he made even the smallest mistake. To make matters more difficult, he realized there was a message just below the surface of the reaction that if he made a mistake, something terrible was going to happen.

Paul's father was a career Marine. Paul clearly loved and respected him a great deal. When he was a child, his father was a big presence in his life. For his Dad, there was the Marine way and the wrong way—and nothing in-between. Moreover, it was emphasized to Paul how important it was to do it the Marine way (that is to say, the "right" way). Either this message was delivered harshly too frequently, or the young Paul over-generalized it and took it very personally when it was delivered by his father. Why wouldn't he, since it came from this strong-minded, big presence in his childhood. At any rate, when the young Paul didn't get it just right and the strong message was delivered once again by Dad, a powerful fear of not getting something right was embedded in his neural firing patterns. We can be fairly certain also that he, as a child, drew the usual conclusions that were also stored, something like "I let my father down. I keep making mistakes because I am not smart enough or *because* there is something wrong with me!"

In realizing these connections, Paul was able to begin the process of disengaging from his unhealthy reactivity around making mistakes. By practicing mindfulness, he was able to slow down the process and affirm for himself that mistakes are inevitable. "To err is human," after all. Although he still wanted to get things right, he was more able to be kind to himself when he did make a mistake. Moreover, he began to break through the message that if he made a mistake, something disastrous was going to happen. This might be true if you are a Marine training to fly a military helicopter. Lives depend on that; and if a mistake is made, something terrible could happen. But not all mistakes are the same. The consequences are not the same, for example, for absent-mindedly tipping over a glass of water as they are for incorrectly following the procedures for landing a helicopter.

Mike's challenging conditioning developed in a different way. At the time I was working with him, Mike was a man in his mid-thirties who had risen quite quickly in his career field. He came to me because his happiness was being undermined by a powerful tendency to engage in what he called "what-if negative thinking."

His mind was constantly anticipating all the possible dangers and negative events that might occur in his life. His pattern reminded me of something that Mark Twain supposedly said: "I have had a lot of tragedy in my life . . . and some of it actually happened!"

To make the pattern even more challenging, not only did Mike so often become engaged in negative anticipation, he then felt compelled to develop a detailed plan for all the possible dangers that might occur. As you might imagine, this took a great deal of energy and consumed a lot of his attention, distracting him from his work, his family and generally undermining his happiness.

When we face fearful experiences as children, we all develop coping strategies to manage, as well as we can at those young ages, the fear and the circumstances that stimulate it. The difficulty is that we are only children. We have limited options available to us and do not yet have well-developed intellectual capacities that would enable us to sort out the whole situation in a logical or analytical way. The coping mechanisms developed early on are the best we can do, given our age and abilities;

but they are often very ineffective or have big negative side effects. Even if they work somewhat for awhile, they often break down totally at some point. Mike's pattern of what-if negative anticipation and the need to develop a strategy for every anticipated negative event arose out of feeling unsafe earlier in life. Both the constant anticipation and the compulsive development of detailed strategies were coping mechanisms designed to ease his anxieties and to help him feel safe. Of course, despite all the effort, he never really felt safe. Therefore, his brain just kept on ceaselessly anticipating and painstakingly developing plans.

As I have said before, there is always more than one aspect to the development of our unhealthy conditioning, but one part of Mike's home environment during his early formative years was significant. As with Jane above, Mike has had a generally positive relationship with his mother throughout his life; but in creating his life narrative and looking for connections, he realized again that his mother had always been an out-loud obsessive worrier. There was constant chatter in the house about something that wasn't going right for her or that she was anxious about. Remember that the evolving brain of the child mirrors the neural biology of the primary caretakers. In other words, the child's brain develops neural firing patterns that model or reflect the neural firing patterns of the parent. What is the message that Mike's alarm system was so frequently taking in: "Watch out! Something terrible is going to happen. Be careful! There is danger right around the corner. Be alert! Be vigilant! Be prepared . . . always!"

With all the messages Mike's young brain received (and there were others that complemented the messages from his mother's pattern), his alarm system became hyper-alert to possible dangers and was overzealous in reacting to the moment-to-moment stimuli in his life. The coping mechanisms he developed early on in an effort to give him a sense of safety never really worked in the face of his anxiety about the dangers he might confront. Therefore, the alarm system and the coping mechanism were on overdrive a great deal of the time.

Heartbreaking Explicitly Negative Messages

In my own example and in the other examples described above, one of the most painful aspects of the information that is stored in the brain is the conclusion the child draws about himself, conclusions that are drawn because the child doesn't have the ability to sort out the actions of the primary caretakers or the family dynamics generally. It is not hard to see why the child takes the painful experiences personally and often draws a negative conclusion about himself. Most of us have a strong natural tendency to react this way. Sometimes, however, the child does not have to draw any conclusion about himself at all, because the message comes in loud and clear. Virtually everyone has heard them directed to others, heard about them or experienced them personally.

I had a particularly poignant example of these direct messages and the impact they have from a workshop I led for counselors, social workers and psychologists in December of 2005. One of the participants left the following letter for me at the end of the workshop.

Terry,

My neck is chronically on the verge of spasm. This condition is growing since my very early 20s. I fear a total lock-up in neck mobility. No medical reason or treatment available that I can find.

I recently learned about torture being defined as using methods to maximize the terror of the prisoner and causing permanent changes to his psyche.

Dad died when I was three. Mom dropped me off wherever she could to be free of me, at least until I was 8. I stayed with my Dad's brother when I was 7. One evening he placed me on the dinner table naked. With his wife's assistance, he threatened me with a large knife. I tried to leave my body. I knew I was going to die. He talked to me for 20 minutes or more. He said I was a bad boy and he would contact

God and send me to Hell if I ever did anything that anyone disapproved of and he found out about it.

Bob

It is heart-breaking that such messages are delivered to children, but we all know they are. There is no way that children can sort out these messages or insulate themselves from them. Unless the parent or other caretaker makes a significant effort to help the child dispel them, the child will take in the messages as true. The child will not be able to see that the message arises from the caretaker's own conditioning or that it is not really a true reflection on the child's basic nature. Physician and researcher Bruce Lipton describes it this way:

> ... While almost all organisms have to actually experience the stimuli of life first-hand, the human brain's ability to 'learn' perceptions is so advanced that we can actually acquire perceptions indirectly from teachers. Once we accept the perceptions of others as 'truths,' *their* perceptions become hardwired into our own brains, becoming *our* *'truths.'* Here's where the problem arises: what if our teachers' perceptions are inaccurate? In such cases, our brains are then downloaded with misperceptions.
> . . . [T]he programmed misperceptions in our subconscious mind are not 'monitored' and will habitually engage us in inappropriate and limiting behaviors. (Emphasis in the original.)[42]

BIG "T" TRAUMA AND LITTLE "T" TRAUMA

The Diagnostic and Statistical Manual of Mental Disorders, the primary reference utilized by mental health professionals in assessing the mental states of clients, defines trauma as ". . . [a] direct personal experience of an event that involves actual or threatened death or serious injury, or other threat to one's personal integrity; or witnessing an event that involves, death, injury, or a threat to the physical integrity of another person;

or learning about unexpected or violent death, serious harm, or threat of death or injury experienced by a family member or other close associate."[43] In a simpler way, we might say that trauma involves a significant threat to one's physical, emotional or mental safety in the face of helplessness.

Mental health professionals who work in the trauma sometimes speak of "big T trauma" and "little t trauma." We can all identify examples of big T trauma: serious accidents, death of a parent or other loved one, sexual, physical and/or emotional abuse. The letter left for me from Bob that I quoted above illustrates how emotional abuse can be very traumatic for the child without involving any physical or sexual abuse. Sexual, physical or emotional abuse by a parent or other caretaker is particularly traumatic for the child because it is, in effect, a profound double-whammy. Not only is it terrifying, but the source of the terror is coming from a person that the child depends on and wants to trust. The child instinctively knows that her life depends, at least in part, on this person; but it is this very person who is breaching her trust and causing such a powerful experience of terror and danger.

These traumatic experiences can lead to a condition many people have now heard of: post-traumatic stress disorder ("PTSD"). Bessel A.van der Kolk, one of the highly respected experts in the area of trauma, briefly describes this condition as follows:

> After people have been traumatized, certain feelings, sensations, or actions can, without apparent rhyme or reason, generate a predictable set of emotional or physical responses that are utterly irrelevant to what is occurring in the present. These reactions seem to occur in people with PTSD because neuronal networks in the brain are activated by sensations, emotions, of feelings that were experienced during the trauma. A sensory or motor response is then activated that would have been relevant on the original occasion (such as fight, flight or freeze), but fails to resolve the hurt, pain, terror or helplessness

that the person is experiencing, just as it failed to do
so during the trauma itself.[44]

Needless to say, working with trauma that results in PTSD
is a very challenging process that should be supported by a
professional experienced in the area. It is useful, however, to
think about van der Kolk's description of PTSD expansively
and in the context of both big "T" and little "t" trauma. PTSD
is most often diagnosed in people who have experienced big
"T" trauma: horrific wartime conditions, serious accidents,
witnessing the death of another and so on. Putting aside the
usual clinical diagnosis of PTSD for the moment, we can see
how van der Kolk's description of the body's reaction to danger
applies equally to little "t" trauma.

Remember that trauma can be described as a significant
threat to one's physical, emotional or mental safety in a state of
helplessness. For children up to a certain age, many conditions in
their home environment can feel like a significant threat to their
safety in a state of helplessness without the condition falling into
the usual categories of "trauma." A father raging unpredictably
at a mother, a mother frequently being unavailable to the child
due to the mother's depression and explicitly negative messages
delivered to the child in an angry way can all feel traumatic to
the child and trigger the reactions that van der Kolk describes in
connection with PTSD.

Even relatively ordinary and inevitable occurrences during
childhood can be recorded as little "t" trauma with long-term
effects if the child experiences them in a way that feels like a
threat to the system in a relative condition of helplessness. In his
book, *Trauma Through a Child's Eyes,* Peter Levine recounts the
example of four-year-old Henry who had developed an aversion
to his previously favorite foods of peanut butter and jelly and to
the barking of the family dog. About a year earlier, Henry had
been sitting in his high chair, having a peanut butter and jelly
sandwich. As he held his half-empty glass of milk out for his
mother to fill, he lost his grip and the glass feel to the ground
with a crash, leading to following series of events:

> This startled the dog, causing it to jump backward,
> knocking over the high chair. Henry hit his head
> on the floor and lay there, gasping, unable to catch
> his breath. Mother screamed and the dog started
> barking loudly.[45]

In falling to the ground and temporarily losing his breath, Henry experienced a threat to his safety in a relative condition of helplessness and the event was recorded as a little "t" trauma. As a result, because the survival system of the brain records all the details of such events and associates them with the danger, Henry developed an aversion to his previously favorite foods of peanut butter and jelly, as well as to the barking of the family dog. To Henry's alarm system, these details had now become warning signals of potential danger. Needless to say, many such relatively ordinary but upsetting events occur in a child's early years. They don't all leave such a powerful impact; but as Henry's story illustrates, they certainly can—and many do.

There are a number of important reminders we can draw from this:

1. Children, in their vulnerable and dependent states, experience a sense of danger or threat to their safety from a wide variety of experiences in their home environment.

2. Although circumstances may not seem traumatic from the adult perspective, it may still be experienced by the child as very threatening. Stated another way, even though the experience may not fit into the usual categories of "trauma" (big "T" trauma), it still may have been traumatic (little "t" trauma) to the child.

3. Both big "T" and little "t" trauma experienced by the child leave deep imprints on the child consistent with the processes described by van der Kolk with regard to PTSD.

4. It is important to think about our childhood experience from the child's perspective when we are seeking to

make sense of our negative conditioning by exploring our life story.

DELVING INTO YOUR PERSONAL LIFE STORY

As we create our personal life story, and hold it in the context of our understanding of the hard-wired functioning of the brain's alarm system, it enables us to make more sense of the habits and patterns that undermine our happiness. Our look at the alarm system helped us to understand "the hardware" of this part of the brain's processes. Developing our life story clarifies how the hardware of the alarm system was programmed with "the software" evolving from our life experience. Understanding how the universal hardware of our alarm system and the personal software from our life experience function together gives us a clear view of those patterns, habits and reactions that so sweep away our best intentions. Seeing our negative patterns in this holistic manner enables us to effectively apply mindfulness practice to intervene on the old negative patterns and to choose new and healthier ways of thinking, acting and being. In the process, we are literally changing the conditioned neurological patterns in our brain.

Siegel and Hartzell have a lovely way of describing this process:

> Reflecting on your childhood experiences can help you make sense of your life. Since the events of your childhood can't be altered, why is such reflection helpful? A deeper self-understanding changes who you are. Making sense of your life enables you to understand others more fully and gives you the possibility of choosing your behaviors and opening your mind to a fuller range of experiences. . . .
>
> Our life stories can evolve as we grow throughout the life span. The capacity to integrate the past, present and future allows us to move into more coherent levels of self-knowledge.[46]

As I said earlier, creating an overview of your life story does not mean re-living every horrible event you might have experienced. Instead, it is a process of imagining how your child-self would have reacted to your primary caretakers and your home environment. In this process of reflection, it is important to bring, as much as you can, a sympathetic attitude about your parents or other caretakers. This is not about blame. As a counselor in one of my workshops said to me recently, "It is a fact-finding mission, not a fault-finding mission."

As far as I know, there are no perfect parents, just as there are very few (or possibly no) fully and consistently enlightened individuals. Even when their reactions toward us fell far short of being affirming or nurturing, our parents did the best they could, given their own entrenched conditioning. You may not be ready to forgive your parents for some of their behavior, but I encourage you to focus on understanding and making sense of your life experience, instead of on blame for your parents' possible short-comings.

Reflecting on our life experience can be difficult. You may feel vulnerable as you look back or may even feel ashamed of certain of your own behaviors. This is natural. Of course, if you feel too overwhelmed by the process, you should consider proceeding with the support of an experienced counselor or other helping professional.

Embracing our whole life story can be stressful at first; but it leads to greater insight about our conditioning. With new understanding, we are more able to soften our hearts and be more compassionate toward ourselves. As the formation of our negative conditioning makes more sense, we can identify it more clearly, disengage more easily and invest in new ways of reacting.

Set forth below is a contemplative exercise for reflecting on your life story. Even if you don't have specific memories in response to one of the questions, you can approach the exercise by imagining how you might have reacted to certain conditions in your home. Using your imagination starts with identifying your parents' patterns or habits that you noticed after you became an adult. Think about how those patterns were reflected (or are still reflected) in the behavior of your parents individually and in their reactions to each other. For example, was your father a black-and-white thinker, was your mother anxious, did your mother and father argue a lot, was either one of them a yeller or someone who fell into unpredictable rages?

It is a pretty safe bet that the patterns and habits you noticed were present and impactful in your home environment when you were growing up. Consequently, even if you don't have specific memories or images from your childhood, you can imagine how your child-self would have felt or reacted to your parents' patterns and habits you noticed later on. You can ask yourself what messages you probably would have taken in, what conclusions you might have drawn and what coping mechanisms you might have developed from the patterns and behavior of your parents

CONTEMPLATIVE EXERCISE REGARDING YOUR LIFE STORY

INSTRUCTIONS

Sit in a quiet place with a notepad. Lightly close your eyes or look down with a relaxed, unfocused gaze. Bring your attention to your exhale and take a few relaxing breaths. Stay with the relaxing breaths until you feel you have settled a bit.

Set an intention or aspiration to bring as much kindness and compassion to yourself and your family members as you reflect on the questions.

Contemplative exercises are much more about asking questions than about pressing for immediate or specific answers. Go through the exercise by reading the questions, experimenting with repeating them to yourself several times in a relaxed way, and then just leave some space. Try not to think too much or strain to come up with specific responses or memories. Instead, simply return to the relaxing breath and see what arises in your mind. This allows your intuition and your mind to work together to reveal useful information in response to the questions.

Don't try to do too many questions at one time. Reflect on only as many of the questions as are comfortable for you. If you feel saturated or overwhelmed at any time, stop and return to the exercise at a later time.

Experiment with writing brief notes or reflections as you recall memories or receive information in response to the questions. The notes do not in any way have to be articulate or fully formed thoughts. They are just for you. After a day or more, go back and review your notes as you continue to reflect on how your earlier experience is connected to and influences your present view of yourself, the ways in which your alarm system gets triggered and your patterns of behavior and speech.

If, at any time, this exercise becomes overwhelming, **Stop.** If efforts to reflect on the questions continue to be overwhelming, I strongly urge you to consult with a counselor. An experienced mental health professional can provide the support and safety you may need to continue with the process of making sense of your history and integrating it in an effective way with your growth process.

QUESTIONS FOR REFLECTION[47]

1. *What was it like growing up in your home environment? Who were the principal players in the environment?*

2. *How would you describe your mother's personality?*

3. *How did you get along with your mother in your childhood?*

4. *How would you describe your father's personality?*

5. *How did you get along with your father in your childhood?*

6. *How did your relationships with your mother and father differ? How were they similar?*

7. *Did you ever feel rejected or threatened by either of your parents in your childhood? Do you feel that any of these experiences continue to influence your life? If they do, how would you describe that influence?*

8. *How did your parents discipline you as a child? How do you feel that impacted on your childhood experience?*

9. *If you feel you received messages about yourself or your place in the world from your mother or father, what would those messages be? How have those messages influenced your life?*

10. *Did any loved one die during your childhood? What was that like at the time? Did anyone help you understand or process that experience?*

11. *When you were distressed, afraid or unhappy as a child, how did your mother and father react to you?*

12. *If you had difficult experiences during your childhood, were there individuals other than your parents that were supportive of you? If so, what impact did the relationships with those individuals have on you at the time?*

13. *How have your childhood experiences influenced your relationships with others as you have grown up? Have you noticed that you try to be or act in a certain way, or try*

not to act in a specific way, as a result of your childhood experiences?

14. Do you feel that you developed any coping mechanisms as a child to help you feel safe, or to deal with a sense of rejection, or to help you fit in or avoid personal risk? Do those coping mechanisms still have an impact on your life? Do they work? Do they have negative side effects?

15. Are there any themes or messages that you have been able to recognize in your emotional reaction patterns? When do you remember first experiencing or recognizing these themes or messages? Are there any images or memories that seem to be connected with these themes or messages?

16. What impact do you feel your childhood experience has had on your adult life generally?

CHAPTER 7

Step Five:
Insight Development...
Identifying Old Messages
or Conclusions
and Exploding Old Myths

LEARNING FROM OUR LIFE STORIES

As we saw in the last chapter, creating our life stories, seeing our whole life experience in a holistic and coherent way, reveals core messages and themes essential to understanding the negative emotional patterns that continue to undermine our happiness. The core messages often reveal themselves, like a sudden beam of light, from the memories of our early experiences, from the personalities of family members or from the energetic nature of the environments in which we lived. It may not be easy to touch in on these old experiences or to see these core themes; but I am reminded once again about the great psychiatrist Carl Jung's comment that "our suffering comes from those unfaced, untouched places in ourselves."

Once we have the courage to face these core themes and experiences, our healing can really begin. There are many references in the metaphysical literature about facing our inner demons and bringing them to light. Shining the light of day on them, in itself, softens their power over us and begins the process of transformation.

More specifically, with our basic understanding of the storage and triggering mechanisms of the brain's alarm system, seeing the connections between our earlier life experiences and our present moment reactivity offers several distinct advantages in the process of transforming our negative conditioning. It is useful to reflect on those advantages for a few moments.

1. Applying our understanding of brain function to the core themes underlying our negative conditioning enables us to be kinder to ourselves, to soften around self-judgment. Many times clients and workshop participants have expressed to me something like the following: "I have had this negative pattern all my life and it has been so confusing. For the first time, it is beginning to make sense to me. I have always felt, somewhere deep in my heart, that there was something basically wrong with me, some defect—and now I can begin to realize that that is not true at all!"

2. By placing our negative reactivity in the context of our life story and seeing the connectivity of it all, we can more clearly see the present-day triggers that activate the old messages and that often move us toward an emotional hijacking. Identifying the triggers more clearly enables us to anticipate them more skillfully. As we stabilize our mindfulness practice of identifying the triggers, we become less vulnerable to them and can more skillfully manage the huge waves of potentially-controlling emotion that sweep over us when the brain's alarm system has been activated.

3. As we more skillfully manage the powerful emotions, and practice our self-soothing or self-regulation techniques, space opens us up for choosing a different reaction to our old happiness-undermining patterns. I call this a "creativity gap"—a space in which we can increasingly become creative with our choice of words and actions. This is, of course, the whole purpose of the **Stop-Breathe-Reflect-Choose** mindfulness technique discussed in Chapter Three.

4. All these advantages flow together and support each other. As we utilize them and integrate them into our on-going, day-to-day mindfulness practice, the neural connections in our brains that store the old negative messages (and the pain, lack of safety, helplessness and hopelessness that travel with them) begin to loosen. Slowly, slowly, slowly we are literally changing our brains and developing new neural connections that better support a lasting happiness. One commentator in the award-winning movie *What the Bleep!? Do We Know!?* states it this way:

> We also know that nerve cells that don't fire together, no longer wire together. They lose their long-term relationship because every time we interrupt the thought process, that produces a chemical response in the body. Every time we interrupt it, the nerve cells that are connected to each other start breaking the long-term relationship. When we start interrupting and observing, not by stimulus and response in an automatic reaction, but by observing the effect it has, then we are no longer the body/mind/emotions consciousness that's responding to its environment as if it's automatic.
>
> * * *
>
> We're in completely new territory in our brain. We're re-wiring the brain, literally re-connecting to a new concept. Then, ultimately, it changes us from the inside out.[48]

Step Five of developing mindfulness refers to insight development. By delving into our life stories and creating a coherent autobiographical narratives, we have the opportunity to re-frame the old themes and core messages that unavoidably emerged from our early history. We will explore this re-framing initially by returning to Sue's story.

SUE'S STORY RE-FRAMED

As you recall, Sue came to me for counseling initially to work on an old pattern that was very disruptive to her sense of self and her relationships. As she described it, she frequently found herself becoming "near-hysterical" if any man that she was interested in withdrew attention or affection from her. As she created her life story in counseling, she remembered the specific incident from age six that I described in Chapter Four. In recalling that memory, she discovered the tip of the iceberg that enabled us to look below the surface of her conscious awareness. Taking advantage of that opportunity, we discovered a whole matrix of components embedded in her neural firing patterns that became the guides for our further work. To refresh your recollection, those components are set forth below.

Information Components	Energy/Emotional Components
Nobody listens to me!	Pain
Nobody pays attention to me!	Lack of safety
Why? Sue's early conclusion:	Confusion
Because I am not good enough!	Helplessness
Because I am not important!	

Sue loved her family. She instinctively felt that they loved her. At age six (and younger), she had not yet developed reflective abilities that would have enabled her to sort out the whole situation. In fact, in the normal course of brain maturation, she would not develop those abilities for some years yet. When, in her perception, her family members frequently didn't listen or pay attention to her, she drew the conclusion that her experience of not receiving attention from the people she loved must be *because* there was something wrong with her. *This was a totally understandable reaction to a given set of circumstances* encountered by the young Sue; but, guess what (!)—her conclusion was simply *wrong*.

Although she might have over-generalized it, her subjective experience that her family did not give her the on-going, attention she yearned for had some truth to it; but her conclusion—namely, that the reason for the lack of attention was because she was not good enough—was inaccurate. Her cause-and-effect conclusion was the best her child-self could do at the time. It resulted from her inability to see the whole set of circumstances and to analyze it accurately. Despite its inaccuracy, the conclusion was deeply embedded in her neural firing patterns and became her reality.

The experience of frequently receiving little attention was powerful for the young Sue. It made her feel very unsafe, and why wouldn't it? Young children are in a life-and-death struggle for survival. Tragically, children who do not receive sufficient nurturing and attention do die. Moreover, we know clearly from study after study that the "failure to thrive" syndrome largely results from insufficient attention and nurturing. Young children don't intellectually "know" this, but there is an instinctual awareness of it that has emerged from the long process of evolution. Therefore, when Sue didn't get the attention she deserved, there was good reason for her to feel overwhelmed, helpless and endangered. Given the strength of this, the recording (i.e., learning and memory) functions of her brain's alarm system reacted with something like: "This is really important. I had better store it with the strong energy it deserves so if anything like this happens again, I can alert the whole system to protect itself."

As a result, the neurons that stored this whole set of experiences had strong connections. Since Sue's family rarely listened or attended to her emotional needs, the neural firing patterns storing the information and energy/emotional components from these experiences were frequently activated. Remember Hebb's axiom in neuroscience from earlier in the book: neurons that fire together wire together. Every time this neural firing pattern was triggered, it was strengthened! Another way of saying this is that every time that particular neural firing pattern was triggered, it became more sensitive to future stimuli from the environment and more likely to being triggered again.

With each repeated triggering of the neural firing pattern, Sue's early conclusion about herself was confirmed and became even stronger. This is an unavoidable result even though the bottom-line message that " I am not good enough" was based on a wholly inaccurate conclusion—a myth. Over time, this myth evolved into a bias or filter through which Sue interpreted her experience in the world. Ultimately, it became a state of mind—a dominant belief, lurking below the surface of her conscious awareness, of not being good enough.

Sue is not unique. In fact, this same dynamic operates for all of us, each in our own personal way, with regard to our negative conditioning. The progression can be summarized as follows:

1. Early childhood experiences of risk or danger →
2. Negative message or conclusion about self →
3. Strong embedding of the message/conclusion and energetic/emotional components in organized neural firing patterns (NFP) →
4. Frequent triggering of the NFP in response to new experiences →
5. Strengthening of the NFP and the negative message/conclusion about self →
6. Greater probability that the NFP will be triggered again in the future →
7. Further strengthening of the NFP and negative message/conclusion with each new triggering →
8. Emergence of a bias or filter based on the negative message/conclusion (in other words, a tendency to interpret our experience through the bias or filter) →
9. Emergence over time of a state of mind about self (for example, the shame of not being good enough)

By having the courage to face her undermining pattern directly, Sue had the opportunity to explode the old myths about herself. Let's go back and look at the situation again, this time with the full perspective of the adult view. Sue came to realize that her father was an alcoholic, caught up in his own conditioning and suffering, with little energy or attention left over for her. Her mother was clearly worn out by the challenges of raising five children in a chaotic environment, complicated by the alcoholism of her husband. It is quite possible that her mother also suffered from some amount of depression, making her attention to Sue even more inconsistent or unreliable. What about the four older brothers? They probably were having their own tough time finding their way in that environment. At any rate, older brothers often don't pay much attention to younger sisters in the early years of childhood, unless they want something from them or are teasing them.

From this viewpoint, the whole landscape looks very different than it could have possibly looked to the young Sue, yearning—as all children do—for attention from her loved ones. With this perspective, encountered for the first time in the process of making sense of her life story, Sue was able to intellectually see that her belief system about herself, carried for so many years, was based on a conclusion about her early experiences that, although understandable from the child's view, was simply wrong. The fact that she didn't receive the consistent attention from her family was a result of the family dynamics and the struggles of each individual family member, and not because she wasn't good enough or because she didn't deserve the attention. Put more bluntly, the lack of consistent attention had nothing to do with her basic worth or basic goodness.

I do not want to be misleading here. This realization was not the end of Sue's work. It was, however, a wonderful stage in moving toward transformation of the old pattern that undermined her sense of self. The re-framing of her childhood memory became a significant building block in the process of creating a new and stable foundation for supporting her happiness. I clearly remember what she told me after we had been working together for awhile. She came to my office for a session and announced:

"I am really beginning to get it up here (pointing to her head); but I don't yet believe it down here (pointing to her heart)."

Despite the rueful look on her face, I was thrilled! "Terrific!" I responded. "Just keep working with all the elements of your mindfulness practice and, sooner or later, the head and the heart will come together."

EXPLODING THE MYTHS OF OTHER STORIES

Let's return to my story and those of the clients discussed in the last chapter for more examples of how new insights emerge from making sense of our life stories and re-framing our early experiences from an adult's perspective. As in Sue's case, what we so often discover when we engage in this process is that the negative messages and conclusions about ourselves—the myths we have been living with for so many years—are simply not supported by the objective evidence.

In the example from my own life, as you recall, I had this unfortunate habit of reacting with great aggravation (or even insult) to any directive or suggestive comment my first wife made to me about something I was doing around the house. The negative messages lurking just below the surface of my reaction were that I did not know what I was doing, or was not capable, or—worse yet—that I was not smart. Realizing that I had modeled my father's neural firing patterns from his reaction to my mother correcting him was an enlightening realization for me. This realization also opened the opportunity to look even more closely at my pattern and ask whether my negative messages were supported by the evidence on the ground. As I did that, it helped me to further re-frame that whole set of circumstances surrounding the pattern and deepen my insight about the myths I had been carrying (and believing!) in my mind.

The truth of my first marriage was this: my wife and I shared responsibility for the domestic duties of maintaining a house. If anything, I may have been more domestically oriented than she was in some respects. As a result, I had a lot of experience in all the usual tasks of cooking, doing the laundry, housecleaning, etc. As I looked at it objectively from the adult's perspective (and not from the view of the little boy who identified with his Dad when he was corrected by his Mom), it was clear that I did know what I was doing around the house—and that I was capable most of the time! (Let's leave sewing out of that. For some reason, I never picked up that little skill.)

As for the broader message of not being smart, as I began to see the whole picture more clearly, it just seemed a little silly. These realizations did not wipe away my old pattern of reactivity, like some wand instantly sprinkling magic dust over me and transforming the mindset I had held for so many years; but the insights were like a vaccination, making me less vulnerable to becoming completely caught up in the old negative emotions.

Jane's little-girl self had concluded from the lack of unqualified compliments from her mother that she could never get anything right, that she really somehow just didn't measure up. As she connected her over-reaction to criticism at work with her painful childhood experiences, she could see that although her early conclusions about herself were understandable from the child's limited view, they did not take into account her mother's conditioning and how it impacted on her. As a child, she could not have seen how her mother's controlling nature left her relatively incapable of being satisfied with anything someone else did. Her mother's pattern of so frequently qualifying a supposed complement with a "but" statement had everything to do with her mother's conditioning and very little to do with whether Jane had done her best or done something well under all the circumstances.

Although Jane's old negative conclusion about herself made it very difficult for her to see, the objective evidence was that she had done many things well. The old belief system embedded in her neural firing patterns obscured her view and undermined her confidence. The truth was that she was a valued employee who performed well at work. Weaving all this insight together enabled her to be kinder to herself, realize her contribution in the workplace and calm her reaction to the constructive criticism that is always a part of growing in our jobs. The result, of course, was that she was much happier at work—and in life generally.

Mike's case is an interesting example of the subtle insights that can emerge from making sense of one's life story. As a result of the influences of his mother's conditioning (interpersonal neurobiology once again hard at work!), Mike's alarm system developed a hyper-vigilance and was frequently operating on overdrive, relentlessly churning out messages that there is danger around every corner. Mike's coping mechanism, begun at a very early age in an effort to help him feel safe in the midst of this constant anticipation of danger, was to develop a detailed plan for all the dangerous events that arose in this "what-if" negative thinking.

In making sense of his life story, Mike confronted the challenge of sorting through the nuances of the old messages. The fact is that, as we experience life in the 21st century, the world does present us with many possible dangers. Part of Mike's early message was not altogether wrong. We could get hit by lightening at any time or die in a plane crash; but the odds of that happening in our life are in the millions. The objective evidence from his life helped Mike work through this. When he could release himself from the captivating power of his old messages, he readily admitted that the vast majority of the dangers his churning mind worked so hard to anticipate had never befallen him.

In fact, even a quick overview of his life at the time we were working together provided evidence that he could relax. He had a loving wife, a delightful young daughter and a strong marriage. He was a good father and a highly-valued professional who had risen quickly in his organization. In the midst of all the possible dangers in this world, he had a stable life that was working well, one that many Americans would readily envy. The objective evidence affirmed, as it so often does, that his personal circumstances were not really the problem. It was his state of mind, conditioned at an early age, that was causing his suffering.

Still, there was this dilemma. Even with his new found insights, there was the reality that the world does present dangers, that the future is unpredictable and that living always, inevitably, involves uncertainties. Mike began to realize that his task had to shift. His old coping mechanism of trying to eliminate uncertainties by endless anticipation and planning did not work—and could never work. As difficult as it was, he had to stop trying to do the impossible. And here is a basic truth for every human on the planet: the task is not to eliminate uncertainty from our lives because (to say it again) it cannot be done; the task is to change our relationship to uncertainty. To put it more directly, the task is to change our state of mind about uncertainty. This is a very big job, indeed—a life-long process. With the insights gained from creating a more coherent life story, Mike was much better equipped to be engaged with this challenge.

THE TENDENCY TO DRAW NEGATIVE CONCLUSIONS ABOUT OURSELVES

From the case studies we have considered so far, we have seen that the child's interpretation of his experiences frequently results in negative conclusions about himself. The negative conclusions take many different forms; but at their core, they generally can be distilled down to something like: "I am just not good enough." or "There is something basically wrong with me or with my experience in the world." As we have seen, these core negative messages about the self often evolve into states of mind, or deeply embedded belief systems, about who we are. The negative belief systems about the self are often below our conscious awareness. Like some secret psychological enemy agent, they undermine our self-esteem and our happiness, even though we may not be aware of their operation or even their existence.

To be able to effectively move forward with the challenging process of dismantling our negative belief systems, we need all the insight and tools available to us. It is helpful, then, to understand more clearly why this tendency to draw negative conclusions about ourselves is so common. Child development experts have explored this a great deal and their research offers helpful insights.

Infants are masters at detecting the emotional states of their caregivers. In fact, they depend on this skill in learning about the new world they are discovering and in determining what is safe and what is not. In the infant's first several years, the emotional state of his mother is vitally important. An experiment called the visual cliff demonstrates this.[49] A baby who can crawl but has not yet learned to walk is placed at one end of a table with his mother at the other end. The first half of the table is made of wood; the second half consists of Plexiglas. Crawling toward his mother, the baby confronts a dilemma. When he reaches the edge of the Plexiglas, he cannot tell whether this clear substance is safe. Invariably, he looks to his mother's face for clues. If his mother's expression is calm and reassuring, he continues over the visual cliff and on to his mother. If his mother appears alarmed, he usually stops and cries.

The infant's constant monitoring of his mother's face and emotional state is not only his main guide about his safety; it is also the main source of information about himself and his experience. The mother's emotional state and expression either affirms the infant's sense of himself and his experience or it undermines it. With this in mind, consider the general experience of the pre-mobile infant in the early months of his life. In a household that is attentive, he hears a relatively consistent stream of affirmations, expressions like how cute and adorable he is, how much his mother (and other caregivers) love him, etc. These expressions instinctively affirm his sense of self and a sense that all is well with his experience. This can change dramatically when he learns to walk.

Excited by his new mobility and fascinated with the larger environment it has made available to him, the toddler's natural instinct is to explore with tremendous energy and enthusiasm. Due to his limited experience, he is often unaware of the risks his mobility exposes him to or the adult order that he may disrupt. All this frequently brings him into potential conflict with his parents, as they keep a sharp eye both on the toddler's safety and the order they seek to maintain in the home. Whereas he was showered with affirmations in his pre-walking days, he is now met with frequent prohibitions: *"No! No! No!"* One researcher has reported that the mother of an eleven-to-seventeen month old child expresses a prohibition on the average of every nine minutes.

As child development specialist Joseph Chilton Pearce explains, this places the toddler in a significantly conflicted position:

> Again, the confusion and depression in the child come from two powerful encoded directives: The first is that the bond with the caregiver must be maintained at all costs. The second is that the world must be explored and knowledge of it must be built at all costs. The mother, with whom the child is compelled to bond, is the major support, mentor, and guide in the toddler's world exploration and learning. When the child, who is also compelled by nature's imperative to explore his world, is threatened by the same caregiver when he does just this, the contradiction is profound. . . . The resulting ambiguity drives the first major wedge in the toddler's mind, which, over time, becomes a gaping chasm.[50]

Drawing further on the extensive work of researcher Allan Schore, Pearce goes on to explain that the startling prohibitions from the mother (and other caregivers as well) can result in an internal imprint of shame that has a lasting effect on the toddler's sense of self and his interpretation of his experience in the world:

> As the child reaches out to explore, the signal from his internal mentation is: *'Stop. You are no good.*

If you do this, you will be looked at and despised.'
(Emphasis in the original.)[51]

Psychologist Louis Cozolino agrees that the sudden onslaught of "No!" from his parents as he begins to walk, when nothing has changed in his perspective and desire to explore, is often confusing to the toddler. It is easy to see how he can misinterpret his parents' prohibitions as a comment on him and his experience, instead of an effort to keep him safe:

> . . . Affection and attunement, experienced as unconditional during the first year, come to be tied to specific types of behavior.
> Shame, appearing early in the second year of life, is a powerful inhibitory emotion and a primary mechanism of social control.[52]

There is undoubtedly a certain amount of self-doubt that is innate to being alive in the human condition; but as you can see from the above discussion, any innate doubt is almost inevitably amplified by the infant very early in life as a result of his instinctive interpretations of his interactions with his primary caregivers. Once those interpretations are internalized and embedded in the neural firing patterns of his brain, the sense of not being good enough or of shame is likely to be activated and strengthened as the child reacts to and interprets his on-going experiences.

There are powerful messages in our culture that so frequently reinforce these internalized negative conclusions about self. These messages implying judgments of who we are, of our abilities and our condition, are all around us. We cannot avoid them and we cannot avoid internalizing some part of the judgments. In addition, our competitiveness leads to a pervasive tendency to compare ourselves with others—and to judge ourselves as a result of the comparisons.

I have a very sweet client who frequently brings in magazines for our waiting room. Sometimes she includes magazines about fitness or diet that invariably have air-brushed photos of young adults (often young women in bikinis) who look terrific and have "the perfect body." What is the message that virtually screams at you from the cover? "If you don't look like this, there must be something wrong with you! You just aren't good enough! You are not valued!" Although I appreciate my client's generosity and kindness, after she leaves the office, I throw out those kinds of magazines. They are just one more example of the heavy implied judgments that reaffirm our negative messages and intensify our self-doubt.

Understanding the unavoidable forces that lead to and strengthen the internalized negative messages about ourselves reinforces several important points as we continue building a foundation for a lasting happiness. Just because these internalized negative messages feel so real, **does not mean they are true**. The fact that they have become a part of our belief system does not mean that there is something basically wrong with us, or that we are defective in some way. Rather, we can see that these negative conclusions are an inevitable result of the way our hardwired brain interprets our interactions with our primary caregivers and our experiences. Finally, understanding the power of this dynamic reminds us that we have to be both patient and conscientious as we apply our mindfulness practice to slowly dismantle the deeply-embedded negative myths about ourselves.

THE CHALLENGE OF EXPLICITLY NEGATIVE MESSAGES

In the preceding section, we explored the basic tendency of the child to draw negative conclusions about himself from his interactions with his parents. We all know, however, that although parents do the best they can within the context of their own conditioning, they sometimes say horrible things to their children. No conclusion needs to be drawn by the child to form a negative image of himself; the message is loud and clear that something is basically wrong with him:

> If you don't get an A on that test, you are going
> to end up in the gutter.

You're so stupid! You never get anything right.

I can't believe how lazy you are! You are never
    going to amount to anything.

Stop crying! You're such a sissy!

You're totally worthless!

You're a piece of #@$%!

I had one wonderful female client in her forties who had a pervasive internalized message that she had done something wrong. As is often the case, this core belief about herself had become a filter or bias through which she interpreted her adult experience in relationships. She didn't come to this mistaken belief through an interpretation of her own. Her mother was only a teenager when she was born and her mother was very angry that having a baby at such an early age had changed her life so dramatically and resulted in giving up a normal teenager's life. As a result of her youth and her anger, my client's mother was constantly telling her daughter that every little upset or thing that went wrong was the daughter's fault. The message was both harsh and constant. Needless to say, it had a powerful impact on my client and became her core negative belief about herself well into adulthood.

As we now know from our study of the child's developing brain, a child cannot protect himself from this kind of explicitly negative message. The information in such messages is powerfully embedded in organizing neural firing patterns and conditions the child's emerging sense of self. Because the child does not have the ability to evaluate the messages for their truth, they become, over time, a part of his belief system, even though the messages are false.

As with the negative conclusions about the self drawn by the child, these false messages must be identified and confronted if we are to build a foundation for a lasting happiness. Once again, our mindfulness practice provides us with a path for doing just that.

APPLYING MINDFULNESS PRACTICE TO THE
NEGATIVE MYTHS ABOUT OURSELVES

There are several stages to the process of applying our mindfulness practice to the negative myths about ourselves.

1. Identifying the myths.

In the Contemplative Exercise Regarding Your Life Story at the end of the last chapter, I encouraged you to review your early history in a way that would safely enable you to identify the impact your caretakers and your home environment had on your emerging self-identity. Many of the questions for review were designed to help you discover conclusions and messages about yourself you may have understandably internalized. If you didn't have the time to do the exercise earlier, please go back and look at the questions for review now. We cannot challenge and explode these old conclusions and messages if we are not clear about what is getting triggered in our brain.

In reviewing your childhood experiences, it may be possible to go a bit deeper now. One way of doing this is to look at your present strong emotional reaction patterns (such as arisings of fear, anxiety or anger) and ask, "What conclusions or messages might be fueling my reaction just below my conscious awareness?" Another way of asking this is: "What is the subtext to my strong emotional reaction?" As you may recall from our earlier exploration of one of my patterns, just below the surface of my reaction of aggravation toward my first wife when she made a directive comment to me was the following subtext: "What! You don't think I know what I am doing! You don't think I am capable! You don't think I am smart!" Realizing the subtext of our negative reactions leads to useful insights about what is really driving our reaction.

2. Confronting and exploding the myths

In all the case examples explored in this chapter, the individuals were able to confront the belief systems that had emerged from the old conclusions and messages about themselves and to really test them for their veracity. By viewing the childhood experiences with the resources of the adult perspective, new insights were gained. The experiences were often seen very differently and re-framed. Sue, for example, realized—for the first time—that the fact that her family frequently didn't pay attention or listen to her (a true fact) was not because she wasn't good enough or didn't deserve it (an inaccurate conclusion). Rather, the lack of attention to her was a result of a chaotic home environment, in which all of the family members were caught up in their own conditioning and suffering.

This review and re-framing is essential. Otherwise, the neural firing patterns that store the old inaccurate conclusions and false messages will continue to be triggered and, without any insight to challenge them, keep on spewing out their inaccurate undermining messages and energies. Even after we have brought the old messages to the light of our awareness, gained new insights about them and begun to develop a response that better serves us (and is a more true reflection of who we are), the old habits of the brain will not die easily. They will continue to snip at our new insights in an effort to pull us back into the old view of ourselves. Now, however, we will be ready. We will have the powerful tool of mindfulness to help us hold our ground and move forward with our happiness project.

At the end of this chapter is a Contemplative Exercise Regarding Re-Framing Old Conclusions and False Messages. I encourage you to do this exercise now. It will provide a basis for applying your mindfulness practice to the negative myths about yourself.

3. Practice, practice, practice

As I have mentioned earlier, the good news about the brain is its plasticity, its ability to be re-molded over the entire course of a lifetime. We can change our brains so that the old negative conclusions about ourselves no longer have the same power over us. However, a major theme of this book, as you well know by now, is that the magic wand we all wish for does not exist. The process of dismantling the old negative belief systems requires attention, focus and whatever effort we are able to bring to it in the present context of our lives. This is an "inconvenient truth"; but what are the alternatives: more unhappiness, more discomfort with our sense of self, more limitations on our true potential, more disconnection from the profound preciousness available to us all in this experience of being human. It really doesn't sound very attractive.

In *The Quantum Brain*, Jeffrey Satinover confronts this inconvenient truth with a sense of realism. He reminds us that we can take advantage of the plasticity of the brain to transform old patterns—that is, "to teach an old dog new tricks"—but that the process requires determination:

> The solution to the old-dog problem is practical and pedestrian: repetition, perseverance, courage, willingness to start all over again. New patterns may be embedded in a fresh network relatively quickly [i.e., the emerging brain of a young child]. When a network is already converged to a specific set of patterns [i.e., the brain of an adult], . . . it will require many more repetitions to 'overlearn' a new—especially a contradictory—pattern.
> . . . If the new pattern is repeated deliberately, diligently and frequently; and if the old pattern is willfully avoided for a long time . . . then even very old habits of thought, feeling and action will slowly weaken as the newer ones grow strong.[53]

So, how do we apply mindfulness practice to the false myths about ourselves and begin to dismantle the belief systems they support? The raw material for your personal practice comes from the contemplative exercises at the end of both the last and this chapter. These exercises can help you to identify at least some of the false messages about yourself that have been unconsciously triggered for so long. Then we return to the technique that is so useful in so many situations: **Stop-Breathe-Reflect-Choose.**

Let's explore this in more detail. As you have discovered, the negative conclusions and messages about yourself—the myths—are often lurking below the surface and intensifying your negative emotional reaction patterns. With this insight in mind, you can practice Stop-Breathe-Reflect-Choose with renewed motivation and enthusiasm. You can observe the wisdom of the body to reveal the first warning signals that a powerful old pattern has been triggered. The alarm bell may come in the form of churning in the stomach, heat in the body, racing heartbeats, a rising tone of our voice, or an energy of anxiety, fear, anger, aggravation, etc. You are training yourself to nurture the witnessing quality of your awareness so that you can notice these warning signals as they arise. The witnessing awareness reminds you to **Stop:** Pay attention! You may be moving in the direction of an emotional hijacking.

You know, of course, that the **Breathe** stage of the technique is so important. If you don't apply your self-regulation techniques and settle yourself down, you will not be thinking clearly and will not be able to effectively apply the rest of our mindfulness practice. This is not your imagination. It is a neurological fact that once the brain's alarm system is activated, you risk losing access to your most sophisticated reflective and analytical abilities.

Having settled yourself as well as you can, you come to the **Reflect** stage. Here is where you can really apply your new insights. From the two contemplation exercises, you have more clearly identified the negative conclusions and messages about yourself that were embedded in your neural firing patterns as a child. From the adult perspective, you have begun to see them in a new light, to re-frame them in a form that is more truly reflective of the broader dynamics of your childhood experience, not limited by the understandably narrow view of the child. The Reflect stage now becomes a self-dialogue, reminding you, over and over, of your new insights.

Years ago, one of my clients summed it up beautifully. He was approaching a challenging situation and was feeling quite anxious about it. Recognizing his anxiety during a session, he spontaneously blurted out, "I realize that I just have to talk myself into a better way of thinking about this!" I felt like jumping out of my chair and giving him a big hug. It was such a wonderful reflection of how the Stop-Breathe-Reflect-Choose technique, and his mindfulness practice generally, had become an integrated resource for him.

To use Sue's case as an example, the internal dialogue might go something like the following if her emotional reaction pattern was triggered by the old belief that "nobody pays attention to me because I am not good enough":

> I've seen this pattern before. I know where it is coming from. That old neural firing pattern is trying to convince me that an inaccurate conclusion I drew in my childhood is still true. It wasn't true then and it isn't true now. That was then and this is now. People do listen to me. And if they don't, it isn't because I am not good enough or don't deserve attention. I am getting emotional because those old experiences felt so horrible back then. I was a child and couldn't sort it all out, so I felt so helpless. I have all my resources as an adult now—and besides, I can now see that the conclusion I drew about myself when I was young was just not true.

That might seem like a long inner dialogue to have when you are in the middle of dealing with a difficult situation. It is rather long, but remember what you are doing. You are identifying an old belief system that has been powerful for a long time, disengaging from it by applying your insight and creating a new foundation for your sense of self and for your happiness. To use Jeffrey Satinover's words, you are doing the hard work that "turns the fourth brain from a mass of randomness into an intellect of dazzling capacity."

The truth is that when you first try to practice in this way, you may very well not have the space for this inner dialogue until your emotional reaction has run its course. Until you have practiced nurturing the witness for awhile, you may only notice what just happened after the fact. That's O.K! Even if you did not catch yourself in the middle of the reaction, you can still review the situation, apply your insights and have your inner dialogue. At that moment, you are acting as your own personal counselor or coach. This process creates the foundation for seeing the reaction more quickly as you continue to practice.

If you are able to reach the Reflect stage in the course of a triggered reaction, the inner dialogue prepares you for the **Choose** stage of the technique: What is the best, most effective choice you can make under the circumstances? As I have said before, often a part of the best choice is to use restraint and be very careful about the words and actions that follow.

After your practice has stabilized and you have gone through your personal dialogue many times in response to the old myths and energies, it is helpful to distill the dialogue down to a short statement or phrase that encapsulates all the understanding and new insights about the old pattern. The word "mantra" means protector of the mind. This short statement then becomes a mantra that protects your mind from the old negative pattern as you respond to each of the arisings with your personalized antidote of the mantra. With practice, you might then discover that something like the following happens. The old message gets triggered and arises like a balloon floating into your awareness. You apply the antidote of the mantra that acts like a pin pricking and deflating the balloon. As a result, the old message increasingly just evaporates into the larger space of your awareness.

It is important to develop a short-form response, a mantra, that speaks to you in a personal way. One way of approaching this is to ask, "What is the heart of the response that I want to make to that old negative message?" or "What is the core message that I want to strengthen in my new neural firing pattern, my new default mode?"

For Sue, it was something like, "People do pay attention to me because I deserve it!" Remember Mike's story? When his "what-if" negative thinking grabbed his attention, his old coping mechanism to try to keep himself safe was to develop a detailed plan for every possible challenging event that could happen. When he was ready to develop and apply a short-form mantra, it became, "I can handle whatever arises. I'll be O.K." This antidote broke through the old impulse to anticipate far into the future and plan for every possible event and constantly reaffirmed the core message of his new insights.

Recent neuroscience research emphasizes that you are doing something very important when you respond consciously to the triggering of the old negative messages and the fearful energies activated with them. Every time the old memory is triggered, it is updated. Scientists now know that this updating process—or "reconsolidation," as it is often called—is accomplished by chemical changes in the neurons that store the memory. In other words, the memory is re-written slightly and stored anew every time it is triggered. The next time that memory is activated, it will appear as last updated and reconsolidated.

If we are merely caught in the old fear-based memory, it is strengthened. Here's the pay-off. Every time we consciously respond to the old negative messages and energies, as by having the inner dialogue in the Reflect phase of the practice or by applying the short-form mantra, the reconsolidation process is impacted by our conscious response and the memory is re-encoded with less power over us. The conscious response affects the memory on a cellular level so that the old fear-based message is weakened and will be less able to dominate our experience the next time it is triggered.[54] With each such reconsolidation of the old memory, we are moving closer to our goal of changing the neural wiring in our brain in ways that support a more durable positive state of mind. In this sense, we are strengthening our immunity to the old fear-based negative messages.

When you don't have the stability of mind to reach the inner dialogue or apply the mantra until after the emotional reaction has subsided, you can do three kind and generous things for yourself:

(1) don't beat up yourself for not catching the emotional reaction earlier;

(2) take delight in the fact that you awakened once again, that your inner wisdom has now kicked in and allowed you to see your earlier reaction with insight; and

(3) set the aspiration to strengthen the inner dialogue you are now having and use it as a foundation for waking up more promptly the next time.

Consistent repetition over time is the essence of any practice. That principle certainly applies to our mindfulness practice and the creation of healthier states of mind. I urge you with all my heart not to think of the many times you will slip into old negative thoughts or reaction patterns as "failures".

As we have discussed at length, we have such a tendency to fall into self-judgment and that fall just adds to the difficulty of our task. The truth is that these slips are not failures. They are a natural and unavoidable aspect of all growth, of all efforts to change old patterns. Once again, we are all in the same boat with this, every one of us. Change simply does not happen in a straight-line fashion. We develop new insights and approaches; we apply them to old patterns; we refine the insights and approaches as we gain experience with them; we forget them altogether at times; we slip back into old patterns; we wake up again, remember, and once again renew our effort to work with (and practice) the new insights and strategies.

A favorite teacher of mine, Pema Chodron, frequently reminds her students that, in the beginning stages of practice, if we can see our old patterns and actively work with them one time out of ten, we should take great delight and feel a certain confidence that we are building something new and wonderful. This is very good advice! If we can bring some amount of focus to that delight, borne out of respect for our courage and inner wisdom, we will avoid that disastrous fall into the pain and shame of self-judgment.

AVOIDING EXPECTATIONS OF PERFECTION

One of the reasons we fall into a depressive self-judgment is that we have unrealistic expectations about what our mindfulness practice will produce. It would be wonderful if all our hard work totally eliminated from our brains an old unhealthy neural firing pattern. If we are conscientious and apply our practice consistently over time, this could happen; but it may not. Remember, the neural firing patterns of the kind we have been reviewing in all the case stories have a long history to them. The negative messages were embedded in our neural firing patterns very early in our lives—and then they were triggered over and over again for years in response to our on-going life experience.

In the very early years of our lives, our growing brains make huge numbers of neural connections as our infant-selves respond to the diverse environments we encounter. As it turns out, not all of these connections are useful and some are not subsequently triggered to any great degree. If particular neural connections are not triggered again, the neural scientists tell us that the brain goes back and "prunes" the unused neural firing patterns. The pruning is the result of "neural Darwinism": if the neural connection is not used, it is cleared away. As adults, the situation is different. The neural firing patterns that store our challenging messages have been triggered many times over the years and are deeply embedded in established neural networks. Consequently, we cannot expect that the brain will prune away these old neural connections.

If the neural networks that house our negative messages are not likely to be eliminated entirely by our mindfulness practice, what changes can we anticipate? In working with this process for years in my own practice and in observing the practice of friends and clients, I can assure you that although "perfection" may not be possible, there is a great deal of transformation that takes place. Once we have the courage to face directly our negative emotional reaction patterns, with all their myths, subtexts and energies, we begin to notice them and intervene more quickly. With each intervention, the neural firing pattern that gives rise to the negative reactivity slowly begins to lose its strength. Over time, the power of the neural firing pattern, its ability to grab and totally dominate both our awareness and our experience, will diminish.

Along the way, of course, we are building and strengthening new neural firing patterns about ourselves and our place in the world that are healthier and more true than the old myths. As we bring both patience and conscientiousness to our practice, we are replacing the old default mode of firing patterns that undermined our happiness with a new default mode that reflects a true sense of self and supports a lasting happiness.

In summary, although we may not achieve perfection and totally eliminate from our brains old negative firing patterns, our mindfulness practice leads to the following positive transformation:

(1) the old pattern begins to lose its strength;

(2) as it slowly loses it strength, its power to dominate our awareness diminishes;

(3) as it loses its power over us, we are able to react to and manage its activation more skillfully;

(4) as we manage its activation more skillfully, the process of transformation accelerates; and

(5) over time, the old negative default mode is triggered less and less frequently and with less and less power.

You may remember the Rumi poem, "The Guesthouse," quoted earlier in the book. In the poem, Rumi wrote about all the automatic thoughts that arrive unexpectedly in our awareness each day. Even with the "dark thought, the shame, the malice," he advised us to "meet them at the door laughing and invite them in." When we can do that, when we can meet our own dark thoughts about ourselves and our place in the world "at the door laughing," we know that all our hard work, all our courageous practice, has really paid off. Hundreds of years ago, Rumi knew that is possible for all of us—and everything we have learned about the brain since his time has confirmed his encouraging message.

Several years ago I had a humorous reminder about both the persistence of our old negative firing patterns and the transformative power of mindfulness practice. My mother and father grew up during the Great Depression. As was the case for millions of Americans during that time, their families had very little money. In fact, a number of times, the only reason they had enough food was because members of their families were farmers and shared some of their harvests with the large circle of the extended family. Mom and Dad went straight from the Depression into the Second World War, another time of great unpredictability and uncertainty. Like many men of his generation coming out of the war, my father's path to security and safety meant earning money.

My father was not in any way an overbearing man with me or my siblings; but interpersonal neurobiology being what it is, his neural firing patterns in this area heavily influenced the development of my own. As a result, a strong message became embedded in my brain that my safety and security depended on money. For many years, I stewed a great deal about money issues. The unexpected bill or the check my wife had not mentioned to me could easily throw me into a tizzy of rumination and worry. This made no logical sense, of course, because I have had the great blessing of a lot of education and have a solid track record of being able to support my loved ones and myself. As we have seen over and over, logic is not involved. This old neural firing pattern had power over me because it mirrored the strong connection money and safety had in my father's neural firing patterns.

At some point years ago, I figured out that this old firing pattern led to a lot of discomfort for me and made no sense. After many years of applying the mindfulness practice we are discussing throughout this book, the old reactivity seemed to have largely disappeared. Then, several years ago, my wife and I were on vacation and stopped into a drug store to pick up a few things. I had only two items, which I had roughly calculated to cost about $3.00. At the check-out counter, the clerk rang up the merchandise and, to my great surprise, the total came to $4.95! Instantly, I could feel a small sensation of gripping arise in my body/mind. If this were a cartoon (which it really was in some respects), the thought bubble above my head would have been, "$4.95! I thought it was going to be only $3.00!" It really had to make me laugh. A whole $1.95 was enough to trigger that old neural firing pattern that still was trying to persuade me to worry about money—or, heaven forbid, I won't be safe. Obviously, the firing pattern that housed the old message wasn't totally gone; it still had enough energy left to trigger a slight sense of being gripped; but, to refer to Rumi again, I could now "meet [it] at the door laughing."

THE SKIRMISH WITHIN: RESISTING THE OLD PATTERNS

It is difficult to fully and accurately capture in a book like this how it feels to apply mindfulness practice to the old negative firing patterns. In the first place, each of us will discover our own unique felt sense of it as we begin to work with our unhealthy emotional reactivity. Second, in reading my descriptions, it can sound like, "Well, we apply the Stop-Breathe-Reflect-Choose practice and we are instantly liberated from the old pattern that had so strongly grabbed our attention." Or: "When we apply the short-form mantra, that balloon with the old disturbing message just disappears."

Wouldn't that be nice! With a lot of practice, that might actually happen; but more often than not, it is a good deal more complicated. Sometimes there is a real internal skirmish going on. We recognize that an old emotional reaction pattern has been triggered and we bring our attention to all the insights we have discovered about it, with the intent to loosen the grip of the old pattern; but there is a real tug-of-war going on between the old messages/emotions and the new insights with our intent to remain balanced.

Let's put this in a specific context by returning to one aspect of my own practice. I shared with you earlier my old pattern of being triggered into aggravation if my wife made a directive comment about something I am doing around the house. I am blessed to have a partner who is very conscientious about her own mindfulness practice. Over the years, we have been conscious of, and helped each other with, our individual negative firing patterns so that their intrusion in our relationship has been greatly minimized. Still, we are like everyone else—not perfect!

Several summers ago we were working in the garden and my wife said something to me about what I was doing. In my perception (and, of course, it is our initial perception that automatically triggers the old firing pattern and gets us into such turmoil), her comment sounded like an instruction with an implied judgment that what I was doing was not quite right. Instantly, I could feel such a heat in my body, fueling the old thoughts: "She's judging me! What right does she have to do that? I can't stand it when she doesn't trust that I know what I am doing!" Because I have had the opportunity to work with this old neural firing pattern for years, the voice of mindfulness still spoke to me in spite of the heat coursing through my body: "I know what is going on. Here's that old pattern again. My wife wasn't intending to judge me or be offensive; I am sure of that."

The point is this: even though my insights and reminders were available to me, I was not immediately "liberated" from the heat of the old pattern. The negative messages were still trying to persuade me of their truth and fill up my whole consciousness. This is what I meant by the skirmish. In a way, the old undermining messages and the new healthier insights were battling it out for control of both my consciousness and my behavior. When this happens, and it will, we need to hold our place, to bring some determination to keeping our focus on the higher ground so that we are not pulled down into the lower road heading toward a full emotional hijacking.

In our garden incident, both my wife and I recognized that a triggering had occurred from the sharp exchange between us and we retreated to different parts of the garden. For the next few minutes, all my attention was directed to my inner skirmish, as I attempted to cool the heat in my body and remember what the higher ground meant to me. "I love this woman and I am not going to let that old neural firing pattern drive my speech or behavior. I am not going to let the heat in my body fuel my response." After staying with my practice for awhile, the heat did subside and I was able to respond to my wife in a way that was consistent with my best intentions. In talking with my wife about this episode recently, she reminded me that I said something like, "It doesn't feel very good, does it, Sweetie?" The acknowledgment of the unpleasant emotional reactivity drew us back together and repaired the disconnection.

I tell this anecdote because I know that even after you have been working with your mindfulness practice for some time, you will have similar experiences. They are normal and unavoidable. Moreover, they illustrate that we are not just coldly and calmly applying some clinical technique and then smoothly going on with our business. Often, we are down in the dirt, dealing with the messiness of our whole history and the complicated nature of being human. As so many teachers have emphasized, it takes courage and perseverance. That is just the nature of the task— and that's O.K. Slowly, slowly, we can work away at it, each of us at our own speed and pace, and the transformation, the more consistent manifestation of our best intentions, will emerge.

The rewards of staying with the skirmish, of holding our balance in the face of the old energies, are profound. In the case of my little story above, it enabled me to stay connected to my wife and to the beautiful environment around us, rather than residing in turmoil for hours (or longer), disconnected from my loved one and from the magical display of color and form enfolding in our garden. In life generally, it is the difference between entrapment in a contracted view of negativity versus remaining in an open, flowing connection to the preciousness of being alive.

RESISTING THE TEMPTATION OF OLD COPING
MECHANISMS

As we have seen, the negative messages and energies first become embedded in our neural firing patterns early in life as our alarm systems react to and record situations in which the child feels unsafe. We then develop coping mechanisms that are a part of our attempt to keep safe in the face of the perceived danger. These coping mechanisms also begin developing in our early years. Although they are the best the child can do, they emerge from the instincts of the young person who does not yet have the ability to sort it all out or see the perceived danger from a larger perspective, supported by analytical resources and greater experience in the world. As a result, although these coping mechanisms may enable the individual to "get by" for some period of time extending well into adulthood, they generally have significant negative side effects that undermine the full development of the individual's capacities. Often, the coping mechanisms really don't work well at all in helping the person stay safe or, even if they do work somewhat, they break down totally at some point.

In his presentations, psychiatrist Dan Siegel sometimes talks about a case history that illustrates the deficiencies of coping mechanisms developed by the child.[55] A mother and her 12-year-old son came to his office for help because the son had decided not to eat any solid foods. In talking about the situation, the mother and son related the following story. About six months earlier, the family had been out to eat and the son choked on his food. It was sufficiently serious that his father had to give the Heimlich maneuver to clear the blockage in the son's throat. After that, the son decided that he wanted to eat only soft foods. Unfortunately, a few weeks after that incident, the son had another choking experience at home. Although not as serious as the first one, it was still startling to the child. Following that episode, the son refused to eat any solid foods and began taking in only liquids. Needless to say, his parents were quite concerned. When Dan asked the boy why he was doing this, he replied that he "just thought it was better."

Before doing anything else, Dan did a short teaching about the alarm system. He explained to the boy that there is a part of our brain he referred to as SAM and that it is SAM's job to try to keep us safe. SAM is always Scanning our environment for information, Appraising that information for possible signs of danger or risk to us and Motiving us to protect ourselves if SAM determines that we are in danger. SAM is our friend, Dan continued, and is doing the best he can; but we need to understand that he makes mistakes and comes up with strategies that really don't work very well. We should respect SAM's efforts and be friendly to him, but we also need to take another look and see if we can design a strategy for keeping safe that works better overall or doesn't have significant negative side effects.

As Dan suggested to the 12-year-old boy, it is extremely useful to take a clear and honest look at our coping mechanisms without beating up on ourselves if we discover that our reliance on them for so many years has really not served us very well. When we do look, it is a common experience to see, often for the first time, that our coping mechanisms have actually led to a great deal of discomfort or unhappiness. Mike's case story is a good example of that. In an effort to respond to his hyper-vigilant alarm system, he began developing a detailed plan for dealing with each anticipated danger. As a result, he was distracted from the rest of his life and dwelled even more on the possibility of something tragic happening to him or his family.

Coping mechanisms are widely diverse since each of us reacts to our experiences in our own personal way. They may be obvious, such as the person with obsessive/compulsive tendencies who washes his hands an excessive number of times each day in an effort to protect himself from germ contamination. Washing one's hands frequently is, of course, a good idea in support of health; but the inability to find a balance with it, or with other obsessive practices, can be very undermining to one's daily experience. Other coping strategies may be more difficult to identify.

Years ago in one of my cardiac rehabilitation classes, a woman shared that she had grown up in a chaotic and disorderly environment in which she frequently felt unsafe. In the process of discussing how the brain responds to such experiences, she realized that for her whole adult life she did not feel comfortable until she had vacuumed, dusted and otherwise cleaned the whole house—on a daily basis! It was clear to her that this was an effort to ward off the old feelings of unsafety she had felt so powerfully as a child in her chaotic home environment. She acknowledged that she would never be a messy housekeeper but that she did not want to keep repeating the old pattern that took so much time and energy and kept her from other activities she enjoyed.

At the time of this writing, I have a client who "hates" social situations and avoids them if at all possible. In reviewing her life story, one of the messages that emerged from her early experiences, both at home and in the first few years at school, was that she "just didn't fit in." As you might imagine, this made her feel very unsafe and left a powerful impact on her sense of self and her place in the world. It is perfectly logical, given how the alarm system (SAM) works, that she would avoid social situations years later in an effort to keep herself safe and not risk feeling that old painful and helpless energy of not fitting in. Although this coping mechanism seemed to work on one level, it kept her trapped in fear, limited her experiences in life and distracted her from doing the real work that would eventually enable her to transform the old messages and negative energies.

Anger is often a coping mechanism designed to defend the self from internal messages and energies that seem impossible to bear. A client in his mid-forties was concerned about his anger explosions when he came to see me. As a result of his father's excessive discipline, he carried powerful messages about something being wrong with him, as well as profound grief about his father's treatment of him. All this was just too terrifying to face directly. As a result, when the old neural firing patterns that housed these messages and energies were triggered, projection of anger onto someone else protected him from feeling directly the energies that were so terrifying to him. As long as he could vent the energy outward in anger, he did not have to look inside and actually feel the grief and negative messages about himself that were at the heart of the matter. In breaking through this old coping mechanism, he realized that the projection of anger on others only resulted in ultimately feeling worse about himself and distracted him, yet again, from transforming the core messages and energies.

When we have the opportunity to identify the old coping mechanisms and begin to realize that they really do not serve our growth or happiness, there is another challenge. These old responses may not be in our best interests, but they are what we know. They are what we have relied on for years to create some illusion of safety. As a result, even though they may have huge negative side effects, it is often very difficult to let go of them as we begin to develop a more effective response.

The French writer Andre Gide said that "we don't consent to discover new lands without losing sight of shore at first—and for a long time." When we begin to disengage from the old coping mechanisms, we are losing sight of familiar territory and, for some period of time while we are seeking firmer ground, it can definitely feel like we don't know where that new shore is. This is very unsettling. I sometimes describe it to clients this way. In the early stages of letting go of the ineffective coping mechanisms, we are like a trapeze artist who has just let go of the steady grip on one trapeze as he swings out toward another bar coming in his direction. For a time, we don't have a grip on anything and there is no ground under our feet. It is definitely a scary time.

In this process of developing healthier strategies, the temptation to resort to the old coping mechanism will often be very strong. Why wouldn't it be? The old patterns are deeply entrenched in the brain. SAM has motivated us to follow the same responses for many years and it feels like they have given us some sense of safety. And the new approach? Well, the foundation simply isn't strong enough yet for us to be confident about the outcome. Will it really keep us safe? Will it really be better for us? Despite the unsettling nature of this, it is very important eventually to hold our ground and not indulge the old response. If we give in to the urge and fall back on the old coping mechanisms, it only reinforces in our brains the ineffective patterns we have been relying on for years, thereby increasing the challenge of responding in a healthier way. As Carl Jung pointed out many years ago, to move to a new place, you have to sacrifice those parts of yourself that held you in the old place.

As is the case with all of mindfulness practice, slips will occur. The urge to fall back on the old coping mechanism will be too strong and we will resort to the old pattern. It is not that we don't intellectually understand what we are trying to do. Nor is it a matter of being lazy about our growth process. It is simply what we have reviewed many times before, namely, that we will slip into old ineffective ways many times while we slowly gain consistency and confidence in our mindfulness practice.

An analogy that is sometimes used to explain this dynamic goes like this. When we have poison ivy, we have an almost irresistible temptation to scratch the infected area. We have the *information* that the scratching will give us some kind of temporary relief; but we don't yet have the *wisdom* to realize that the scratching will only make the situation worse. So, we keep on giving in to the temptation to scratch and, to continue the analogy, eventually our whole body turns into a bloody, intolerable mess.

Our slips into the old coping mechanisms may give us some temporary relief, but they frequently have significant side effects and cause us additional discomfort—like continuing to scratch the poison ivy. If we are able to recognize, even after the slip, that relying on the ineffective coping mechanism only causes more problems, the slips actually help us strengthen our wisdom that the risks of scratching are greater than not scratching.

Moving Forward

There is a great deal to absorb in this chapter. As always when we are starting in a new direction, it is useful to simplify the process so that we are clear about the first steps. To move forward with your project of creating a foundation for a more lasting happiness, complete the Contemplative Exercise Regarding Re-Framing Old Conclusions and False Messages on the next page. It will lead you through the process of bringing this aspect of your mindfulness practice down into your life. To reiterate a message that cannot be repeated too frequently, open the kindness of your heart to yourself. Remember that, no matter how challenging this process is or how slowly you seem to be moving with it, you are giving yourself and those around you a very precious gift by bringing your attention to it.

CONTEMPLATIVE EXERCISE REGARDING RE-FRAMING OLD CONCLUSIONS AND FALSE MESSAGES

INSTRUCTIONS

Sit in a quiet place with a notepad. Lightly close your eyes or look down with a relaxed, unfocused gaze. Bring your attention to your exhale and take a few relaxing breaths. Stay with the relaxing breaths until you feel you have settled a bit.

Set an intention or aspiration to bring as much kindness and compassion to yourself and your family members as you reflect on the questions.

Contemplative exercises are much more about asking questions than about pressing for immediate or specific answers. Consequently, go through the exercise by reading the questions, experimenting with repeating them to yourself several times in a relaxed way, and then just leave some space. Try not to think too much or strain to come up with specific responses or memories. Instead, simply return to the relaxing breath and see what arises in your mind. This allows your intuition and your mind to work together to reveal useful information in response to the questions.

A significant part of this exercise involves reviewing the circumstances related to the negative conclusions you drew about yourself and any explicitly negative messages that might have been directed to you. Although you may be able to identify negative conclusions or messages, you may not have clear memories of the circumstances involving your parents or other primary caretakers. If this is the case, try the technique described earlier. Think of the personalities, characteristics, style and habits of speech and action of your parents you have noticed since you became an adult and then imagine how your child-self might have reacted to or interpreted such qualities and behaviors in your early years.

Don't try to do too many questions at one time. Reflect on only as many of the questions as are comfortable for you. If you feel saturated or overwhelmed at any time, stop and return to the exercise at a later time.

Experiment with writing brief notes or reflections as you recall memories or receive information in response to the questions. The notes do not have to be articulate or fully formed thoughts. They are just for you. After a day or more, go back and review your notes. Reflect on how your earlier experiences are connected to and influence your present view of yourself. Consider the ways in which you can re-frame the messages and meaning of the earlier experiences. Continue to clarify the insights you want to return to when the old neural firing patterns are triggered.

If, at any time, this exercise is overwhelming, **Stop.** If efforts to reflect on the questions continue to be overwhelming, I strongly urge you to consult with a counselor. An experienced mental health professional can provide the support and safety you may need to continue with the process of making sense of your history, re-framing the meaning of that history and integrating your new insights in an effective way with your growth process.

Before beginning the questions for reflection, list in your notebook any negative conclusions or messages about yourself that emerged from the contemplation exercise at the end of the last chapter.

QUESTIONS FOR REFLECTION

I. *With regard to negative conclusions about yourself:*

   a. *How might your child-self have interpreted the reactions of your parents or other primary caretakers to reach such a conclusion or assumption?*

   b. *What might your child-self have misunderstood or not realized about the situation?*

   c. *How might your child-self have taken personally comments or actions by your parents or other primary caretakers that were not intended to be personal or judgmental?*

   d. *Looking now from an adult perspective at the circumstances that gave rise to the negative conclusions, can you see a possible different meaning or intent in any of the speech or actions of your parents or other primary caretakers?*

2. With regard to explicitly negative messages about yourself:

    a. Do you know anything now about your parents or other primary caretakers that would give a different perspective about any of these negative messages?

    b. Can you begin to at least imagine that these negative messages were the result of the personal suffering or conditioning of your parents or other primary caretakers and not a reflection of your true nature?

    c. Can you begin to at least imagine that just because the negative messages were spoken to or about you does not mean that they were ever true?

3. With regard to both any negative conclusions you drew about yourself and any explicitly negative messages delivered to you, what is the best re-interpretation you can now make of those experiences from an adult perspective?

4. Imagine that a wise, highly-realized being (or the Divine, if you prefer) had viewed all the situations that gave rise to your negative conclusions and/or messages, what advice do you think she or he would give you about them.

5. With regard to each of the negative conclusions or messages about yourself you have identified, and in light of your new

insights about both your personal story and brain functions:

a. *What new insights do you have about yourself?*

b. *What new insights do you have about the way the negative conclusions or messages became a part of your belief system?*

c. *When the old negative conclusions or messages get triggered by your on-going experience in the world, what is the response that best serves your happiness and sense of self? (Be imaginative and come up with the best or healthiest response even if you are not sure it is true. Take the time to reflect on the best response for each of the negative conclusions or messages you have identified and write each response in your notebook.)*

STABILIZING THE INSIGHTS AND THE PRACTICE

After you have completed the exercise, the following steps can help you to stabilize your insights and integrate them into your mindfulness practice.

1. Choose one negative conclusion or message about yourself that you have identified in the two contemplative exercises. It is usually better not to pick the most challenging or painful one in the beginning.

2. Start to work with this negative conclusion or message by applying the Stop-Breathe-Reflect-Choose technique. To strengthen the effectiveness of your practice:

a.   Reflect on the circumstances or situations in which this old conclusion or message is likely to be triggered. This nurtures your "witnessing" awareness and increases your ability to promptly recognize that the old neural firing pattern has been triggered. The more quickly we can do this, of course, the more able we will be to skillfully manage the message and the energy that comes with it.

b.   Review the healthy response to this negative conclusion or message that you wrote in connection with Question 5(c) above. Revise or add to it in any way that makes it even more clear or meaningful to you. This response serves as your inner dialogue in the Reflect part of the practice.

c.   If your healthy response involves a number of insights or reminders, ask yourself this: "What is the core reminder of my healthy response?" If you can, write a short-form response (just a phrase or a short senten ce) that captures the primary insight you want to repeatedly reaffirm in response to the old neural firing pattern.

d.   Write out both the full healthy response and its short version on a 3 x 5 card so that you can carry it with you and actually read it, if you need to, when you get triggered.

3.   Review your 3 x 5 card in the morning and set the intention (1) to notice when the old conclusion or message has been triggered and (2) to apply the Stop-Breathe-Reflect-Choose technique.

4.   Use the in-between spaces of your day (for example, for just a few minutes while you are driving, waiting in line, walking to the bathroom, etc.) to reflect on your healthy response and the new foundation you are building for your happiness.

5. Before you go to sleep, review the day with questions such as: "Did I notice any triggerings of the negative conclusion or message? Did I use my mindfulness practice? If I did, can I take delight that I was able to be mindful? If I can now see that I got triggered and the old energies dominated my consciousness, can I be kind to myself and simply reaffirm my intention to start my mindfulness practice again tomorrow?" Let go of your review of the day, take a few relaxing breaths to settle yourself and drift off to sleep as peacefully as possible.

6. When you feel that your mindfulness practice has become more consistent in noticing and consciously working with the negative conclusion or message, choose another old negative reaction pattern and include it in your practice. I strongly urge you not to put pressure on yourself by setting time frames for this or by thinking that you are not moving fast enough. We are in this for the long haul. It is so important to be comfortable with your own pace and the energy you are able to bring to the practice within the context of the demanding circumstances of your life. Every little bit you can do, no matter how slow the pace may seem, will contribute to the process of literally changing your brain and building new neural firing patterns that better serve your happiness.

CHAPTER 8

Step Six:
New Realities ...
Investing in a New Vision of Self

THE FUNDAMENTAL OBSTACLE TO A LASTING
HAPPINESS: A DISTORTED VISION OF OURSELVES

At the core of our happiness project are the images and beliefs about ourselves. The fundamental obstacle to a lasting and durable happiness is our distorted view of who we are—of our basic nature. Transpersonal psychologist Frances Vaughan succinctly emphasizes this point:

> Since everything in the world is constantly changing, including our states of mind, nothing can guarantee lasting happiness. Only with the relinquishment of illusory self-concepts can the conditions for happiness be established.[56]

Let's briefly review what we have considered so far with regard to our concepts about ourselves. In looking at brain functioning, we learned that the alarm system of the brain is hard-wired to store, from our earliest days, conclusions and messages about ourselves that emerge from the on-going experiences in our home environments. We saw that children have a natural tendency to draw negative conclusions about themselves and that these conclusions generally are experienced with a powerful energy of feeling unsafe, overwhelmed, helpless and/or afraid. Because it is the alarm system's job to record experiences in which we feel in danger, this combination of negative conclusions about ourselves and powerful energies are then strongly embedded in our neural firing patterns. Explicitly negative messages are, of course, stored in the same way, so that the "software" of our brains is programmed with persistent negative images about ourselves.

As we explored the further functioning of the alarm system, we saw that the negative images of ourselves, along with the energies of danger or helplessness, were triggered over and over again as the alarm system constantly took in current stimuli from our environment, scanned our entire memory bank to determine whether there is a link with an earlier experience of danger and then triggered the old neural firing pattern if it found a match— often a loose and sloppy match. Each time the old neural firing pattern was triggered, the neural connection, *and the negative image of ourselves stored in it,* was strengthened. Eventually, that negative image evolved into a state of mind, a bias or a filter that influenced how we saw ourselves and interpreted our experience in the world.

Understanding the basics of the brain's alarm system, and its hard-wired processing of our early experiences, underscored the usefulness of mindfulness practice. Consequently, we considered various stages of developing a mindful approach to the internal negative images of ourselves. We looked below the surface of our thoughts and emotions to identify the core messages that undermined our sense of self. We applied various techniques, such as Stop-Breathe-Reflect-Choose and imagery, to intervene when the old neural firing patterns housing the negative messages were triggered. In doing so, we began the process of disengaging from the unhealthy messages. In an effort to dismantle the belief systems that undermine our happiness, we re-framed the childhood experiences and discovered that the negative messages we absorbed from our primary caretakers had more to do with others' conditioning and very little to do with our own basic nature or basic goodness.

As we continue with our mindfulness practice, and increasingly disengage from the old belief system that something is basically wrong with us, that we are just not good enough, we are often left with a vacuum. If the old concepts and images of ourselves are not true, what is? We need to discover a new, healthier and true vision of ourselves that we can believe in. In the rest of this chapter, we will look to a number of sources to explore the possibility of investing in a new vision of ourselves.

THE TRANSPERSONAL PSYCHOLOGY MOVEMENT

In the late 1960s, a small group of psychologists and writers began to review Western psychology's limited view of human potential. They were motivated by the belief that Western psychology and psychiatry had focused primarily on what is "wrong" with human beings (that is to say, on the pathology of individuals) and had not meaningfully explored our potential for growth, psychological health and exceptional well-being. Building on the work in the early 1960s of humanistic psychology, the movement that came to be known as transpersonal psychology sought to expand our awareness of our true potential as human beings. Ironically, a significant part of the transpersonal movement's teachings came not so much from new discoveries but from fresh recognition of the commonalties and collective wisdom of the world's great spiritual traditions.

One of the movement's initial assumptions is that Western psychology and culture in the 19th and 20th centuries had contributed to an entrapment in a limited view of our potential. Roger Walsh, one of the founders of the transpersonal movement, described it this way:

> Clearly the human condition offers possibilities far beyond those that are usually recognized. From this it follows that what we have called 'normality' is not the peak of human development but rather may represent a form of developmental arrest.
> . . . Indeed the world's wisdom traditions are in widespread agreement that our usual state

> of consciousness is not only suboptimal but
> significantly distorted and dreamlike. . . .
>   Usually the dream goes unrecognized for several
> reasons. We all share in it; we have been hypnotized
> since infancy; and we live—each and every one of
> us—in the biggest cult of all: cult-ure.[57]

The first assumption of transpersonal psychology, that our usual state of consciousness is "suboptimal," initially appears to be somewhat pessimistic; but it is not. The good news is stated in the movement's second assumption:

> The second assumption is that although the
> untrained mind is clouded and out of control, it can
> be trained and clarified, and this training catalyzes
> transpersonal potentials.[58]

Transpersonal psychology emphasizes that our true potential and states of exceptional well-being (for our purposes, a durable and lasting happiness) can be realized by techniques that "are a part of an art and technology that has been refined over thousands of years in hundreds of cultures and constitutes the contemplative core of the world's great religious traditions."[59] From the view of transpersonal psychology, these techniques can be practiced within the context of a specific religious tradition or completely separate from religion. The common elements of the practices identified by the transpersonal movement,[60] and their relationship to mindfulness practice, is set forth below.

1. Ethical training.

Unethical behavior reinforces destructive mental forces and generally results in very distracting and undermining thoughts and emotions. It is difficult to develop a positive image of ourselves when we are distracted by the self-judgment, remorse and/or guilt that result from unethical actions. Put another way, lying or treating our loved ones badly inhibits any effort to maximize our true potential. Ethical behavior, on the other hand, undermines destructive forces and cultivates positive forces.

Through the practice of mindfulness, we are more able to catch up with the automatic, pre-intentional energy of the brain that moves us in the direction of unethical speech and behavior.

2. Attentional training and concentration.

Awareness of mental activity and stabilizing concentration enable the individual to be creative with negative emotions and to nurture positive emotions. As we have seen in so many ways throughout this book, the constant activity generated by the brain, and the unavoidable automatic arisings of emotion, present all of us with an initial challenge if we aspire to transcend the usual suboptimal state of consciousness and live with more awareness. Mindfulness practice offers us clear strategies and techniques for meeting this challenge.

3. Emotional transformation.

Transpersonal psychology emphasizes that there are three significant components of emotional transformation: the reduction of destructive emotions, the cultivation of positive emotions and the cultivation of equanimity. The stages of mindfulness practice we have explored so far are designed to transform the destructive emotions that undermine our sense of self and our happiness. In this process, we have considered mindfulness techniques that enable us (a) to identify destructive emotions that emerge from old neural firing patterns, (b) to intervene in the triggering of such emotions and (c) to begin to free ourselves from their hold on us. In continuing with this process, we cultivate positive emotions as we repeatedly affirm our best intentions and live more intentionally.

4. Motivation.

Ethical behavior, attention training and emotional transformation work together to redirect motivation along healthier and more transpersonal lines. Mindfulness is a path and strategy for working with the first three elements of transpersonal psychology. Our growing experience with mindfulness practice strengthens our belief in ourselves and the possibility of continued meaningful change. Creating an experience of change and seeing its impact on our day-to-day lives, in turn, adds further energy to our motivation and accelerates our movement along the path of our individual growth and transformation.

5. Refining awareness.

Intuitive capacities are cultivated and perception is rendered more sensitive and more appreciative of the freshness of each moment of experience. Mindfulness practice offers the possibility of an expanded, more consistent awareness, uncluttered by the old messages, needless worries and the endless distractions of the brain's automatic, hardwired activity. As a result, we are more able to draw more fully on all our resources—our intuition as well as our intellect—in leading a more intentional and graceful life.

6. Wisdom.

In transpersonal psychology, wisdom emerges from the lifelong processes of personal transformation and leads inevitably to a deeper understanding of the true nature of reality. Mindfulness provides a well-defined path for continuing to work on personal transformation. As we bring our attention and energies to this path, a clearer, more stable and integrated sense of ourselves and our place in the world develops—a sense that is continually refined over time. With persistence, this wisdom becomes the ground on which we live and the true foundation for experiencing a lasting happiness.

Transpersonal psychology offers a very encouraging vision of who we are and what our real potential is. It stands as an impressive body of research, thought and experience that is in stark contrast to the old images of ourselves we have carried for so long. Moreover, the common elements and practices identified by transpersonal psychology to reach our true potential reinforce the mindfulness practices we have been exploring in this book. This strengthens our confidence that we are on the right path and that transformation leading to a more lasting happiness is possible for each of us. The transpersonal movement adopted the message of the ancient wisdom traditions as its own. It is a fitting message for the conclusion of this section:

> The message of the great spiritual traditions can therefore be summarized very easily: Wake up! Wake up from your suboptimal entranced state of consciousness; wake up to your true nature; wake up to the fact that you are more than this body and are not only more than you think but more than you can think . . .[61]

THE TEACHINGS OF THE GREAT SPIRITUAL TRADITIONS

As we saw in the preceding section, the transpersonal movement drew upon certain teachings common to the great spiritual traditions. Although it would be wonderful to do a more thorough exploration of the nature of the human beings as described by these traditions, that is beyond the scope of this book. Still, there are a few examples from several of the traditions' teachings that are useful to explore for the precious light they shed on our search for a new vision of ourselves.

If we look deeply enough, we will find that the ancient wisdom traditions have a very positive and expansive view of our true nature. In the Buddhist tradition, for example, there is the fundamental teaching that each and every one of us has Buddha-nature. What does this mean? Essentially, it reminds us that we all have the potential to be a highly realized and wise being, freed from the suffering that results from the conditioning we have been discussing. Western references to the concept of Buddha-nature sometimes refer to it as "basic goodness." In Buddhist cultures, such as Tibet and most of the Southeast Asian countries, this concept plays out in a way that powerfully supports the individual's sense of self. No culture or tradition gets it all right, of course; but there is an aspect of this Buddhist teaching that tends to be healthier for the individual's sense of self than the comparative tendency in our culture.

Let's start with our culture. In our country, we generally make the following association: bad act or behavior—bad person. In other words, there is often a snap judgment that bad or harmful behavior indicates that there is some character flaw, or more simply, something basically wrong with the person. The pervasive underlying tendency to judge ourselves and others in this way supports and continually gives new energy to the negative images we have of ourselves.

The teachings of the Buddhist tradition generally avoid the harsh negative judgments about the basic nature of the individual. Bad or harmful behavior is certainly not condoned; it is simply subject to the law of karma. Karma is the law of cause and effect. Our harmful behavior is a cause that will definitely, according to the law of karma, have a negative effect on us. We may experience that effect immediately, later in life or even in another lifetime; but we will not be able to avoid the consequences of our harmful or hurtful acts. In the West, we have a saying that is parallel to the law of karma: "You reap what you sow."

The interplay of the concept of Buddha-nature and the law of karma means that the teaching would be something like this: "That was a harmful act and you will have to bear the consequences of your act; but your basic nature, your essence, is still Buddha-nature. It is inexhaustible and no one or no thing, not even your own bad actions, can wipe it away or take it away from you. It may be covered over by your conditioning or your misunderstanding, but it will remain the essence of who you are."

Significantly, there is no word in the Tibetan language for guilt. There is, of course, an unavoidable responsibility for an individual's actions in the Tibetan-Buddhist culture, due to the law of karma. In addition, there is the strong emotion of remorse for one's actions that cause suffering to others; but there is no directly equivalent concept of guilt. Consequently, the heavy weight of guilt that carries such a strong implication of something being wrong with us, that we are simply a bad person, is generally not experienced.

These and other factors indicate that the struggle with low self-esteem, so pervasive in our society, is not transcultural. There is an interesting story from one of the Dalai Lama's early visits to the United States. He was meeting with a group of Americans and a member of the audience asked him what advice he had for the large number of people in our country who suffer from a sense of low self-worth.

The Dalai Lama is universally recognized as a man of profound wisdom and understanding of human nature; but he was puzzled by the question. Although Tibetans have their own challenges, they usually do not carry the type of negative self-concept that many Americans confront. This is not terribly surprising since the Tibetan child will hear over and over again from his earliest days that his basic nature is Buddha-nature, the inexhaustible potential to be a highly realized being. This is his culturally-imposed vision of himself. Because the Dalai Lama had not yet spent much time in the United States, he was still learning about our culture and had not yet become familiar with the self-esteem challenges we face here.

Turning to the Catholic tradition, there is a specific and relatively recent reminder of our true nature. I first heard this in the recording of a workshop led by Father Thomas Keating.[62] Father Keating is an articulate and kind teacher who frequently speaks of the false messages about ourselves that inevitably result from our conditioning. He emphasizes how these negative messages so constantly undermine our happiness. Using the spiritual language of the Christian tradition, he reminds us that from Jesus' profound love for us emerged a wish that we all be happy. There was, of course, a powerful wisdom in this wish, too. Jesus knew that if we were happy, we would treat others more respectfully and lovingly and avoid so much of the suffering that we have traditionally caused one another.

Consequently, Father Keating refers to the process of growth and transformation we are exploring, this happiness project of ours, not as some selfish expenditure of energy, but as a spiritual work that will inevitably benefit all those around us. In relating to our negative messages about ourselves, Father Keating uses the word "renunciation"—renouncing those messages that undermine our happiness. This is a useful word to keep in mind in the context of mindfulness practice. It reminds us that disengaging from the negative messages that undermine our happiness requires firm resolve, a determination to say over and over again that we are no longer going to accept as true the negative messages we have carried for so long.

Father Keating also teaches what he refers to as contemplative prayer. This is a form of meditation that is virtually identical to the one-pointedness or circle meditation described in Chapter Three, except that Father Keating suggests using a word chosen by the practitioner (such as peacefulness, calm, silence, etc.) as the point of focus rather than the breath. Father Keating stresses the importance of meditation in transforming our relationship with our minds. His essential message is that our minds are so busy with thinking, mental churning and the automatic energy of the brain that there is no space for connecting with deeper aspects of ourselves—or with the Divine. Meditation is needed to settle this mental activity and create space for the possibility of these profound connections. If you are interested in pursuing mindfulness practice within the context of the Christian tradition, I am sure that you would find Father Keating's teachings instructive, motivating and inspiring.

I have great respect for Father Keating's teachings. I turned to him because of the following reminder he offers to his listeners. Occasionally, the Pope issues pronouncements that carry the weight of establishing or affirming the dogma (that is, the truth) for the Catholic Church. The Vatican II pronouncements issued in the mid-1960's affirmed that *each of us has the Divinity within*, as well as a connection with the Divinity outside us. Think of that! Isn't that another powerful reminder of our true nature. Shouldn't we be on rooftops with bullhorns shouting,

"You have the Divinity within! I repeat! Pay attention! You have the Divinity within! This is your true nature!" We should take this pronouncement to heart as we continue to invest in a new vision of self.

Turning to another tradition, author and teacher Deepak Chopra offers a vision of the self in his description of soul:

> . . .The same unbounded potential of the infinite spirit also resides in each and every one of us. Our personal soul, which we think of when we think of our 'selves,' is an outcropping of the eternal soul. If we could learn to live from the level of the soul, we would see that the best, most luminous part of ourselves is connected to all the rhythms of the universe. We would truly know ourselves as the miracle-makers we are capable of being.[63]

We could, of course, continue to search for more examples of a true vision of ourselves from the great spiritual traditions, but our exploration would simply lead to more of what the examples above have already illustrated—that our true nature is luminous and powerful and capable of engaging with endless possibilities in beautiful and graceful ways. We might even discover, as difficult as it is to believe in the face of our human frailties, that our nature includes and reflects the Divine. The research and experience of the transpersonal movement leads to this very conclusion:

> We have even begun to suspect that the most profound and radical claims of the perennial philosophy may be correct and that it may in fact be true that
>
> *The kingdom of heaven is within you* (Christianity).
>
> *By understanding the Self all this universe is known* (Upanishads).
>
> *Atman (individual consciousness) and Brahman (universal consciousness) are one* (Vedanta).
>
> *God dwells within you as you* (Yoga).
>
> *Look within, you are the Buddha* (Buddhism).

Heaven, earth and human are of one body
(Neoconfucianism).

Those who know themselves know their God
(Islam).[64]

Resisting Our Greatness

You may remember that in Chapter One, I quoted from Nelson Mandela's 1994 inaugural speech in which he noted the basic human fear of acknowledging the vast potential of our basic nature:

> Our deepest fear is not that we are inadequate. Our deepest fear is that we are powerful beyond measure.
> It is our light, not our darkness, that frightens us.

If we are to be successful in opening up to a new vision of ourselves, and in slowly building a new foundation for the lasting happiness we seek, then we must acknowledge this tendency to resist our greatness. Since the great wisdom traditions have been reminding us for thousands of years of the radiance and goodness of our basic nature, why do we so persistently resist it? Why, as the transpersonal movement emphasizes, do we get so stuck in a "suboptimal state of consciousness"? In the early years of modern American psychology, William James stated that "most people live, whether physically, intellectually or morally, in a very restricted circle of their potential being. They make use of a very small portion of their possible consciousness. . . . We all have reservoirs of life to draw upon, of which we do not dream."[65] Why is this so?

I don't pretend to have all the answers to these important questions, but a significant part of the explanation emerges out of the exploration we have already done. It might be summed up as "the security of the familiar." Let's start by accepting, just as a working hypothesis, that the reminders of the great wisdom traditions, sages, poets and philosophers over the ages are correct, namely, that the essence of our basic nature is unlimited potential. Let's assume for the moment that we come into this world with the capacity to manifest the greatness of this potential. What happens from the first day of our life (and probably beginning even earlier in the womb)?

As we have seen in so many ways, the conditioning of our emerging brains begins immediately. Since our parents have their own limiting conditioning, and since our sense of self is fundamentally "crafted" by them in the early years, our view of ourselves becomes limited and loses sight of the full potential of our basic nature. In looking at the basic functioning of the brain's alarm system and the stories of the individuals mentioned throughout this book, we have touched upon the many ways this conditioned view of ourselves plays out for all of us.

This limited sense of self, this belief system about who we are, is what we know. Even though it is *the* fundamental obstacle to obtaining lasting happiness, even though it has huge negative side effects on the way we experience our lives on a day-to-day basis, we lapse into, and get hooked on, "the security of the familiar." Residing in amnesia about the potential of our basic nature, the security of the familiar drives us to do so many things that logically make no sense. We stay in jobs and relationships far too long when they make us miserable or, even worse, when they further diminish our sense of self. We return to negative habits over and over when they threaten to destroy our health or the last semblance of balance we have in our lives. It's human nature. We cling to what we know out of our understandable fear of what is uncertain. I had a man in a workshop who knew he needed to let go of his anger; but it "scared" him "to death" because without his anger, he didn't know who he was.

For all of us, letting go of this limited sense of self requires venturing into the unfamiliar, what appears to be the unknown, and this presents a barrier of fear. Transpersonal psychologists Frances Vaughn and Roger Walsh, sum it up this way:

> Growth involves movement into the unknown and often requires surrendering familiar ways of being. Consequently, we tend to fear growth. The tragic result, as both psychologists and philosophers have

recognized, is that we actually deny and defend against our greatness and potential. . . .

Defenses against transpersonal development also operate in society. Cultures seem to function not only to educate, but also as collective conspiracies to constrict consciousness. As such they mirror and magnify our individual ambivalence toward transcendence.[66]

We need to face these obstacles to connecting with a new vision of who we are. They are like walls separating us from the possibility of connecting with our true nature, our true potential. For most of us, unlike the Berlin Wall, the walls will not be torn down overnight. The real dismantling of them will occur in the course of persistent mindfulness practice, as we repeatedly identify the old messages that have separated us from our true nature for so long, disengage from them and slowly strengthen our growing insight about who we are. To refer again to Thomas Merton, it is this consistent mindfulness practice that is our vehicle for crossing "the abyss that separates us from ourselves."

Although fully believing in this new vision of ourselves may take some time, and integrating it into how we manifest in the world, will take even more practice, I am challenging you right here and now to open your imagination to the possibility of this new vision being an accurate reflection of who you are. More than twenty-five years ago I read a book that left a great impression on me. It has been so long ago now that I can't remember either the author or the title. What stuck with me was this simple statement: "Imagination is the door to new realities."

The problem is that we do not seriously entertain the reality of our true nature and therefore don't know what is truly possible for us. If this new vision of yourself is difficult to believe, or even seems "far out," I am asking you to open up the door of your imagination, just a little, and imagine the possibility of this new vision of yourself. I am urging you to be curious about your true nature. One way to do that is to reflect on the messages from the great spiritual traditions explored earlier in this chapter. For example, what does it mean that "the kingdom of heaven is within you" or that "God dwells within you" or that "those who know themselves know their God"? It may well take the rest of our lives to more fully understand the meaning of those messages, but we can start being actively curious about them. We can do that by simply reflecting on questions such as:

> What do they offer to me?
>
> How do I understand them (even when my present understanding is vague or not very complete)?
>
> What might they mean to me if I invested in them?

In the midst of the unavoidable nagging doubts about yourself and confusion about the meaning of the wonderful messages from the great spiritual traditions, please take comfort in my assurance that, with the opening of your imagination, the flowering of your curiosity and the growing effect of your mindfulness practice, a new reality will begin to emerge – a growing realization of your own radiant, eternal and pure true nature.

What's the alternative, anyway? Continuing to believe in those conditioned negative messages, that old limited vision of yourself, can only produce one result: more discomfort and suffering. We know that for certain. As a practical matter, it is simply a very bad investment. It is like investing your life savings in Enron the day *after* it declared bankruptcy. There is only one possible result. The energy of the investment is squandered. Making the practical choice and investing, just a little at a time, in the new vision of yourself offers the real possibility of having "the perfect day" I wrote about in a poem some years ago.

> What is a perfect day?
> Is it 24 hours of making all your appointments?
> Or not having to be anywhere on a schedule?
>
> Is it a day without illness?
> Or without sadness, suffering or fear?
> It is a string of moments when you
>   feel good about yourself?

Or a time when you are not thinking
about yourself much at all?

Is it a late afternoon when the wind sings
waves of lights across a pond?
Is it when you can see and hear and feel this
symphony of light and water with your whole being?

Or is it when you simply remember
The wisdom deep in your heart,
And suddenly realize anew who you truly are?

Forgiving Ourselves and Others

If we hope to open more fully to this new vision of
ourselves, we must consider the practice of forgiveness—for
ourselves as well as for others. Harming others and being hurt is
an inevitable part of the human experience. Of course, we would
like to avoid harming and being hurt as much as possible, and
our mindfulness practice will help us minimize that; but those
conditions will occasionally be a part of our lives nevertheless.

Because we are not fully enlightened, we have all acted
inadvertently or unskillfully at times, causing harm to ourselves
and to others. When others have hurt us, we often carry resentment
or anger. The harm we have done to ourselves and others
frequently results in guilt or other emotions that undermine our
sense of self. In both cases, the emotions of resentment, anger,
guilt and harshness close off our hearts to our true nature and
to a full awareness of the incredible possibilities available to us
in each moment. Most of the time, we don't realize that these
powerful emotions directed to others are burning us up—and
literally undermining our health as well. As George Bernard
Shaw supposedly said, "Resentment is like swallowing poison
and waiting for someone else to die."

We have become so accustomed to carrying these dense,
heavy emotions—and to accepting this hardening of our
hearts—that it doesn't occur to us how limiting they are or

that they can be released. In fact, we may even have become convinced that guilt, for example, is an emotion we should live with for years for all the harm we have done. Meditation teacher and writer Sharon Salzberg draws on the Buddhist tradition to make a very useful point about guilt:

> Guilt [in the Buddhist tradition] is considered unskillful, because of the component of lacerating self-hatred in it. We go over and over the harmful thing we have done, continually blaming ourselves, stuck there until we are drained. The result is that we are left with no energy to actually transform our actions. . . .[67]

The central point of this section is this: no matter how justified you feel in carrying the anger or resentment for the hurtful acts of others, no matter how much you believe you deserve the guilt or self-hatred for the harm you have caused, continuing to carry these heavy burdens presents a significant obstacle to achieving lasting happiness. The hard shell around your heart does not serve you. As understandable as it is that your heart has hardened, it is essential to seek to soften it. Creating an aspiration of forgiveness opens the possibility of breaking through the shell and releasing the energy it has consumed all these years to maintain it. As transpersonal psychologist Frances Vaughn has written, "forgiving ourselves for being just as we are is the first step to healing."[68]

You may feel that forgiveness means condoning the hurtful behaviors. It does not. Even though we forgive another, we still oppose destructive acts and take the necessary steps to protect ourselves from further harm. We may also need to take action to prevent the person from harming others. Forgiving ourselves does not mean that it is O.K. to slip back into old behaviors that are hurtful to others or that undermine our own health and happiness. With forgiveness for ourselves, we need to bring determination to learn from our mistakes and set the intention to make more skillful and healthy choices in the future. Mindfulness practice offers a vehicle for manifesting this intention as much as possible.

We have devoted our attention in this chapter to the challenging process of opening to a new vision of ourselves. In order to remove a significant obstacle to that process—and to open your heart to a revitalizing flow of new energy—I encourage you to do the forgiveness meditation set forth below. As with all the meditations in this book, it is a good idea to read through the exercise a couple of times so that you are generally aware of the flow of it. Of course, it is perfectly fine to return to the text in the middle of the meditation until you are accustomed with the practice and can do it totally on your own.

FORGIVENESS MEDITATION

Find a comfortable sitting posture, spine upright, hands held comfortably in your lap or on your knees.

Lightly close your eyes. If closing your eyes is not comfortable for you, look down at the floor with a relaxed, unfocused gaze.

Begin by bringing your attention to your exhale and taking a few relaxing breaths. The relaxing quality of the exhale can be enhanced by drawing together three resources: (1) the natural relaxing quality of the exhale, the quality we experience spontaneously in a sigh, (2) the body-mind communication and (3) your imagination. The power of the body-mind communication is utilized by giving the body direction—simply say silently to yourself, on the exhale, "relax, release, let go," or just one of those words. The power of imagination is utilized by imagining the muscles and tissues of the body relaxing, softening and letting go. Although it may seem a little complicated at first to think of all three of these resources on each exhale, with a little practice it begins to feel very natural to use the three resources at the same time.

Stay with the relaxing breaths until you feel you have settled in a bit. If you become distracted at any time by a thought or emotion (and it is almost certain that you will), simply notice that your mind has wondered off and bring your attention gently back to the exhale.

A very important part of the practice is to watch the temptation to judge yourself. This can happen in many ways: "Oh, I'm distracted; I can't do this right." Or: "I don't like that thought—or that feeling." Here the practice has a simple and repetitious aspect to it: just notice the temptation to judge yourself, your performance in the practice or the process itself, let go of the temptation as well as you can and gently return your attention to the exhale.

Remember that forgiveness is a practice. It may not be effective for you, or seem to create anything new the first time. It is something to work with over time.

First bring your attention to harm you have caused others. We have all hurt others, in thought or word or deed, knowingly and unknowingly. We act unskillfully only for two reasons: out of our pain and out of our fear. We become confused in our pain and act without awareness. Bring to mind a time when you have caused harm or pain to another. It is best to start with a relatively minor incident. As the practice becomes more familiar, and you begin to see that forgiveness is a real possibility, you can gradually include acts of harm that weigh more heavily on your heart.

Have the courage to open your heart to the pain you caused another in the incident you are recalling. Remind yourself that none of us acts from our best intentions all the time and, as much as we try, we all act unskillfully in ways that hurt others. Imagine that the person you hurt in the incident is standing in front of you and ask for forgiveness. Moving from the specific incident to all your unskillful acts, ask for forgiveness from all those whom you may have hurt by your words or deeds. Imagine what it would feel like to be truly forgiven. Rest for a few moments in the sense of being forgiven.

Now direct your attention to yourself. We have all been so hard on ourselves. We have judged ourselves relentlessly. Many times we have not taken care of ourselves; we have not respected our needs; we have not protected ourselves from danger. To forgive is to soften the barrier around your heart, to let yourself more fully into your heart.

Bring to mind one aspect of how you have not treated yourself well and ask for forgiveness. Stay with this until you can feel some softening in your judgment of yourself. If no softening occurs, simply set the intention to nurture the possibility of forgiving yourself in the future. Now expand your awareness to all the ways—out of your fear and pain and unknowing, out of neglect or dishonesty—you have hurt your body, heart or mind, for the many ways you have not taken care of yourself, and ask for forgiveness for your sweet, precious self.

This may be hard, but you can do it. You have the power to accept who you are and you can begin doing it right now. Let your heart be as soft as it can. You deserve to be forgiven. Forgiveness lets you open, to escape from the hard shell around your heart and to more fully connect with your own radiant nature.

At the very least, imagine what it would feel like to truly forgive yourself. Rest in the soothing light of that imagined forgiveness. Reflect on the energy that would be released if you let go of the heavy anchor of judgment you carry in your heart.

Finally, direct your attention to the wounds and sorrows you have suffered at the hands of others. All the hurts you have held with such tenacity only serve to harden your own heart. Bring to mind a person who has hurt you and whom you have not forgiven. Again, it is best not to start with hurts that have been the most wounding.

Feel the places in your heart or your mind where you hold resentment or anger for this person and touch them with kindness. Remind yourself that these emotions, as understandable as they are, only serve to burden and limit you. In this sense, forgiveness for another is, in the first instance, an act of kindness for yourself. See if it is time to forgive and let go of the heaviness in your heart. If not, set the aspiration to forgive in the future.

Rest in the healing light of forgiveness. If the meditation was difficult for you and you have not felt ready to forgive yourself or others, take pride in the courage you have had to even approach the hurts you have experienced and caused. Please know that your courage will eventually lead to a further softening of your heart and a release of heavy, burdensome energy from your mind, emotions and body. Before you close the meditation, open your imagination to the possibility of that softening and release—and rest in the comfort it offers you.[69]

CHAPTER 9

Step Seven:
A Personal Strategy...
Developing a Clear Plan for Mindfulness Practice

A PERSONAL STORY

Many years ago my wife and I made one of our several trips to Nepal and India. We were in Katmandu, the capital of Nepal. At the time, Katmandu was a city of about 100,000, with another 150,000 or so living in the surrounding valleys; but it was not a city that an American could easily visualize. It had the feel and look of a town out of another age. There were a few buildings that pulled our thoughts to the current century, but it was impossible to fully believe in them, as they were swallowed up by sights and sounds that were not easily placed in the modern age. The diverse pulse of this ageless community instantly drew us into its rhythm. On even a short walk through its dirt streets, our senses were enlivened in ways that would be impossible at home. It is difficult to describe the display of it all, the feeling of amazement it evoked. As a friend from another trip to Nepal once said: "How do you describe the taste of mustard to someone who has never tasted it?"

The details may not capture the magic we felt in being there, but they do begin to build a mosaic that reflects some of the experience of the place. On one early-morning walk, we were treated with all the following sights: bicycle rickshaws piled high with freshly slaughtered goat meat; porters with long bamboo sticks over their shoulders, balanced at both ends with baskets filled with live chickens huddled passively together; children, usually bare-footed, with radiant smiles that instantly melt your heart; outdoor haircutters kneeling at the edge of the street while they worked on their customers; rock crushers breaking up individual stones into gravel for a new building to fill the place of one fallen to time; women in every imaginable dress, often beautiful saris or brightly-colored cloth wrapped and draped in styles consistent with ethnic traditions; wool beaters sitting in the street with long sticks, rhythmically beating piles of rough wool; medieval-looking stone and wood buildings decorated with intricately carved windows and doors; and small shops of all kinds, more like caves dug out of the surface of the ancient buildings, stuffed with all the goods of ordinary Nepali life. Entering into this scene often felt like a creative dream exploring a new and fascinating world.

My wife and I were especially impressed with the obvious seamlessness between the ordinary activities of the Nepalis' personal lives and their spiritual practices. Of course, there were the congregations of large temples and religious statues in places like Durbar Square, the spiritual center of old Katmandu; but small temples, shrines and beautifully carved spiritual images dotted the streets. They were a constant reminder of spirit where passers-by connected with their spirituality by touching their forehead, bowing, ringing bells, saying a blessing or a prayer or simply paying quick homage to their favorite deity as they went about the business of their day.

On one of our last days in Katmandu, my wife and I and were sitting on the rooftop of the Tibet Guest House where we were staying. With magnificent views of the bustling old city below us and Himalayan peaks in the distance, we marveled at the small spiritual practices we had so often witnessed in the streets. It seemed to us that the Nepali people were "touching in" with their spirituality during the flow of their days in a way that was like connecting the dots with something larger than their ordinary tasks and responsibilities. The more frequently they connected the dots of mindful spirit, the more likely they were to be in connection with this "something larger" throughout the course of daily activities.

It was also clear to us that this practice of touching in had a naturalness to it. With repetition over time, it simply became a part of how they lived and did not require great discipline or setting of priorities. Just as Americans might brush their teeth several times a day in the natural flow of our lives, without much struggle or planning, the practice of touching in with spirit we had witnessed on the streets of Nepal was just the way many Nepalis lived.

On that glorious morning in that magical place in the middle of old Katmandu, my wife and I committed ourselves to looking for ways to support our meditation and mindfulness by "touching in" with practice during the course of what we knew would be our busy lives once we returned home. The first possibility that occurred to us, as we sat on that rooftop, was to take a small pause before we ate a meal, a pause that might be filled with a blessing or a connection with our gratitude or might simply be a moment of mindfulness before we began eating. It seemed like a good start.

I tell this story because those lessons from Nepal have proved to be so important over the years. As we begin to consider the concept of personal practice in this chapter, I encourage you to be especially kind to yourself and think small. Bringing even modest elements of practice into your life, returned to consistently, will begin to shift something and "connect the dots" of mindfulness. Over time, this touching in will strengthen the foundation that is the essential support for the lasting happiness we seek. Moreover, I can assure you with great confidence that even the most modest practice, returned to repeatedly, will naturally and organically lead to other practices, opening you more consistently to the profound preciousness of being alive.

APPROACHING PRACTICE

We have explored a great deal in the first six steps to mindfulness. Now it is time to begin to clarify how we bring all the ideas, concepts and techniques down into our lives. In essence, we are seeking to develop a mindfulness practice that enables us to develop our full potential, to weed out the old patterns that obstruct the manifestation of that potential and to refine a belief system that supports it. Neurologist Bruce Lipton states the reason for this in very clear terms:

> Learning to harness your mind to promote growth is the secret of life, which is why I called this book *The Biology of Belief*. Of course the secret of life is not a secret at all. Teachers like Buddha and Jesus have been telling us the same story for millennia. Now science is pointing in the same direction. It is not our genes but our beliefs that control our lives . . . Oh ye of little belief![70]

We all have flashes of realization when, all of a sudden, connecting with something true in ourselves and in our lives feels clear and real. I read several years ago that Huston Smith, one of the foremost scholars in the world's great spiritual traditions, noted that the task is to extend and stabilize these "flashes of illumination into abiding light." Practice, supported by consistency and perseverance, leads us into that abiding light—a light that consistently reveals the best course through the landscapes of our lives. The sages throughout the centuries have been urging us to move in the direction of practice. More recently the transpersonal psychology movement again affirmed the necessity of this conclusion:

> Given that there exist developmental possibilities far beyond those we have taken to be the ceiling of human potential, and that these possibilities include enlightenment, the obvious practical question is, 'How can we realize these potentials for ourselves?' The answer is that one takes up a practice . . . .[71]

When we begin to think of developing a practice, the possibilities are immense—so much so that it is easy to get overwhelmed. "Where do I start?" Not being able to answer that question with confidence, the tendency is to become mired in the endless possibilities and not to start at all. In the next section, I will suggest a format for organizing a potential practice based on the material we have explored so far with the first six steps to mindfulness.

As I mentioned earlier, the Buddhist tradition defines two broad classes of practice: formal and informal practice. Formal practice is when we set aside all our other activities and bring our attention to some technique designed to strengthen the skills and cultivate the qualities of being that support the manifestation of our highest potential. Informal practice, then, is the rest of our life. The purpose of formal practice is not to just have a nice relaxing experience—which we may or may not have in any given practice session. The aspiration is much greater than that. It is to inform the way we live.

Consequently, the practitioner is constantly trying to build a bridge between the formal practice and how she lives. The crucial questions become: "How is my formal practice informing the rest of my life? How is it changing the way I experience my day-to-day activities? How is it supporting my growth toward my full potential?" Stating it more simply, the Dalai Lama says that if practitioners are not experiencing more happiness, they should take a close look at their practice. The Buddhist teacher Tenzin Wangyal describes it this way:

> The gap from the opening of your heart and seeing the fruits in results in your daily life is a very important gap to bridge. . . . We must create bridges between practice and our behavior, making changes in our lives. Perhaps we experience love, but it is only half-ripened, and so a little encouragement to manifest that love would be nice. If you can manifest love in your kitchen or your workplace or with colleagues or with your family, if love can manifest in those

particular situations where it seems necessary, that
will be a practice.[72]

So we have formal and informal practice. The Buddhist
tradition also talks about "practicing in the gaps." Essentially,
this is a process of bringing your attention to some type of
practice in the in-between spaces of your day or when you are
doing routine activities. One example would be doing some
conscious breathing and intentionally evoking the relaxation
response while you are walking from the car to your place of
work. I refer to this type of practice as "semi-formal practice."
In the outline we are creating, those will be the three classes of
practice: formal, informal and semi-formal practice.

Under each category, there are two basic focus areas:

1. The reduction of negative emotions (such as fear, anger,
    jealousy, etc.), negative conclusions about ourselves and
    belief systems that undermine our happiness, and
2. The cultivation of positive emotions (such as love, joy,
    compassion, etc.), visions or images about ourselves
    and belief systems that support our happiness.

In other words, the two focus areas are the transformation of
negative states and the cultivation of positive states. There are,
of course, other ways that we could define the focus of practice;
but this straightforward approach is very inclusive and is an
easy way to think about the intention of practice.

I encourage you to think about those two aspects of
mindfulness as a format for your growth. As you integrate
practice into your lives, it is very useful to occasionally assess
whether there is balance between the two. In our culture, we so
often are attracted to the problems that we neglect the cultivation
of positive states. Our happiness project is best served when we
devote a roughly equal amount of attention both to working
through problems and to cultivating those positive states and
qualities that sustain us.

AN OUTLINE OF POTENTIAL PRACTICE

Set out below is an outline of potential practices. Please do not let it intimidate you. We will break it down into small pieces leading to straightforward choices as we move forward with the chapter.

I. Formal Practice: setting aside time for practice
   A. Meditation
      1. Sitting meditation
      2. Walking meditation
      3. Meditative body scans
      4. Meditative yoga, tai chi, qi gong
   B. Visualization and imagery
   C. Prayer and blessings
II. Semi-Formal Practice: practicing in the gaps
   A. Conscious breathing
   B. The ten-second body scan and relaxation exercise
   C. Positive imagery
   D. Affirmations and mantras
   E. The setting of intentions and aspirations
III. Informal Practice: living mindfully
   A. Watching the mind and emotions throughout the day
   B. Settling negative emotions as they arise
   C. Returning from distractedness to awareness
   D. Shifting from contractedness to openness
   E. Noticing and loosening from judgment of yourself and others
   F. Manifesting love and kindness for yourself and others

(As will be discussed below, the Stop-Breathe-Reflect-Choose practice offers a practical technique with all these aspects of living mindfully.)

Of course, the outline is not meant to be exhaustive. We could always add much more to it; but even in this brief form, it illustrates both the wide variety of practices available to us and the complexity of choices confronting us. Before we move to simplifying the choices, I would like comment on the three major aspects of practice.

Formal Practice

It is very challenging, in the context of our busy lives and with the pressures of our culture in the twenty-first century, to set aside time for formal practice. We certainly can bring more mindfulness into our lives without formal practice; but formal practice is a powerful stabilizer that continually strengthens the foundation of mindfulness. It is an accelerator in this big project of working with the mind and emotions to create a more lasting happiness. As the Dalai Lama has emphasized, "The main emphasis in Buddhism is to transform the mind and transformation of the mind depends on meditation." If you feel it is the right time to bring some formal practice into your life, or if you are already engaged with formal practice but want to extend it or be more consistent, there are certain supports that are very helpful.

The most ideal support is to have a teacher or mentor who can provide guidance, insight about your practice and inspiration. When the Dalai Lama was asked whether it is necessary to have a teacher to reach enlightenment, he replied, "No, but it certainly saves a lot of time!" It's interesting, isn't it, that we so value the experience and guidance of skillful teachers throughout our formal education; but once we finish our schooling, we have the naïve impression that we should be able to navigate the life-long process of our growth on our own.

With mindfulness and our happiness project generally, it is so beneficial to receive the guidance of someone more experienced in the journey than we are. As the Dalai Lama was implying, such a teacher or mentor can be a guiding light illuminating the path. Of course, the teacher cannot do the work for us, but she or he can steer us clear of dead ends, help us refine and make sense of our practice and provide endless amounts of motivation and inspiration.

It may take a long time, years even, to find a teacher with whom you connect—someone who you feel is authentic and credible and, probably most importantly, someone who touches your heart. Often the discovery of a teacher results from a combination of relaxed, non-hurried exploration and reading or listening to recordings of many teachers' ideas and perspectives. In the case of my two primary teachers, I was hooked on one the first time I heard him speak live at a public lecture. It wasn't so much what he said. I can't remember anything from the subject of the talk at this point; but his personal presence was so moving and inspiring to me that I knew I had made an important connection. That was almost thirty years ago and the inspiration I felt on first hearing him, along with the substance of his wonderful teachings, continues to be a powerful force in my life.

Since 2003, I have had a more up-close-and-personal relationship with another teacher. I found him through reading a book that I felt was extremely clear and authentic. When I sought him out and attended one of his weekend workshops, it was immediately clear that I had made another important connection with someone who could help me strengthen my personal practice and my growth process.

Although it might be awhile before you discover someone who inspires and motivates you in a way you cannot ignore, there is probably a meditation group somewhere not too far from where you live that could be a wonderful support for your formal practice. A community of practitioners offers energy and motivation for your practice through support, guidance and companionship. As the revered teacher Thich Nhat Hanh and many others have frequently said, it is very difficult to maintain the consistency of formal practice without such a community. Being a part of such a community also has a way of leading the practitioner to authentic and very experienced teachers.

Whether or not you have a teacher or become affiliated with a group of practitioners, there are other supports that are helpful in maintaining a personal formal practice. Most of us are accustomed to the nature of practice in some form. Practicing a musical instrument, a sport, a craft or a new profession has given us a sense for the challenges and rewards of bringing consistent attention to a practice. Formal meditation practice is supported by the same foundations, qualities and attributes. To begin or enhance your practice, consider the following attributes and qualities. With great kindness for yourself and what you may already be doing, ask whether any of these supports and qualities deserve new or more attention.

Basic supports	Qualities
• A supportive and pleasing place	Determination
• The right equipment to support a stable and comfortable posture	Courage
	Patience
• The right time: the time of day that best fits your life	Perseverance
	Kindness for self
• Scheduling: deciding *in advance* on your practice time	Energy or passion (for growth, happiness or liberation)

Creating a pleasing and supportive place in your home or apartment for your personal practice can be a really fun thing to do. Ideally, it would be a quiet place away from the general hustle and bustle, maybe in a corner of your bedroom or even in an attic or a basement if they are comfortable spaces. Experiment with creating a personal altar with images and objects that are important to you. If you are practicing within a specific religious tradition, they could be spiritual images; but they could just as well be photos of loved ones, a beautiful stone or a small art piece that touches something in you. Open your imagination to create a little environment that moves and inspires you in some way. Then it will always be pleasing to return to your place of practice—and that environment will also be a reminder of your practice every time you pass by it.

Your creation does not have to be grandiose or complicated. When we lived in a relatively small house some years ago, my wife created her altar on a wooden board set on top of her dresser in the bedroom. When she sat down for meditation, she opened one of the drawers on the dresser, set the wooden board on the open drawer so that her altar was right at eye level during her practice—so simple but very sweet.

In my experience, the most important support for consistent formal practice is finding the time for practice that best fits into your life and committing yourself in advance to practice at that time. Like many other activities that are designed to maintain balance in our lives—exercising, for example—if we don't make a commitment in advance, but instead try to decide on a daily basis, far too frequently the best intention to practice gets swept away by the pressure of tasks and obligations.

Everyone has to find her or his own time; but for my wife and me (and for many others), the best time is shortly after waking up in the morning. For years, our routine has been to wake up, have a glass of juice or water and then to sit down immediately for practice. With work schedules and children, this may be challenging. It may be necessary to get to bed a bit earlier or to "sacrifice" a few minutes of sleep in the morning. An important shift took place for my wife when she realized that "to sacrifice" meant "to make sacred" and that she was making something sacred of those few minutes of sleep she had given up for her practice.

While we are talking about time, try not to be obsessive or compulsive about your practice time. We have such a tendency to focus on quantity or rigid thinking about practice, whether it is an exercise program, a musical instrument or meditation practice. "Oh, if I can't walk for a half an hour today, I might as well not walk at all!" Did you ever find yourself falling into that trap? Of course, it would be nice to meditate for twenty minutes or more every day; but it is the consistency, not the quantity, that is important. If you only have time to be engaged with your formal practice on a given day for five minutes, terrific! Doing even that brings more stability to your foundation.

The outline above touches lightly on the tremendous variety of techniques and elements available to you for formal practice. At first, it is important to keep it simple while you are building a foundation for practice; but you can still be creative within a basic construct. One way to do this is to think of a beginning, middle and end to formal practice, even if you are starting out with only ten or fifteen minutes. For example, a short, straight-forward practice might look like this:

Beginning: Conscious breathing and body
              3 minutes relaxation

Middle: One-pointedness meditation
              10 minutes (Circle of Liberation)

End: Prayer, blessings, intention
              2 minutes or aspiration setting

The conscious breathing and body relaxation is a wonderful way to settle in and prepare the body for the rest of the meditation. It also sharpens your awareness of what is happening in the body and strengthens your skill set for releasing tension, stressful energy and contraction during the course of our day.

I am frequently asked by individuals who want to start a formal meditation practice how they will know when they have meditated for fifteen minutes or whatever time length they are choosing. When first starting to practice, it is helpful to set a timer so you don't have to wonder about the passage of time. As you become more familiar with your practice, you will develop a natural sense of when it is time to close your practice for that session.

In Chapter Three, we explored the many qualities and skills we are nurturing in the Circle of Liberation practice: attention, concentration, patience, endurance, acceptance, gentleness, kindness, letting go, equanimity and a more insightful understanding of our own mind. Just think of how beautifully each one of these supports living with effectiveness, harmony and grace. Here again is the bridge between formal practice and the rest of our lives. In doing formal practice, these qualities and skills are strengthened and become more available to us as we confront the challenges of daily living.

A short ending of prayer, blessings and/or setting of intention creates positive conditions for entering into your day. Repeated consistently and mindfully, such an ending also begins to shift the old and tedious mindset that is your default mode and replaces it with a mindset that serves you much better. In the process, you are literally (slowly, slowly) changing your brain. The ending is also a place where you can be creative in a very personal way. I have made up prayers and blessings over the years that I have used at the end of my practice. When I have included a specific prayer or blessing for some period of time, I will create a new ending, sometimes with something I have written or with a lovely piece I have discovered in my reading. I would like to share two of my prayers with you here.

Prayer for the New Day

With the dawn of the new morning,
May I remember with gratitude
The preciousness of each day.

Gazing out to the vast expanse of space,
May I remember that among the millions
Of planets warmed by a universe of
stars,
We have been given the opportunity
To explore our soul, expand our spirit
    and share our love.

As I walk through this day,
Buffeted by the winds of chaos and challenge,
May I honor my fears, doubts and
    confusions
As an essential part of my humanity.
May I find the vision to see
The beauty in the briefest of moments
    and in the most simple occurrences.

May I cultivate my love
So that others around me may feel its
    warmth.
May I nurture my compassion
So that my community may be more
    whole.
May I explore my sense of wonder
So that others may experience its joy.

Teachers, loved ones and wise spirit
    gone before

Please take heed of me.
From this morning and with each new
    day,
May I have the strength
To listen to the truths of my inner voice.
May I have the courage
To live with an open heart.
May I have the clear light of mind
To see the blessings of this moment.

Prayer for Love

With each breath I give thanks for my loved ones.
May I find the courage to bring to them each day
An open heart free of judgment and full of
    kindness.

With awareness of impermanence clearly in mind,
May I fill every greeting with love and
    compassion.
May I approach every separation
With a heart at peace with our parting.

With the blessings of love constantly in my awareness,
With gratitude for the love I have received from
    others,
May I find the wisdom to greet each new person
    with acceptance and friendliness,
Knowing that they have the same wish for happiness
    as those already in my heart.

Semi-formal Practice

In addition to formal practice (or even if we are not able to set aside time for formal practice), we can still work into our lives moments of focused practice, often in the "in-between spaces" that naturally occur during the day. Semi-formal practice—or "practicing in the gaps"—nurtures our ability to touch and affirm something important and significantly strengthens our foundation of mindfulness. The beauty and efficiency of semi-formal practice in our 24/7 culture is that it is totally guilt free. We don't have to worry that we should be doing something supposedly more "productive" because we are bringing ourselves to practice in the flow of our day without setting aside any additional time to do it. Tenzin Wangyal has this to say about practicing in the gaps:

> I'm not saying formal practice is not important. It
> is. But we expand our notion of practice in order to
> bring the results into everyday life. If we look closely
> at our lives, we always have time to practice.[73]

Set forth below are just a few ideas for semi-formal practice. It is important to be gentle with yourself. If any of the ideas appeal to you, pick just one and commit yourself to practicing it for a couple of weeks before adding something else:

- As you walk to the car or public transportation to go to work, notice with focused awareness something special or new about the morning: a flower that bloomed, the sounds of the birds, the wind, the warmth of the sun, the color in the landscape or the sky. Allow yourself to open as fully as possible to connecting, without thoughts or mental commentary. In other words, cultivate the openness of connecting directly with your moment-to-moment experience.

- Use the time travelling to work or other activities to check in with your body, mind and emotions. Settle yourself and spend a few minutes doing some conscious breathing.

- Use the walk from the car to your work or other activity to focus on your breath and disengage from thoughts for a few moments, opening your awareness to just a bit more spaciousness.

- When you arrive at work or are about to begin a project, take a brief pause to breathe consciously and relax your body before beginning.

- Use the walk to the bathroom, or to any other location during the day, to focus on conscious breathing to settle the busy mind, any unsettled emotions and any hectic or stressful energy.

- Convert waiting times into a few moments of mindfulness practice—for example, at the bank, in the grocery store, waiting on hold on the phone, at a red light or in a traffic jam. Let go of any impatience or agitation and consciously breathe back into balance and mindfulness.

- In returning home from work or other activities, use part of the travel time to make the transition mindfully. Check in with your mind/body/emotions and settle any tension or stress that you are carrying from the day. Set an intention about the attitude you would like to cultivate for the evening.

- As you begin to drift off to sleep, take a few relaxing breaths to once again settle the mind, body and emotions in preparation for a restful night of sleep.

Informal Practice

Simply put, informal practice is the art of living more mindfully. It sounds like a good idea, and it certainly is; but with all that we have explored, we know how difficult it is to do it consistently. With the magnitude of the challenge, *it is so useful to view life as a practice*. Everything you encounter then becomes an opportunity to work with the challenges of being human, to face them skillfully and honestly and to increasingly think, speak and act in a way that serves your happiness and benefits both yourself and others. This is the heart of mindfulness!

Under "Informal Practice" in the outline of practice above, I listed a number of aspects of bringing mindfulness into the flow of our day: watching the mind and emotions, settling negative emotions, returning from distractedness to awareness, shifting from contractedness to openness, loosening around judgment and manifesting love and kindness toward yourself and others. Once again, it sounds great; but how do you actually go about such a big task? It is important to remember that whatever formal and semi-formal practice you are able to do slowly creates a foundation for all aspects of living mindfully. Those two forms of practice can be seen as an accelerator in your movement along the mindfulness path. Every time you do even a little of either formal or semi-formal practice, it strengthens your "mindfulness muscles" so that they will be stronger supports for the ultimate goal of living more mindfully. With that in mind, let's be very clear and practical about informal practice—that is, living more mindfully.

The Stop-Breathe-Reflect-Choose practice can serve as the vehicle for doing all the things listed under informal practice in the outline above. Moreover, it is a straight-forward technique that is inclusive enough to bring together all the six steps to mindfulness we have explored in this book. Let's look in more detail of how this works.

Stop

The Stop aspect of the technique brings into play the witness of Step One discussed in Chapter Three in connection with the Circle of Liberation. We are noticing what is going on in our inner landscape—our body, mind and emotions—with awareness. In the process of stopping and noticing, we are switching from the automatic pilot mode to mindfulness. We are waking up once again. We are opening to a more spacious awareness, to a higher state of consciousness.

Breathe

The Breathe aspect of the technique activates all the self-regulation practices we explored in Step Three (see Chapter Five). We know that settling the negative emotions and energies (such as anxiety, fear, anger, agitation, impatience, tension, etc.) is essential, not only because they don't feel good and are unhealthy, but also because we will not have all our mental resources (logic, reflection, analytic abilities, etc.) available to us while those negative energies are coursing through our body.

Reflect

The Reflect aspect invokes a number of the steps. It draws on the insight about our brain explored in Step Two (Chapter Four) to make sense of our whole life story (Step Four in Chapter Six), to repeatedly explode the myths and negative messages about ourselves we have been carrying for so long (Step Five in Chapter Seven) and to invest in new realities and belief systems that support our happiness and are a more true reflection of who we are (Step Six in Chapter Eight).

Choose

The Stop-Breathe-Reflect stages create the best possible conditions for then making choices in our thoughts, speech and actions that truly serve our lasting happiness and therefore benefit both ourselves and others.

The point is simply this: by returning over and over again to the Stop-Breathe-Reflect-Choose practice whenever you get stuck, contracted or immersed in negative emotions, you are practicing the essential aspects of mindfulness and building a process that, over time, will be more spontaneous. Just like conscientiously practicing a sport, you will gradually evolve from being awkward and somewhat confused about what you are doing to being more and more effortlessly in the flow of the game.

A SIMPLIFIED APPROACH TO PRACTICE

We have explored a great deal of material, lots of possibilities for practice; and you may be feeling a little adrift. Of course, you may sort through all this material to refine your present practice or to creatively design a clear way to start your practice. That's wonderful! To help with that process, set out below is an approach that incorporates the basic elements we have explored. Although it has a simple structure, it is comprehensive and is a great start for building a strong foundation of mindfulness. Better yet: it doesn't take much time.

The structure of this practice is built on the four major transitions of our day.[74] It looks like this:

Transition	Practice	Time
#1: From sleep to awake	Focus attention on a positive image	30 seconds
	Formal practice: body relaxation and Circle Meditation, prayer, blessing and/or intention setting	15 minutes
#2: From home to the world	Conscious breathing and setting intention for the day	3 minutes
#3: From the world to home	Conscious breathing, body relaxation and setting intention for the evening	3 minutes
#4 From awake to sleep	Review of the day, letting go, conscious	3 minutes

breathing and body

relaxation

In less than twenty-five minutes a day, this format brings together the elements of formal and semi-formal practice to strengthen your mindfulness foundation, settle the inevitable triggering of stressful reactions in the body/mind/emotion complex and create positive conditions for living mindfully. Naturally, you would want to add to this the Stop-Breathe-Reflect-Choose practice as you notice that you are caught in some negative energy or emotion during the course of the day.

A format such as this also weaves the thread of mindfulness through the course of the day. The bell of mindfulness is struck at the very beginning of the morning and continues to reverberate during the day as you touch back into your practice at each of the transition points. The trick is to remember to return to the practice. A useful aid in the beginning is to write the elements of your practice on index cards or post-it notes and leave them in places where you will inevitably see them: on the bathroom mirror, on your screen-saver, in your car and in some conspicuous spot at your workplace.

COMMITTING YOURSELF AND GETTING STARTED

Now is the time to begin creating a new experience. Reading this or any other similar book is a good start; but whatever value it has slowly slips away if you don't put it into practice. I am as guilty as anyone. Many times I have read an interesting book with great insights and ideas, put it down and simply moved on to something else. It's not necessarily conscious, but just below the surface is the reaction or thought that the material was interesting, that I know it now or am at least fairly familiar with it—and that somehow it will automatically flow into my life. If only it were so easy! You have spent significant time reading this book. Please don't let whatever value it has had for you slip away. Take what you can and begin to practice the creation of a new experience right now. This is the way you will create the lasting happiness you deserve.

At the end of this chapter is an Action Plan we used at the cardiac rehabilitation program where I taught for years. For the people in the program, change was so important to avoid further life-threatening cardiac events. For the rest of us, change is equally important if we are to manifest our full potential and truly experience the preciousness of the human experience. The Action Plan is a helpful tool in starting just where you are and committing yourself to adding something, however modest, to your effort to live in a mindful way. If you already have a practice, the Action Plan can be used to refine and expand it.

Here are a few suggestions for carrying out your action plan successfully.

1. **Start modestly.** The form itself encourages you to be kind to yourself and start easily with something you are confident you can accomplish. This builds a history of success that motivates further effort.

2. **Be consistent.** Once you have your plan, try not to make any exceptions for the time period you have established. It takes the discipline of consistency over time to build a positive habit. Once the new practice is established, the need for exertion of discipline diminishes.

3. **Be forgiving of yourself.** Even with a strong intention, we are still imperfect humans. It is inevitable that you will not carry out your plan perfectly. When this happens, practice kindness for yourself and loosen around any self-judgment. This is such an important part of all mindfulness practice. Sometimes you will notice only after the fact that you got stuck in a negative emotion or other old pattern. Be especially careful of self-judgment here. It's O.K. It will happen; but when you eventually notice, your mindfulness has awakened again. Take delight in that, even if you wish it had awakened earlier. Late or not, by noticing, you have strength-

ened your ability to witness your inner landscape and to return to awareness.

4. **Just start over**. This flows from the previous suggestion. When you notice that you have fallen short and loosen from self-judgment, all the energy of judgment is released to the task at hand: *just begin again*. The Circle of Liberation is a wonderful reminder of this. It is never a matter of staying in the practice all the time, of staying open and aware totally consistently. From what the traditional teachings tell us, even those few beings who attain full enlightenment get momentarily caught in distraction from time to time. When it happens to you and you notice it, you can simply return to mindfulness one more time by bringing your mind home.

5. **Be patient.** We all would like a quick fix, the silver bullet (or pill) that would just make everything all right. For all the reasons we have explored, we have to let go of this illusion. We are in for the long haul, the life-long practice of moving gradually along the path. If we are patient and conscientious, positive change will occur. All the great teachers and highly realized beings over the centuries have given us this strong assurance.

I once heard the Dalai Lama tell a personal story that reflects all these suggestions. The story is a wonderful commentary on the nature of practice generally. He began his training when he was recognized as the Dalai Lama at age three and taken to the traditional home of the Dalai Lamas, the Potala Palace in Lhasa, the capital of Tibet. He said that he wasn't really interested in his training for years and preferred to play with the men who cleaned the palace or to look out from the palace and watch all the activity in the city below. By the time he was in his early teens, he began to realize that the teachings of his mentors had value; but when he was fifteen, China invaded Tibet. As the spiritual and political leader of Tibet, much of his energies over the next ten years were consumed with trying to work skillfully with the occupation of his country.

In 1959, at the age of 24, he was forced to secretly flee Tibet and relocate in India. More than 100,000 Tibetans followed him over the next few years and, once again, much of his energies had to be directed to establishing a community-in-exile for his people. By the time he was in his thirties, the Dalai Lama said, he really began to get more seriously committed to his studies and practice; but over the next thirty years there was precious little time in the midst of all his other duties and responsibilities. Of course, he continued to practice as much as he could. When I heard him tell this story, he was in his early sixties. He concluded by saying, "Now, if I just had more time, I think I might be able to make some progress!" The patience and humility in the Dalai Lama's account are powerful reminders for all of us as we bring whatever effort we can to our practice.

A LAST WORD ABOUT PRACTICE

It is so easy to fall into doubt about our practice. "Is it working? In the face of all my other responsibilities of work, family, householding, etc., should I really be taking the time for it? Do I deserve to take the time for it?" Moments of doubt will inevitably arise. When they do, it is so important to remember the overview of what we are doing. We have been focusing on the process of creating a lasting happiness for ourselves through the path of mindfulness, but the project is not an isolated one. As we come back to our practice over and over again, the ripples of our effort touch everything in our personal environment.

As Father Keating reminds us, with our growing clarity about what truly supports our happiness, we gradually become more consistently loving and kind to our children and other loved ones. We become more patient and generous of spirit with our friends and work colleagues. We become less judgmental and accepting of even the most challenging people.

Prof. Robert Thurman of Columbia University and many others have written about the "inner revolution" that is essential if we are to shift the balance of energies on this small planet of ours from destructive and depleting to nurturing and replenishing.[75]

There are many things that we cannot do on our own. We can't stop wars overnight. We can't immediately stop practices of others that pollute our environment. We cannot protect all the children in the world from violence and hunger. But there is one thing we can do. We can bring energy, each in our modest way and in the context of our busy lives, to our personal inner revolution. No matter how insignificant our effort may seem, it is a valuable part of the global shifts we long for. Even if we don't feel optimistic that such shifts will dramatically occur in our lifetime, we have to realize that our small stream of energy flows into a much larger ocean that will continue to grow in size long after we are gone. Every bit literally does count.

So, in the face of doubt, we can always mindfully remind ourselves. Our practice will produce positive change. From our greater happiness will flow an energy that nurtures and supports the happiness of others. As more and more individuals make their own contributions to this momentum of change, one day we will reach a tipping point and significant shifts will occur. No one expected the Berlin Wall to come down when it did; but one day, the tipping point was unexpectedly reached and overnight, magically, the wall was gone and a whole new era in Europe began. More recently, one courageous street vendor in Tunisia protested against the conditions in his country by setting himself on fire and his dramatic action ignited a wave of change throughout the region. No one expected the "Arab spring" to happen when it did; but a tipping point of conditions had been reached and suddenly an amazing wave of incredible change swept over many countries.

We don't have to take all this need for change on ourselves. All we have to do—and it is a big enough challenge in itself—is to return over and over again to our mindfulness practice. The rest will take care of itself. Unexpected and beautiful shifts will occur, in our own lives and in the world generally—and we will have been a part of their creation.

ACTION PLAN FOR PERSONAL PRACTICE

(*Formal, Semi-formal and/or Informal*)[76]

Action plan for the next two weeks:

— Something you want to do.

— Something reasonable you can do the next two weeks.

— Something behavior specific.

— Caution: you must be 70% sure you can complete or consistently carry out your plan for it to be reasonable.

I want to _____

_____

_____

_____

for the next two weeks.

How much or often? _____

When? _____

Are you 70% sure you can carry out your plan during the next two weeks? If not, be kind to yourself and revise the plan so that it better fits into your life.

CHAPTER 10

Further Along the Path of Mindfulness...
Cultivating Joy, Opening to Love

As I said in the Preface, I believe we have the opportunity to minimize our suffering and to cultivate a life profoundly enriched by love, joy and lasting happiness. Although I am very optimistic about this opportunity, I am also realistic. What we are really talking about is transformation and transformation is a life-long process. For anyone who enters this path, there will be ups and downs. Even if you enter the path with great energy and enthusiasm, there will be times when you will lose heart, when you will think that you are not getting anywhere. There will be times when you feel you had dealt with an old issue, message, pattern or challenge, and—all of a sudden—you realize that it has grabbed you once again.

As my first meditation teacher said, walking this path is like climbing a mountain. Sometimes we are walking up the mountain and we really think we are getting somewhere. Other times, we are simply walking around and around, covering old and familiar ground—or we may even have slipped down the slope and have to climb up again just to reach where we previously were. Over time, though, we slowly make it farther up the mountain where the air is more pure, the view more magnificent and our perspective is increasingly clear.

I think of the Seven Steps as resources that we are drawing on over and over again. When we have explored them and deepened our familiarity with each of the seven resources, we draw on them as needed. At times our attention will be more on some of the resources than on others. Eventually, they will begin to flow together in such a way that focusing on one or two of the resources will inevitably invoke and support the strengthening of all the resources. Cultivating the ability to witness our inner landscape of thoughts and emotions, for example, inevitably leads to working with self-regulation and exposing the old messages that undermine our happiness. In this way, the Seven Steps are interdependent. Whenever we work with one of the steps, we are bringing energy to the whole bundle of resources and increasingly building a cohesive foundation for the happiness we deserve. In the process, our mindfulness practice begins to draw seamlessly on the resources we need at a particular time.

The Circle of Liberation reminds us that mindfulness practice is not about staying on the straight and narrow path all the time. **It is always about returning.** At some point, we realize we have slipped, fallen asleep or got caught in some old pattern—and we simply wake up to mindfulness once again. We make the switch from automatic pilot to mindfulness. Rather than judging ourselves for getting caught in the old pattern, no matter how many times it has grabbed us, we take delight in the fact that we have awakened, that our inner wisdom has spoken to us.

There is a wonderful saying in the Buddhist tradition that goes something like this: "When mind is fully luminous, delusion is cut at its very root." There is so much humility in this saying. It is reminding us that even when mind is fully enlightened, the illusions of old messages and patterns still arise; but they are seen quickly for what they are and are "cut at their root." I find this reminder very comforting. We can be kind to ourselves when illusions grab us and simply renew our practice of seeing them for what they are and working with them skillfully.

Having made it this far in our exploration, you now know that there are clear steps you can take, that there is a defined path you can travel. You can open your imagination a little wider to the truth that more lasting happiness is possible for you. I encourage you to invest in this truth. As you do, there will be a natural passion emerging for your mindfulness practice. You will begin to see whatever life throws at you as an opportunity to practice, to be as intentional as possible, to make choices that serve you and all those around you. Even with all the challenges we face in this dysfunctional world, your passion for the practice and its benefits will spontaneously give birth to more and more delight—and that will further inspire your practice.

Now that you can see that there are clear steps you can take, that there is a defined path you can travel, can you open your imagination a little wider to the truth that greater happiness is possible for you? If you can, there will be a natural passion emerging for your mindfulness practice. You will be drawn to it and look for ways to keep refining and expanding it. (This may mean, by the way, that you will shift some of your attention and energies from your old, historical interests to more exploration of your practice.) Even with all the challenges, your passion for the practice and its fruits will spontaneously give birth to delight—and that will further inspire your practice.

In an important way, building your own mindfulness practice is a process for slowly taking back your life. In this 24/7 world we live in, we are so consumed by the struggle to juggle demanding jobs, the constant deluge of e-mails, voice-mail and all sorts of new information, children and/or other family obligations, household responsibilities, a little self-care and maybe even some leisure time. The "struggle to juggle" can drive us into automatic pilot mode a good deal of the time. Mindfulness helps to make sense of it all, to see it from a bigger perspective. As we strengthen our mindfulness practice, we are more immune from the stressful 24/7 messages in our culture. We are more able to be conscious creators. We intentionally create a balance that works better and feels more satisfying. In this sense, we are taking back our lives from the compulsive, and sometimes crazy, energies around us.

I realize that the lasting happiness we have explored throughout this book may exist only in your imagination at this point, but I am urging you to believe in that imagination, to believe that it is possible for you. I am also encouraging you to be patient. The Dalai Lama offers this reminder about transforming the mind in the service of nurturing true happiness:

> One thing you should remember is that mental transformations take time and are not easy. I think some people from the West, where technology is so good, think that everything is automatic. You should not expect this spiritual transformation to take place within a short period; that is impossible. Keep it in your mind and make a constant effort.[77]

PRESENCE: THE STATE OF BEING FOR EXPANDED JOY

I believe in the grand aspiration, the big vision of what is possible for us. This may be the only life we have in this human form—or at least the only one we can remember. Why not have the grand aspiration? Even if we don't fully manifest it, just opening ourselves to a big vision creates the possibility of making some part of it a reality. In the last two sections of this book, I am going to briefly explore two grand aspirations that are available to us all.

Mindfulness practice builds confidence. We begin to believe in ourselves and in our place in the world. As we repeatedly return to mindfulness, we more frequently remember who we truly are and what we are creating. We don't take the old messages and illusions so seriously. When they arise, as they always will, we can smile at them with a kinder heart from the foundation of our mindfulness practice.

Referring again to the metaphor used by my first meditation teacher, as we continue our walk up the mountain, we have a better view of the whole landscape. We begin to see the big view more clearly—the view of ourselves, the true nature of reality and the beauty of everything that lies before us. It takes time for this view to emerge; but as it does, everything makes more sense. I think of how my old messages are now seen in this big view with a whole new perspective. I think of a dear friend who struggled his whole life with depression and self-esteem issues. As his practice strengthened and this larger view became more clear, the depression and other issues faded into this clear view of the truth. They may not have faded from the picture altogether, but they are held in the loving context of this larger view.

All this enables us to relax with ourselves and our lives as they are at the present moment. We become more fully present with what is actually happening. We are more settled, not so consumed by compulsive thinking and not so vulnerable to the distracting energies of negative emotions. In this place of greater settledness, we have more access to our full resources. Our intuition and our inner wisdom are more able to complement the power of our intellect in a harmony that increases our clarity and confidence. Life simply flows more easily and lasting happiness becomes more of a reality.

Being more fully present, undistracted by all the obstacles to our happiness, offers the possibility of an expanded experience of joy. Presence enables us to more profoundly connect with the preciousness of being alive, to experience the joy and wonder that is always available to us. We all know this experience, even if it only occurs occasionally. I recently led a client through a guided meditation and visualization in which I asked him to search his memory bank for an experience that was extremely positive for him. After we completed the meditation, I asked him if anything had come up and he described the following experience.

It was more than twenty-five years earlier when he and the woman he eventually married were first falling in love. They were hiking early in the morning in the Rocky Mountains and arrived at the top of a ridge, at about 12,000 feet, just as the sun was cresting the mountains in front of them. All the conditions—being with the woman he was beginning to love, the mountains, the sunrise—brought him to undistracted presence and connection with the power and beauty of the moment. He didn't have to think about it or create it. He was simply spontaneously fully open to joy and love. It was such a moving experience that I got goose bumps just listening to it. At times like those, there is no analyzing the experience, no naming it or telling stories about it in our mind. We are simply filled with joy.

Maybe you have had such experiences when you felt truly held and loved or when you connected with the radiant nature of a baby or with your love of nature—or in the ecstasy of sexual union with a lover. These experiences usually arise spontaneously and often surprise us. We might think of them as "dumb-luck joy." We stumble on to them or they emerge suddenly out of special conditions, as they did for my client. It is so important to not let these moments of grace pass too lightly. Whether it is "dumb-luck joy" or not, such moments deserve our attention. It is so useful to consciously take note of them, to cultivate our familiarity with them.

The truth is this: our mindfulness practice eventually enables us to be more fully present with each moment of our experience. As we become more present, joy is there. Put another way, as our practice enables us to relax into a more settled state of being, we more consistently connect with the truth and beauty available in every moment. This is the experience of pervasive joy. Maybe we sense it in the crisp wind of a fall day, the magical unfolding of a flower blossom, the sweet scent of newly-cut grass, the glance of our beloved, the most insignificant movement of our own precious body or simply in the lush energy of the air we breath thousands of times a day. There it is: joy! As we become more familiar with joy, as we cultivate the presence that gives us access to it, we begin to discover it everywhere.

So there is the grand aspiration of opening more consistently to joy. Of course, it is not possible for us all the time. We have to think and plan. We have to accomplish things and take care of our responsibilities. We are drawn to ruminating at length about the small details of our lives and to get lost in mindless distractions of all sorts. Nevertheless, by returning to mindfulness practice once again, we can settle down in the midst of it all and be more present with whatever is happening. In that more relaxed presence, the precious energy of joy is always there.

SPACIOUSNESS: THE OPENING TO PERVASIVE LOVE

Father Keating reminds us that "awareness of the ground of our being is the ultimate source of security, love and freedom. If we stop thinking long enough, this relationship begins to insinuate itself into our awareness."[78] The energy of love is one way to think of the ground of our being. I am not talking here of romantic love or the love we may feel for a single person. This love is much bigger. It is the all-pervasive energy of love that permeates every part of our existence. Opening to this vast love gives us the sense of being held in the arms of love no matter what is happening. The aspiration to experience this kind of love is truly grand. As with any of the grand aspirations, we should not let our present limitations convince us that the experience is entirely out of our reach.

Mindfulness practice offers us the possibility of manifesting some part of this grand aspiration. Notice that Father Keating said that "if we stop thinking long enough," our relationship to the ground of our being will begin "to insinuate itself into our awareness." The contemplative prayer taught by Father Keating, and its close-cousin the Circle of Liberation meditation presented in this book, both are the first steps to taming the automatic energies of our mind and being more conscious of when thinking is useful and when it is not.

With conscientious practice, we begin to let go of needless thinking and open to the natural state of our minds: spaciousness. We allow our attention to expand as broadly as possible. We imagine or experience awareness as boundless. It is in this spacious awareness that the pervasive energy of love is available to us. We may not be able to describe it, or explain it, or even to understand it fully; but it is there. A few years ago I wrote a poem that was my modest attempt to penetrate the nature of this vast love:

What Is This Love

What is the nature of this love? he asked.

It is the experience of wordless expression, she
    replied.

Of heart on fire,

Of mind free from the cage of self.

Where does this come from?

It comes from nowhere—

And everywhere.

It is the space from which all creation emerges.

How do I understand this love?

It is neither understandable nor incomprehensible.

It cannot be thought,

But it can be known.

What do I do with this love? he asked.

There is nothing to do, she answered.

When grace opens you to its radiant space,

There is only the effortless being of Light.

But what if I find myself afraid and closed to
    this space? he sighed.

Then there is only to forgive yourself—

And smile.

This love waits with endless patience
    for your return.

We may not be able to open at will to this ground of our
being, this vast love; but mindfulness practice, once again,
offers a path for creating the right conditions for opening to it.
This truly grand aspiration has been experienced by authentic
practitioners for many centuries. A full discussion of the area is

beyond the scope of this book, but let's briefly explore one aspect of the practice that can lead to realizing this grand aspiration.

Over time, conscientious mindfulness and meditation practice inevitably leads to glimpses of what the Buddhist tradition refers to as sky-like mind. The basic nature of the sky remains the same no matter what passes through it. A dark cloud may temporarily change the appearance of the sky, but it doesn't change its nature. The sky doesn't hold on to or try to control whatever passes through it. It doesn't prefer one type of cloud to another or rain to rainbows. Its nature remains consistent. In mindfulness practice, then, the aspiration here is to maintain an awareness that is open and spacious like the sky, that is less and less vulnerable to being changed by whatever arises in our thoughts, emotions or sensations.

Here is a specific example of how this might play out. I had a bout of cancer a long time ago; my father died of cancer; and for a number years, I led weekly meditation and healing sessions at a cancer support center. With that much of a personal relationship with cancer, it is virtually unavoidable that anxiety about cancer occasionally arises in my mindscreen. "Gee, what is that lump in my throat?" or "Boy, that lymph gland seems awfully swollen!" In the absence of sky-like mind, my awareness could easily contract down around that thought and the accompanying anxiety. My view of the whole landscape would be limited and the anxiety could dominate my whole experience until it settled down. Simply stated, my awareness, open just one moment before, would be totally changed.

On the other hand, if I were fortunate to hold some semblance of sky-like mind, the arising of anxiety would not change the basic nature of my awareness or dominate my whole experience. With sky-like mind, I could take notice of the cloud of anxiety passing through and choose my response. Maybe I would need to take a moment to remind myself that my cancer was many years ago and that I am doing the best I can to avoid any recurrence. On another occasion, nothing more may be needed. The anxiety would be present in my awareness, but I could just let it be as

I went on with the business at hand. In either case, the open nature of my awareness would not change.

Cultivating the spacious awareness of sky-like mind strengthens our psychological immune system. With sky-like mind, even if old messages and negative energies arise, we are less vulnerable to them and more able to maintain our balance. In the process, we are able to live with more intentionality. But there is more that becomes available as we abide in sky-like mind. In this open and spacious awareness are the conditions for connecting with something deeper in ourselves—and something greater than ourselves. It is within the spaciousness of the natural state of mind that the pervasive energy of love becomes apparent to us—and is available to hold and comfort us in the face of the great challenges of being alive in the 21st century.

I called this a grand aspiration for good reason. At this moment in your life, it may seem far too grandiose and out of reach, but I assure you it is possible. With patience for ourselves and conscientiousness for our mindfulness practice, it is truly possible for each and every one of us to gradually cultivate this open and spacious awareness.

If you are passionate about your own happiness, about expanding joy and connecting with the vast and perfect love that is available to you, if in your wildest imagination you can accept my assurances that this is all possible for you, I encourage you to gradually expand and refine your practice in whatever way is possible in your life, one gentle step at a time. Find an experienced teacher or mentor for guidance and inspiration. Delve more deeply into the teachings of a tradition that inspires you to clarify your insight and wisdom. Seek out a community of like-minded practitioners as a marvelous support for moving forward with your own process. A teacher, an authentic tradition of teachings and a community are all sources of inspiration. Inspiration, literally taken, means "to breathe in." All these sources of inspiration help us to breathe in the energy of our practice and to return over and over again to practice as a sustaining force in our lives.

Finally, I share one more of my poems as an encouragement to invest in what is really possible for you through your practice of mindfulness: the lasting happiness you deserve.

A Love So Vast

What if there was a love so vast
There was no place it couldn't find you?
Would you recoil in the face of its awesome power?
Would you shrink back into that small place inside
    you,
That cave where you have hidden many times before,
Fearing someone would see you out in the open,
That you would lose that contracted idea of yourself
You have desperately protected for so long?

Or would you do something very different,
Something brilliant?
Would you let the radiance of this vast love
Burn through the last of your armor?
Would you call to the magical child
Who has been sleeping in your heart,
And shout with giddy delight,
"I am here! I am ready now!"

Can you imagine how glorious that would be?
Released from the darkness of your cave,
Your eyes would see gold in every heart.
Freed from the weighty burden of your shield,
Your limbs could carry any suffering.
Held in the warmth of this love,
Every fall would be just a playful tumble.

Do you want the rays of this vast love
　to shine through you?
Do you want to sing with the sweet harmonies
　of this love?
Do you want the passion of this love to light
　the fire of inspiration in you?
Do you want the ecstasy of this love to bless
　your every movement?

All your life you have yearned for this.
Are you finally ready to let in this vast love?

　　　　Be brilliant.
　　　　Just open.
　　　　It is here for you.
　　　　Now!

MINDFULNESS AND CHILDREN

In the workshops I lead for mental health professionals, I am often asked about the possibility of using mindfulness techniques and strategies with children. In my view, creatively introducing mindfulness to children is a tremendous gift to them. As you may recall from the discussion of Emotional Intelligence by Daniel Goleman earlier in the book, we do not devote a great deal of energy to educating our children about emotional intelligence. As a result, when children are caught in emotional hijackings—an unavoidable and perfectly natural situation— they have no foundation for managing them. As we all know, this frequently leads to significant disruption in families, classrooms and in the interpersonal relations of children of all ages. By skillfully bringing mindfulness practices into their lives, we are nurturing the growth of their emotional intelligence.

Of course, whatever is done in this area needs to be adapted to the capacities and developmental levels of the children involved; but even very basic approaches can help them learn that they have a choice about their challenging emotions and about their behaviors when they get caught in those emotions.

What a wonderful foundation to begin developing early on in children's lives.

In one of my workshops last year, a counselor shared a heart-warming example of how even very young children can learn mindfulness. She said that she had had her first child, a daughter, about two years before. From about the time her daughter was six months old, she began a practice of frequently doing two things (along with other nurturing, of course) when her daughter became upset. With her palms out in front of her, face down, she let out an audible exhale with the sound "ah" and slightly bent her knees to settle into the sigh. Over time, it helped her daughter settle down.

The counselor went on to tell us that when she gets upset, her daughter has a tendency to say, "Mommy," and make the same exhale sound and body movement that she learned from her mother. Think of how wonderful that is! At two years old, this little girl understands that she has a choice about her emotions and has an effective practice to regulate challenging arisings and self-soothe—a practice she knows so well that she even reminds her mother of it. That is a terrific beginning for cultivating emotional intelligence using mindfulness. We can all imagine how well this basic foundation will serve her as she gets older and learns to expand and refine her mindfulness skills.

Set forth below are resources for bring mindfulness concepts and practices to children. It is not an exhaustive list, but it will help you get started if you are interested in this aspect of mindfulness.

Books

> Allen, J., Klein, R. (1996). *Ready, Set, Relax: A Research-Based Program of Relaxation, Learning and Self-Esteem for Children.* Inner Coaching, 1108 Western Avenue, Watertown, WI 53094.

> Bothmer, S. (2003). *Creating the Peaceable Classroom: Techniques to Calm, Uplift and Focus Teachers and*

Students. Zephyr Press, Box 66006, Tucson, AZ 85728 (1-800-232-2187).

Fontana, D., Slack, I. (1997). *Teaching Meditation to Children: A Practical Guide to the Use and Benefits of Meditation Techniques.* Element Books, 160 North Washington Street, Boston, MA 02114.

Fox, A., Kirschner R. (2005). *Too Stressed to Think: A Teen Guide to Staying Sane When Life Makes You Crazy.* Free Spirit Publishing, 217 Fifth Avenue North, Suite 200, Minneapolis, MN 55401 (612-338-2068).

Greco, L. A. and Hayes, S. C. (Editors), *Acceptance and Mindfulness Treatments for Children and Adolescents: A Practitioners Guide.* (New Harbinger Publications: Oakland, CA, 2008.)

Greenland, S. *The Mindful Child: How to Help Your Kid Manage Stress and Become Happier, Kinder and More Compassionate.* (Free Press: New York, 2010.)

Hipp, E. (1995). *Fighting Invisible Tigers: A Stress Management Guide for Teens.* Free Spirit Publishing, 217 Fifth Avenue North Suite 200, Minneapolis, MN 55401 (612-338-2068).

Lite, L. (1996). *A Boy and a Bear: The Children's Relaxation Book.* Specialty Press, 300 N.W. 70th Avenue, Suite 102, Plantation, FL 33317 (954-792-8100).

MacLean, K. (2004). *Peaceful Piggy Meditation.* Albert Whitman and Company, 63400 Oakton Street, Morton Grove, IL 60053. www.albertwhitman.com.

Powell, M. *Stress Relief: The Ultimate Teen Guide.* (The Scarecrow Press: Lanham, MD, 2002.)

Smith, S. (2001). *Meditations for Children*. FPMT Education Services, 125B La Posta Road, Taos, NM 87571.

Useful Websites

innerkids. org

heartmath.org (see especially the Emotional Security Tool Kit)

CDs

Meditations for Children. FPMT Education Services, 125B La Posta Road, Taos, NM 87571.

Ready... Set... Release! Music and Relaxation Exercises for Children. Inner Coaching, 1108 Western Avenue, Watertown, WI 53094 (920-262-0439).

Programs

Child Development Project, Eric Schaps, Development Studies Center, Oakland, CA.

Paths. Mark Greenberg, Fast Track Project. University of Wisconsin.

Seattle Social Development Project, David Hawkins, Social Development Research Group, University of Washington.

The Improving Social Awareness-Social Problem Solving Project. Maurice Elias, Rutgers University.

Yale-New Haven Social Competence Program, Roger Weissberg, University of Illinois at Chicago.

APPENDIX II

Books

There are so many authentic teachers and writers who have something to add to our understanding about the topics we have explored in this book that it would be challenging to compile an exhaustive list. The list set forth below is a limited selection of some of my favorites. I have deliberately kept it short so that you would not be overwhelmed by the volume of material if you wanted to pursue further reading.

Mindfulness

> Tara Bennett-Goleman, *Emotional Alchemy: How the Mind Can Heal the Heart* (New York: Harmony Books, 2001).

> Jon Kabat-Zinn, *Full Catastrophe Living: Using the Wisdom of Your Body and Mind to Face Stress, Pain and Illness* (New York: Dell Publishing, 1990).

> Thich Nhat Hanh, *Peace Is Every Step: The Path of Mindfulness in Everyday Life* (New York: Bantam Books, 1991).

Meditation

Jack Kornfield, *Meditation for Beginners* (Boulder, Colorado: Sounds True, Inc., 2004) (includes CD with guided meditations).

Sharon Salzberg, *The Force of Kindness: Change Your Life with Love & Compassion* (Boulder, Colorado: Sounds True, Inc., 2005) (includes CD with guided meditations).

Jean Smith (Editor), *Breath Sweeps the Mind: A First Guide to Meditation Practice* (New York: Riverhead Books, 1998).

Shinzen Young, *Break Through Pain: A Step-by-Step Mindfulness Meditation Program for Transforming Chronic and Acute Pain* (Boulder, Colorado: Sounds True, Inc., 2004) (includes CD with guided meditations).

Neuroscience

Sharon Begley, *Train Your Mind, Change Your Brain: How a New Science Reveals Our Extraordinary Potential to Transform Ourselves* (New York: Ballantine Books, 2007).

Daniel Goleman, *Emotional Intelligence: Why It Can Matter More Than IQ* (New York: Bantam Books, 1994).

Daniel Goleman, *Social Intelligence: The New Science of Human Relationships* (New York: Bantam Books, 2006).

John J. Ratey, *A User's Guide to the Brain: Perception, Attention, and the Four Theaters of the Brain* (New York: Vintage Books, 2001).

Daniel Siegel, *The Developing Mind: How Relationships and the Brain Interact to Shape Who We Are* (New York: Guilford Press, 1999).

Daniel Siegel and Mary Hartzell, *Parenting from the Inside Out: How a Deeper Self-Understanding Can Help You Raise Children Who Thrive* (New York: Teremy P. Tarcher/Penguin, 2003).

Daniel Siegel, *The Mindful Brain: Reflection and Attunement in the Cultivation of Well-Being.* (Norton and Company: New York, 2007.)

Daniel Siegel, *Mindsight: The New Science of Personal Transformation.* (Bantam Books: New York, 2010.)

Personal Spirituality
(with emphasis on mindfulness and meditation)

Rabbi David A. Cooper, *The Handbook of Jewish Meditation Practices: A Guide for Enriching the Sabbath and Other Days of your Life.* (Jewish Lights Publishing: Woodstock, Vermont, 2000.)

James Finley, *Christian Meditation: Experiencing the Presence of God.* (Harper Collins Publishers: New York, 2004.)

Jack Kornfield, *A Path with Heart: A Guide Through the Perils and Promises of Spiritual Life* (New York: Bantam Books, 1993).

Jack Kornfield, *The Wise Heart: A Guide to the Universal Teachings of Buddhist Psychology.* (Bantam Books: New York, 2008.)

Related Topics

Bruce Lipton, *The Biology of Belief: Unleashing the Power of Consciousness, Matter and Miracles* (Santa Rosa, California: Mountain of Love/Elite Books, 2005).

Joseph Chilton Pearce, *The Biology of Transcendence: A Blueprint of the Human Spirit* (Rochester, Vermont: Park Street Press, 2002).

John Welwood, *Love and Awakening: Discovering the Sacred Path of Intimate Relationship* (New York: Harper Collins, 1996).

John Welwood, *Perfect Love, Imperfect Relationships: Healing the Wound of the Heart* (Boston: Trumpeter Books, 2006).

APPENDIX III

CONTEMPLATIVE PRAYER RESOURCES

If you are interested in pursuing meditation practices within the Christian tradition, the following organizations are good sources of information about programs and teachings:

Contemplative Outreach, Ltd.
10 Park Place, Suite B
Box 737
Butler, NJ 07405
973-838-3384

Mastery Foundation
1 Charlton Court #1
San Francisco, CA 94123
708-338-9128

Contemplative Outreach of Southern
California
The Parrish of St. Matthew
1031 Bienvenida Ave.
Pacific Palisades, CA 90272
310-573-7422

St. Benedict's Monastery
1012 Monastery Rd.
Snowmass, CO 81653
970-927-1162

USEFUL WEBSITES

The following are just a few of the websites that are useful in obtaining more information about resources and programs related to the topics explored in this book.

www.umassmed.edu/cfm: Mindfulness-based stress reduction material and programs (This is the website for The Center for Mindfulness in Medicine, Health Care and Society that evolved from the programs started by Jon Kabat-Zinn more than twenty-five years ago at the University of Massachusetts Medical School in Worcester, Massachusetts.)

www.meditationandpsychotherapy.org: Institute for Meditation and Psychotherapy

www.soundstrue.com: recorded talks and presentations by experienced speakers and teachers in many areas, including meditation, mindfulness, psychology, Buddhism and spirituality generally

www.eomega.org: Omega Institute, in Rhinebeck, New York, one of the premier centers for holistic studies offering weekend and week-long programs led by experienced presenters in the areas, among others, of mindfulness, meditation and personal growth

www.dharma.org: Insight Meditation Society, Barre, Vermont, a residential center founded in 1976, offering retreats and meditation programs in the Buddhist tradition

www.spiritrock.org: Spirit Rock, Woodacre, California, offering classes, day-long programs and residential retreats in the practice of insight meditation and mindfulness awareness

www.mindandlife.org: articles, conferences, research, etc., involving meditation, mindfulness and science (This is the organization that, among other things, organizes the Mind and Life Conferences approximately every two years, involving dialogue between the Dalai Lama and top Western experts in the areas of mindfulness, meditation, neuroscience, emotions, consciousness, etc. The last such conference was held in Washington, D.C. in November, 2005.)

www.inquiringmind.com: journal relating to mindfulness and mindful living

www.dharmaseed.org: talks and presentations by mindfulness teachers

www.tricycle.com and www.shambhalasun.com: Buddhist magazines

www.SnowLionPub.com and
www.Wisdompubs.org: meditation, mindfulness and Buddhist books

ENDNOTES

Chapter One

1. Jon Gertner, "The Futile Pursuit of Happiness," *The New York Times Magazine* (September 7, 2003), pp. 116-128.

2. Eric Weiner, "Be Like Bhutan," *New York Times*, November 13, 2006, p. A17.

3. I first heard this story from the recording of a set of teachings by Jack Kornfield entitled *The Inner Art of Meditation* available from Sounds True, Box 8010, Boulder Colorado 80306 (www.soundstrue.com).

4. Frances Vaughn, *The Inward Arc: Healing & Wholeness in Psychotherapy & Spirituality* (Boston and London: Shambhala, 1986), p. 91.

5. Omega Institute near Rhinebeck, New York, is a wonderful adult learning center. Many nationally recognized teachers in diverse areas (e.g., art, music, dance, theater, energy work, spiritual practice, relationships and much more) lead workshops there from spring through the fall. To obtain more information

about Omega's programs, visit its website at www. eomega.org or call 1-800-944-1001.

6. Jon Kabat-Zinn is the founder of the Center for Mindfulness in Medicine, Health Care and Society at the University of Massachusetts Medical Center. The Center has on-going programs in mindfulness-based stress reduction, in addition to training programs for individuals who wish to teach mindfulness-based stress reduction or use its approaches in medical or mental health settings. Information about the Center's activities can be obtained from their website: www.umassmed. edu/cfm. For a comprehensive presentation of Jon's work in the area of mindfulness, see his classic book, *Full Catastrophe Living: Using the Wisdom of your Body to Face Stress, Pain and Illness* (New York: Dell Publishing, 1990).

7. A psychologist in one of my workshops suggested that this excerpt from Nelson Mandela's speech was originally from Marianne Williamson's book *A Return to Love* (New York: Harper Perennial, 1992). Although there is certainly the same sentiment in *A Return to Love* (see, for example, pages 276-279), I have been unable to confirm that the quote from Mandela's speech was taken from Williamson's book.

8. This material is from a presentation by Richard Davidson at Investigating the Mind 2005: The Science and Clinical Applications of Meditation, held at the DAR Constitution Hall in Washington, D.C., November 8, 9 & 10, 2005. The conference was organized and presented by the Mind and Life Institute. For articles, conferences, research, etc., involving meditation, mindfulness and science, see the Institute's website at www.mindandlife.org.

Chapter Two

9. Father Thomas Keating is a wonderful teacher of meditative and contemplative practices in the Christian tradition. He directs retreats in the practice of Centering Prayer, a cornerstone of Christian contemplative practice. His many books include *Open Mind, Open Heart; The Mystery of Christ; The Human Condition;* and *Intimacy with God.* Recordings of his teachings can be obtained from Sounds True (www.soundstrue.com). Information regarding Christian-based meditation can also be obtained from Contemplative Outreach, Ltd., 10 Park Place, Suite B, Box 737, Butler, New Jersey 07405 (973-838-3384) and St. Benedict's Monastery, 1012 Monastery Read, Snowmass, Colorado 81653 (970-927-1162.

10. Christopher K. Germer, Ronald D. Siegel and Paul R. Fulton (editors), *Mindfulness and Psychotherapy* (New York: The Guilford Press, 2005), p. 9.

11. Jon Kabat-Zinn, *Full Catastrophe Living: Using the Wisdom of Your Body and Mind to Face Stress, Pain and Illness* (New York: Dell Publishing, 1990), p.2.

12. Thich Nhat Hanh, *The Miracle of Mindfulness* (Boston: Beacon Press, 1975), p.14.

13. From a set of recorded teachings by Jack Kornfield entitled *The Inner Art of Meditation* (available from Sounds True: www.soundstrue.com).

14. John Welwood, *Love and Awakening: Discovering the Sacred Path of Intimate Relationship* (New York: Harper Collins Publishers, 1996), pp.12-13. Welwood is a creative thinker and articulate writer. For another wonderful book by him about the wound of the heart, our yearning for love and thoughts about a love that is always

available to us, see *Perfect Love, Imperfect Relationships* (Boston: Trumpeter Books, 2006).

15. Ibid., p.15.

16. Jean Smith (Editor), *Breath Sweeps the Mind: A First Guide to Mediation Practice* (New York: The Berkley Publishing Group, 1998), p.17.

17. Kornfield, *The Inner Art of Meditation*. See Note 3 above.

18. Coleman Banks (Translator), *The Essential Rumi* (San Francisco: Harper Publishing, 2004), p. 109.

19. Karme Choling Newsletter (Spring 2005), p 1. Karme Choling is a meditation and retreat center in Barnet, Vermont. For information about the Center's programs, visit its website at www.karmecholing.org or call 802-633-2384.

Chapter Three

20. John J. Ratey, *A User's Guide to the Brain: Perception, Attention, and the Four Theaters of the Brain* (New York: Vintage Books, 2001), p.133.

21. *Harvard Women's Health Watch* (Volume 11, Number 6: February, 2004), p.1.

22. See Herbert Benson with Miriam Z. Klipper, *The Relaxation Response* (New York: Avon Books, 1975).

23. Smith, *Breath Sweeps the Mind*, p. 20

24. William James, *Principles Of Psychology* (New York: Dover, 1890), p.424.

25. The basic structure of this technique was adapted and modified from a stress-reduction approach utilized in the work of Herbert Benson and the staff at the Mind/

CULTIVATING LASTING HAPPINESS 295

Body Medical Institute of New England Deaconess Hospital and Harvard Medical School. See Herbert Benson and Eileen M. Stuart, *The Wellness Book: The Comprehensive Guide to Maintaining Health and Treating Stress-Related Illness* (New York: Fireside, 1993), p. 184-185.

Chapter Four

26. For a more detailed description of the parts of the brain, using your hand as a model, see Daniel Siegel and Mary Hartzell, *Parenting from the Inside Out: How a Deeper Self-Understanding Can Help You Raise Children Who Thrive* (New York: Jeremy Tarcher/Penguin, 2003), pp. 171-180.

27. When the alarm system is triggered and the mind/body shifts into the protection mode, processes and behaviors that support cellular replacement, vitality and growth (the "growth mode") are blocked or inhibited. For a description of the interplay between the protection and the growth modes, see Bruce Lipton, *The Biology of Belief: Unleashing the Power of Consciousness, Matter and Miracles* (Santa Rosa, California: Mountain of Love/ Elite Books, 2005), pp. 145-154.

28. For an excellent discussion of an "Anatomy of an Emotional Hijacking," see Daniel Goleman, *Emotional Intelligence: Why It Can Matter More Than IQ* (New York: Bantam Books, 1995), pp. 13-29.

29. Louis J. Cozolino, *The Neuroscience of Psychotherapy: Building and Rebuilding the Human Brain* (New York: W.W. Norton & Company, 2002), p. 163.

30. Sharon Begley, *Train Your Mind, Change Your Brain: How a New Science Reveals our Extraordinary Potential to Transform Ourselves* (New York: Ballantine Books, 2007), p. 5.

31. Jeffrey Schwartz and Sharon Begley, *The Mind & The Brain: Neuroplasticity and the Power of Mental Force* (New York: Regan Books, 2002), p. 224

32. Ibid.

Chapter Five

33. See note 28.

34. Goleman, *Emotional Intelligence*, p. 14.

35. For information regarding various programs and research studies involving emotional intelligence educational programs for children, see Goleman, *Emotional Intelligence*, pp. 305-309.

36. This summary is from a presentation by Prof. Robert Sapolsky of Stanford University at the Investigating the Mind 2005 Conference referred to in note 8. Prof. Sapolsky is an expert on the effects of stress.

37. John Ekman, Editor, *Emotional Awareness: Overcoming the Obstacles to Psychological Balance and Compassion – A Conversation between The Dalai Lama and Paul Ekman, PhD.* (New York: Times Books, Henry Holt and Company, 2008), at p. 68.

38. Andrew Newberg and Mark Waldman, *How God Changes Your Brain: Breakthrough Findings from a Leading Neuroscientist* (New York: Ballantine Books, 2009) at p. 19.

39. This technique was adapted from an approach described by Joseph Chilton Pearce in his book *The Biology of Transcendence: A Blueprint of the Human Spirit* (Rochester, Vermont: Park Street Press, 2002), pp. 213-214. The technique described by Pearce is part of a HeartMath "mind tool" called FreezeFrame.

Chapter Six

40. Daniel Siegel, *The Developing Mind: How Relationships and the Brain Interact to Shape Who We Are* (New York: The Guilford Press, 1999), p. 21.

41. Siegel and Hartzell, *Parenting from the Inside Out*, p. 34.

42. Lipton, *The Biology of Belief*, p. 134,

43. American Psychiatric Association: *Diagnostic and Statistical Manual of Mental Disorders,* Fourth Edition. Washington, DC, American Psychiatric Association, 1994, p. 424.

44. Bassel A. van der Kolk, *EMDR: Promises for a Paradigm Shift* (New York: APA Press, 2002), pp. 59-60.

45. Peter Levine, *Trauma Through a Child's Eyes* (Berkeley, CA: North Atlantic Books, 2011), at 12.

46. Siegel and Hartzell, *Parenting from the Inside Out*, p.123.

47. Certain of the questions for reflection have been adapted from Siegel and Hartzell, *Parenting from the Inside Out*, pp. 133-134.

Chapter Seven

48. Dr. Joseph Dispenza, *What the Bleep!? Do We Know!?,* Captured Light & Lord of the Wind Films, LLC (2004). For more information about the movie and the commentators in the film, go to www.whatthebleep.com.

49. For a description of the visual cliff scenario and an infant's sensitivity to minute changes in the expressions of others, see Thomas Lewis, Fari Amini and Richard

Lannon, *A General Theory of Love* (New York: Vintage Books), pp. 60-65.

50. Joseph Chilton Pearce, *The Biology of Transcendence: A Blueprint of the Human Spirit* (Rochester, Vermont: Park Street Press), p. 138.

51. Ibid., p. 140.

52. Cozolono, *The Neuroscience of Psychotherapy*, pp. 193-194.

53. Jeffrey Satinover, *The Quantum Brain: The Search for Freedom and the Next Generation of Man* (New York: John Wiley and Sons, Inc., 2001), p. 49.

54. See Daniel Goleman, *Social Intelligence: The New Science of Human Relationships* (New York: Bantam Books, 2006), pp. 78-79.

55. From a presentation made by Daniel Siegel on October 16, 2005 in a telephone course presented by *Psychotherapy Networker* entitled *The Brain-Savvy Clinician: A Practical Approach.* Siegel frequently presents such courses on various aspects of neuroscience and therapeutic growth. For more information about such courses, go to www.psychotherapynetworker.org.

Chapter Eight

56. Vaughan, *The Inward Arc*, p.88.

57. Roger Walsh, "The Transpersonal Movement: A History and State of the Art," *The Journal of Transpersonal Psychology*, Volume 25, Issue 2 (1993), pp. 130-131.

58. Frances Vaughan and Roger Walsh, "The Art of Transcendence: An Introduction to Common Elements of Transpersonal Practice," *The Journal of Transpersonal Psychology*, Volume 25, Issue 1, p. 2.

59. Ibid., pp. 1-2.

60. Ibid., pp. 3-6.

61. Walsh, "The Transpersonal Movement," p. 131.

62. This recorded teaching by Father Thomas Keating is entitled "Contemplative Prayer: Traditional Christian Meditations for Opening to the Divine" (Boulder: Sounds True, 1995). For more information regarding the availability of this and other teachings by Father Keating, go to www.soundstrue.com.

63. Deepak Chopra, *The Spontaneous Fulfillment of Desire: Harnessing the Infinite Power of Coincidence* (New York: Harmony Books, 2003), pp. 76- 77.

64. Walsh, "The Transpersonal Movement," pp. 135-136.

65. Vaughan & Walsh, "The Art of Transcendence," p. 1.

66. Frances Vaughan and Roger Walsh (Editors), *Paths Beyond Ego: The Transpersonal Vision* (Los Angeles: Jeremy P. Tarcher, Inc., 1993), p.110.

67. Sharon Salzberg, *The Force of Kindness: Change your Life with Love & Compassion* (Boulder: Sounds True, Inc., 2005), p. 20.

68. Vaughan, *The Inward Arc*, p.56.

69. Parts of this forgiveness meditation were adapted from a meditation recorded by Jack Kornfield in *Meditation for Beginners: Six Guided Meditations for Insight, Inner Clarity, and Cultivating a Compassionate Heart* (Boulder: Sounds True, Inc., 2004), CD, Meditation #5.

Chapter Nine

70. Lipton, *The Biology of Belief*, p. 144.

71. Walsh, "The History of the Transpersonal Movement," p. 131.

72. From the newsletter of the Ligmincha Institute for the Study of the Religions and Cultures of Tibet founded by Geshe Tenzin Wangyal Rinpoche, December, 1, 2005, p.2. Ligmincha Institute offers retreat programs at its Dharma Center at Serenity Ridge, Nelson County, Virginia and teachings by Geshe Tenzin Wangyal at various locations in the United States, Mexico and Europe. For more information about the programs at Serenity Ridge and teachings in other locations, go to www.ligmincha.org or call 1-434-977-6161.

73. Ibid., p.3.

74. The idea for the structure of this practice comes from a teaching by Tenzin Wangyal Rinpoche at Omega Institute in Rhinebeck, New York, on July 29, 2006.

75. See Robert Thurman, *Inner Revolution: Life, Liberty and the Pursuit of Real Happiness* (New York: Riverhead Books, 1998).

76. The Action Plan has been used for years at *Turning Point*, the cardiac rehabilitation program offered by Maine Medical Center in Portland, Maine, where I previously taught. It is an effective tool for initiating action in connection with a plan for health. I have not been able to determine the original source of the Action Plan form.

Chapter Ten

77. His Holiness the Dalai Lama, *The Dalai Lama's Little Book of Wisdom* (New York: Barnes & Noble, 1995), p. 124.

78. From a presentation by Father Thomas Keating at the Mind and Life 2005 Conference referred to in Note 8.

INDEX

A

acceptance, 3, 43, 77, 81-83, 252, 255, 281, 303
Action Plan, 262, 266, 300, 303
A Love So Vast, 277, 303
amygdala, 98, 99, 108, 109, 113, 117, 119, 135, 303
anchoring, 142, 303
attention, 3, 5, 6, 12, 32, 34, 37, 44, 47, 50, 54-56, 62-64, 66, 69-71, 73-78, 81, 83, 85-91, 93, 101, 109-113, 115, 117, 130-132, 135-144, 146, 147, 150, 156, 160, 170, 178, 179, 181, 192-196, 202, 203, 210, 211, 223, 224, 229, 236-239, 245, 246, 250, 252, 260, 268, 269, 272, 273, 284, 294, 303

B

Benson, 68, 294, 295, 303
Big "T" trauma, 163-166, 303

brain,
        magical brain, 96, 303
brainstem, 97, 98, 108, 116, 303
Buddhist tradition, 55, 62, 94, 225, 226, 235, 245, 246, 268, 275, 290, 303

C

Christian tradition, 227, 228, 287, 293, 303
Circle of Liberation, 64-67, 72, 73, 76-78, 80, 82-85, 252, 258, 263, 268, 273, 303
compassion, 9, 10, 23, 40, 77, 81-83, 85, 129, 153, 170, 211, 246, 254, 255, 284, 296, 299, 303
concentration, 67, 77, 78, 223, 252, 303
Contemplative Exercise Regarding Re-Framing Old Conclusions, 192, 210, 211, 303

Contemplative Exercise Regarding Your Life Story, 170, 191, 303

contemplative prayer, 228, 273, 287, 299, 303

coping mechanism, 161, 184, 185, 197, 207-209, 303

cortex, 62, 97-99, 103, 108, 116, 119, 124, 125, 135, 303

Course in Miracles, 39, 304

D

Dalai Lama, v, 8-11, 23, 94, 137, 227, 245, 248, 263, 264, 270, 290, 296, 301, 304

dumb-luck joy, 272, 304

E

emotional hijacking, 108, 109, 111, 113, 118, 123-126, 128-134, 143, 159, 176, 194, 203, 295, 304

emotional intelligence, v, 125, 126, 128, 143, 279, 280, 284, 295, 296, 304

emotional transformation, 223, 304

endurance, 77, 79, 80, 83, 85, 252, 304

equanimity, 77, 82, 83, 85, 223, 252, 304

F

Fachidiot, 125, 304

forgiveness, 234-240, 299, 304

G

Guest House, 242, 304

Gurdieff, 46, 304

H

Hebb's axiom, 111, 179, 304

I

imagery, 135-138, 141, 142, 145, 220, 247, 304

impact bias, 27, 304

implicit memory, 104, 106, 107, 111, 118, 120, 304

J

joy, 3, 5, 7, 12, 14, 15, 38, 49, 246, 254, 267, 270-273, 276, 304

K

karma, 226, 304

kindness, iii, 3, 16, 23, 24, 38, 55-57, 65, 74, 75, 77, 81-83, 85, 153, 170, 189, 210, 211, 239, 247, 250, 252, 255, 258, 262, 284, 299, 304

L

Ladakh, 139

life story, vii, 20, 151-153, 156-158, 167, 168, 170, 176, 178, 181, 184, 185, 191, 207, 259, 303, 304

limbic region, 98, 99, 108, 116, 117, 135, 304

Lipton, 163, 244, 285, 295, 297, 299, 304

little "t" trauma, 163-166, 304

M

meditation, v, 8, 30, 40, 51, 62, 66, 75, 81, 86, 132, 145, 146, 228, 235, 236, 240, 243, 247-252, 260, 267, 270, 271, 273, 275, 281, 284, 285, 287, 289-294, 299, 304

messages, 20, 21, 28, 32, 33, 35, 50, 56, 80, 90, 112, 115, 116, 118, 135, 152, 155, 157-159, 161-163, 165, 169, 172, 173, 175-178,

182, 184, 185, 188-194, 197, 199, 202, 203, 205, 207, 208, 210-215, 219, 220, 224, 227, 228, 232, 233, 259, 268-271, 276, 304, 305
mindfulness, v, vii, 1, 3-6, 9, 12-16, 19
    as a path of healing, 47, 50, 58, 304
    as a practice, 51, 257, 304
    definitions, 43, 59, 81, 304
    Mindfulness in Daily Practice, 90, 304
    Mindfulness in Everyday Life, 283, 304
    Mindfulness in Relationships, 91, 304
    Seven Steps to Mindfulness, 19, 58, 59, 84, 304
motivation, 12, 57, 58, 68, 77, 194, 223, 224, 249, 304
Mullah Nasruddin, 28, 29, 305

N
negative messages, 20, 32, 33, 35, 56, 80, 116, 162, 165, 177, 182, 185, 189, 197, 199, 203, 205, 208, 211, 214, 220, 227, 228, 233, 259, 305
Nepal, 31, 241, 243, 305
neural Darwinism, 199, 305
New Realities, vii, 21, 47, 219, 232, 259, 305

O
Obstacle One, 25, 305
Obstacle Two, 25, 305
Obstacle Three, 32, 305
Obstacle Four, 33, 305

Obstacle Five, 35, 305
Obstacle Six, 36, 305

P
patience, 3, 53, 54, 56, 57, 65, 76, 77, 79, 80, 83, 85, 144, 200, 250, 252, 264, 274, 276, 305
plasticity, 20, 114, 115, 155, 192, 193, 305
practice,
    formal practice, 66, 67, 79, 80, 85, 86, 245, 247-252, 256, 260, 305
    informal practice, 66, 85, 86, 245-247, 257, 258, 305
    self-regulation practice, 132, 144, 145, 149, 305
    semi-formal practice, 246, 247, 256, 258, 261, 305
Prayer for Love, 255, 305
presence, 8, 9, 31, 49, 55, 58, 73, 77, 78, 81, 83, 85, 159, 249, 270-273, 285, 305
pruning, 199, 305

R
Ratey, J., 305
reconsolidation, 197, 305
Relaxation Exercise, 67, 68, 87, 132, 247, 305
restraint, 8, 124, 133, 134, 156, 196, 305
Rumi, 57, 200, 202, 294, 305

S
Safe Place Visualization, 145, 146, 305
SAM, 206-208, 305
self-regulation, vii, 20, 68, 123, 128, 130, 132-137, 139, 142-145, 149, 176, 194,

259, 268, 305
Siegel, D., 305
sky-like mind, 275, 276, 305
spaciousness, 19, 52, 61, 257,
        273, 276, 305
Step One, vii, 19, 61, 143, 258,
        305
Step Two, vii, 19, 93, 143, 152,
        259, 305
Step Three, vii, 20, 123, 143,
        259, 305
Step Four, vii, 20, 151, 259, 305
Step Five, vii, 20, 175, 177, 259,
        305
Step Six, vii, 21, 219, 259, 305
Step Seven, vii, 21, 241, 305
Stop-Breathe-Reflect-Choose,
        87-89, 95, 113, 120-122,
        131, 156, 176, 193-195,
        202, 215, 216, 220, 247,
        258, 259, 261, 305
stress response, 68, 100, 117,
        127, 130, 305
Sufi tradition, 28, 305

T
Third Zen Patriarch, 56, 305
transpersonal psychology, 221-
        224, 244, 298, 305

V
visual cliff, 186, 297, 305

W
What Is This Love, 274, 305
What the Bleep!? Do We
        Know?, 177, 297, 306
wisdom, 8-12, 15, 16, 37, 40,
        53, 59, 60, 114, 121, 130,
        131, 194, 198, 209, 221,
        224, 225, 227, 230, 234,
        255, 268, 271, 276, 283,
        292, 293, 301, 306

The Witness, vii, 19, 61, 64, 65,
        73, 88, 116, 143, 195,
        258, 306